Apple Training Series

GarageBand 3

Mary Plummer

Apple
Certified

Apple Training Series: GarageBand 3
Mary Plummer
Copyright © 2006 by Mary Plummer

Published by Peachpit Press. For information on Peachpit Press books, contact:

Peachpit Press
1249 Eighth Street
Berkeley, CA 94710
(510) 524-2178 or (800) 283-9444
Fax: (510) 524-2221
http://www.peachpit.com
To report errors, please send a note to errata@peachpit.com.
Peachpit Press is a division of Pearson Education.

Apple Series Editor: Serena Herr
Managing Editor: Nancy Peterson
Development Editor: Justine Withers
Production Editor: Laurie Stewart, Happenstance Type-O-Rama
Technical Reviewer: Victor Gavenda
Copy Editor: Darren Meiss
Compositor: Chris Gillespie, Happenstance Type-O-Rama
Indexer: Joy Dean Lee
Media Production: Eric Geoffroy
Cover Art Direction: Charlene Charles-Will
Cover Illustration: Kent Oberhue
Cover Production: Happenstance Type-O-Rama

ISBN 0-321-42165-5
9 8 7 6 5 4 3 2 1
Printed and bound in the United States of America

Dedicated to the universal language of music, and GarageBand
for bringing the world a little closer one song at a time.

Acknowledgments First and foremost, deepest thanks to my husband and partner, Klark Perez, for your incredible devotion in carrying the weight for both of us and our company InVision Digital and Media Arts while I was writing.

Thanks to Patty Montesion for a career I adore as an Apple Certified Trainer, and the extraordinary opportunity to write this book. Your positive attitude, energy, and enthusiasm for the program that you built from the ground up are one of a kind.

Thank you Xander Soren for first introducing me to GarageBand and keeping me up to speed as it evolves. Also thanks to Apple's GarageBand team for making music production, video scoring, and podcasting fun, easy, and accessible to everyone.

Special thanks to Justine Withers for your invaluable input, patience, and leadership in keeping this book on track and on schedule. Thanks also to Victor Gavenda for your music recording experience. More thanks to Serena Herr, Nancy Peterson, Laurie Stewart, Eric Geoffroy, Darren Meiss, and the rest of the amazing Peachpit Press team for making this book a reality.

Thanks to our friends at Universal Studios Florida for the opportunity to have a production company and training center on the lot. Thank you Speakeasy—Jimmy Kaufholz, Amy Harwood, and Kyle Chason—for lending your original music and interviews.

Extra special thanks to my family for their unconditional love throughout my freelance career. Thanks "Meem," Lee, Dad, Ginny, Chris, Sessely, Jorin, Landon, Kim, Guy, Emily, Chris, Jackson, Gabe, Peg, Jim, Warren, Loretta, Chase, Bill, Paula, Sergio, Virginia, Kent, Klark, Katie, and my dog Niki. Finally, my mother Jane Ann, her mother Betty K., and her mother Kathryn for the musical gift and heirloom—your piano.

Contents at a Glance

Table of Contents

Getting Started

Welcome to the official training course for GarageBand 3, Apple's dynamic music recording and arrangement software. This book is a detailed guide to recording, arranging, and mixing music using GarageBand, your own instrument recordings, and the library of more than 1,000 royalty-free Apple Loops that is included with the software. You'll also learn to use new GarageBand 3 features to create original podcasts, and add music and sound effects to your movies.

Apple Training Series: GarageBand 3 is based on the premise that a training book should go beyond a basic tour of the application by providing you with practical techniques that you will use on a daily basis to add professional-quality music and sound effects to your projects.

Whether you are a seasoned composer or have never written a piece of music before, you'll learn how to use GarageBand for a variety of real-world scenarios including recording, arranging, and mixing music from scratch. You'll work with Real Instruments, MIDI Software Instruments, and prerecorded Apple Loops to edit music and add effects that sweeten your finished projects. Finally, you'll export and work with your finished projects in other iLife applications.

The Methodology

This book emphasizes hands-on training. Each exercise is designed to help you learn the application inside and out, starting with the basic interface and moving on to advanced music editing, arranging, and mixing techniques. If you are new to GarageBand, it would be helpful for you to start at the beginning and progress through each lesson in order, since each lesson builds on information learned in previous ones. If you are already familiar with GarageBand, you can start with any section and focus on that topic.

Course Structure

Each of the ten lessons in this book focuses on a different aspect of creating projects with GarageBand 3. Each lesson expands on the basic concepts of the program, giving you the tools to use GarageBand for your own projects.

The lessons in this book can be informally divided into five sections:

▶   Lessons 1–2: Learning the interface and working in the Timeline.

▶   Lessons 3–6: Arranging music using the different types of GarageBand musical regions, including Software Instruments, Real Instruments, and Apple Loops.

▶   Lesson 7: Mixing and adding effects to complete a project.

▶   Lessons 8–9: Creating original podcasts and scoring movies.

▶   Lesson 10–Appendixes: Exporting and sharing finished projects, JamPacks, and going from GarageBand to Logic Express.

System Requirements

Before beginning to use *Apple Training Series: GarageBand 3*, you should have a working knowledge of your computer and its operating system. Make sure that you know how to use the mouse and the standard menus and commands and also how to open, save, and close files. If you need to review these techniques, see the printed or online documentation included with your system.

Basic system requirements for GarageBand 3 are as follows:

▶ Mac OS X version 10.3.9 or later, Mac OS X version 10.4.4 recommended.

▶ PowerPC G4, Power PC G5, or Intel Core processor.

▶ At least 256 megabytes (MB) of physical RAM, 512 (MB) recommended.

▶ DVD drive required for installation.

▶ In order to make full use of all features of GarageBand, a screen resolution of 1024 × 768 pixels or more is recommended.

▶ Approximately 5 GB of free disk space to install the GarageBand application and media.

System Requirements for Software Instruments

Software Instruments require a Macintosh G4 or G5 and at least 256 MB of physical RAM. (If you are working on a G3, you will not be able to play or record Software Instruments in GarageBand 3. You will be able to open the song; you just won't be able to play it without overloading your processor.)

If you are working with a slower computer, you will find some useful tips and techniques for dealing with slower computers in "Strategies for Minimizing Processor Load" (Bonus Exercises > **Minimizing_Processor_Load.pdf**) on the accompanying DVD.

Hardware Compatibility

GarageBand can operate with any Core Audio- and Core MIDI-compliant audio interface, USB MIDI interface, or even a microphone, keyboard or guitar with the correct adapter. You may need to install additional drivers from the manufacturer of the audio interface in order to provide full Mac OS X support.

For a list of supported audio and MIDI interfaces that work with GarageBand, see the GarageBand Web site at www.apple.com/ilife/garageband/accessories.html.

Installing GarageBand

To install GarageBand, double-click the GarageBand installer and follow the instructions that appear.

If you see a message that you do not have sufficient privileges to install this software, click the lock icon in the installer window and enter an administrator name and password. The administrators of your computer are shown in the Accounts pane of System Preferences.

The installer places the Apple Loops Library and the index to the loops library in /Library/Audio and it places the Instrument Library in /Library/Application Support/GarageBand. Do not move these items from their default locations.

Copying the Lesson Files

This book includes an *ATS_GarageBand_3* DVD containing all the files you'll need to complete the lessons. Inside the GarageBand 3 Lessons folder are Lesson subfolders organized by lesson number. Within each numbered Lesson sub-folder, you will find projects for each exercise.

When you install these files on your computer, it's important to keep all of the numbered Lessons subfolders together in the main Lessons folder on your hard drive. If you copy the Lessons folder directly from the DVD to your hard drive, you should not need to reconnect any media files or have problems opening projects.

Installing the Lesson Files

1   Put the *ATS_GarageBand 3* DVD into your computer's DVD drive.

2   Double-click to open the DVD and drag the GarageBand 3 Lessons folder from the DVD to your computer's desktop.

3   To begin each lesson, launch GarageBand. Then follow the instructions in the exercises to open the project files for that lesson.

About the Apple Training Series

GarageBand is part of the official training series for Apple iLife applications developed by experts in the field and certified by Apple Computer. The lessons are designed to let you learn at your own pace.

For those who prefer to learn in an instructor-led setting, training courses are available at Apple Authorized Training Centers worldwide. These courses, which use the Apple Training Series books as their curriculum, are taught by Apple Certified Trainers and balance concepts and lectures with hands-on labs and exercises. Apple Authorized Training Centers have been carefully selected and have met Apple's highest standards in all areas, including facilities, instructors, course delivery, and infrastructure. The goal of the program is to offer Apple customers, from beginners to the most seasoned professionals, the highest quality training experience.

To find an Authorized Training Center near you, go to www.apple.com/software/pro/training.

Resources

Apple Training Series: GarageBand 3 is not intended to be a comprehensive reference manual, nor does it replace the documentation that comes with the application. For comprehensive information about program features, refer to these resources:

▶ The Reference Guide. Accessed through the GarageBand Help menu, the Reference Guide contains a complete description of all features.

▶ Apple's Web site: www.apple.com.

1

Lesson Files	GarageBand 3 Lessons > Lesson_01 > 1-1 Alaska Sunrise
Time	This lesson takes approximately 1 hour to complete.
Goals	Launch GarageBand
	Explore the GarageBand window
	Navigate in the Timeline
	Work with the transport controls
	Start and stop playback in the Timeline
	Open the editor
	Compare Real Instruments and Software Instruments
	Edit regions in the editor
	Open the Loop Browser in Podcast Sounds view
	Add a video clip from the Media Browser

Working with the Interface

GarageBand is powerful enough to record and mix a professional-sounding music demo, podcast, or video score, yet simple enough that anyone can use it right out of the box.

Over the years, I've worked with many frustrated musicians who bought their first computers and software specifically to try recording their own music. Unfortunately, instead of finding inspiration and a new creative tool, they got more frustrated because the software was way too complicated.

That was before GarageBand. This software is different. You don't have to be a computer major or audio engineer to record music. You don't even have to be a musician. If you can click a mouse, you can turn your Mac into a basic recording studio for music, scoring video, or producing podcasts— it's really that simple.

In this lesson, you'll take a guided tour of the GarageBand basic interface and learn how to use the transport controls and navigate in the Timeline. Along the way, you'll learn some of the new GarageBand features, as well as some useful keyboard shortcuts as you get to know the program.

If you've been working with GarageBand for a while and are already comfortable with the basic interface, editor, and navigation, feel free to jump ahead to Lesson 2.

Before You Start

Before you start, you need to load the GarageBand 3 program onto your hard drive. You also need to copy the GarageBand 3 Lessons folder from the CD in the back of the book to your computer's Desktop.

The instructions for loading the software and files are in "Getting Started," the introduction to this book. After you complete those two steps, you can move forward with this lesson.

Now that you have the GarageBand program and lesson files loaded onto your hard drive, you're ready to begin this lesson.

> **NOTE** ▶ Make sure your screen resolution is set to 1027 × 768 or higher in the display preferences for your computer. If your resolution is below 1027 × 768, you won't be able to see the entire GarageBand window on your screen.

Launching GarageBand

There are three ways to launch GarageBand:

▶ On your hard drive, double-click the GarageBand application icon.

▶ On the Dock, click the GarageBand icon.

▶ Double-click any GarageBand project file.

For this exercise, you'll launch GarageBand by opening a project file.

1   Locate the GarageBand 3 Lessons folder on your computer.

> **NOTE** ▶ If you haven't copied the GarageBand 3 Lessons folder to your hard drive, do so at this time.

2   Select the Lesson_01 folder, then double-click the **1-1 Alaska Sunrise** project file to open the song and launch the program.

An initializing progress window appears, showing that GarageBand is opening the selected project. When GarageBand opens, you will see a large window containing all the elements for the song **1-1 Alaska Sunrise**.

Exploring the GarageBand Window

One of the many advantages of GarageBand is the simplicity of the interface. As with all the iLife applications, GarageBand uses one window as the base of operations. This window is your recording studio.

Let's take a quick tour of the GarageBand window:

▶ Track headers—Show the instrument icon and name to the left of each instrument track. The track headers also include a Mute button to silence a track, a Solo button to silence all other tracks, a Record Enable button (which allows you to record to a specific track), and a Lock button to protect the track and its contents from unintended changes.

▶ Track Mixer—Includes a Volume slider to adjust the track volume and a Pan wheel to adjust the position of the track in the left-to-right stereo field.

▶ Timeline—Acts as your music recording and arranging workspace. The Timeline is made up of horizontal tracks for each individual instrument. The Timeline graphically represents linear time from left to right using a Beat Ruler at the top of the window. The far-left edge of the Timeline represents the beginning of a song.

Timeline

Track headers   Track Mixer

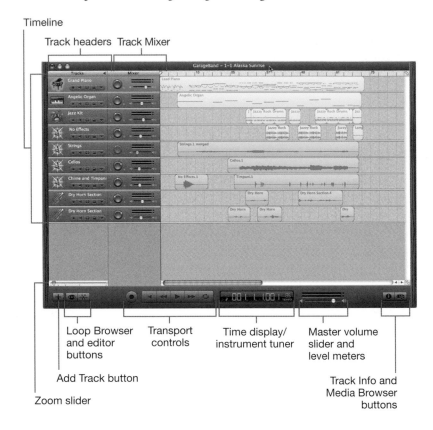

Loop Browser
and editor
buttons

Transport
controls

Time display/
instrument tuner

Master volume
slider and
level meters

Add Track button

Track Info and
Media Browser
buttons

Zoom slider

▶ Zoom slider—Zooms in to or out of the Timeline.

▶ Add Track button—Adds a new track in the Timeline.

▶ Loop Browser button—Opens the Loop Browser.

▶ Editor button—Opens the editor.

▶ Transport controls—Provide the standard recording and playback buttons to navigate in the Timeline, including Record, Go To Beginning, Rewind, Start/Stop Playback, Fast Forward, and Cycle.

▶ Time display—Shows the song's tempo and current playhead position in musical time (measures, beats, ticks) or absolute time (hours, minutes, seconds, fractions).

- ▶ Instrument tuner—Located in the same space as the time display; use it to check the tuning of any Real Instrument, including vocals.

- ▶ Master volume slider—Adjusts the output volume level of the project.

- ▶ Level meters—Indicate the output volume level of a project and include red warning lights if levels are clipping (too loud).

- ▶ Track Info button—Opens the Track Info pane.

- ▶ Media Browser button—Opens the Media Browser pane. The Media Browser is a new feature in GarageBand 3.

Window Basics

GarageBand was designed for Macintosh OS X, and the GarageBand window works the same as other OS X windows. If you're new to the Mac or to OS X, it's a good idea to know the GarageBand window basics.

Close (X) button
Minimize (–) button
Zoom (+) button
Window title bar
Wooden side panels
Resize control

You can use the Zoom, Minimize, and Close buttons to resize the window, minimize it to the Dock, or to close the window and the project. Double-clicking the title bar at the top of the GarageBand window will also minimize the window. You can use the wooden side panels, top edge, or bottom edge to drag the window to a different location on the screen. To resize the entire window, drag the resize control in the lower-right corner of the window.

> **TIP ▶** If you're using a laptop or a large studio display, the Zoom button is a very useful tool to maximize the size of your workspace. Also, any time you can't see the entire window because part of it is offscreen, you can click the Zoom button to bring the entire window into view.

Now that you know how to adjust the full GarageBand window, let's play the project and take a closer look at some other features, starting with the Timeline.

Playing a Song in the Timeline

There are several ways to play a project in the Timeline. In fact, many GarageBand features can be accessed by menu, button, or keyboard shortcut. For example, to play a project you can click the Play button in the transport controls (the mouse method), or you can press the spacebar (the keyboard method). For this exercise, you'll start with the transport control buttons located at the bottom of the GarageBand window, below the Timeline.

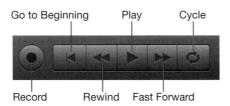

1   In the transport controls, click the Go to Beginning button to move the playhead to the beginning of the song (if it is not already there).

The Go to Beginning button is the first button on the left of the transport controls. It looks like a vertical line with an arrow pointing to the left.

Transport control buttons turn blue when they are active.

2   Click the Play button, located in the middle of the transport controls, to play the project. Listen to the song **1-1 Alaska Sunrise**.

While the song plays, watch the playhead (vertical red line) as it moves left to right along the Timeline.

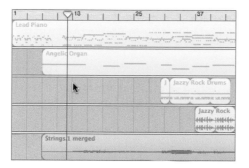

The playhead simultaneously plays whatever regions (musical parts) it scrubs across in the Timeline.

NOTE ▶ If you get a warning message that part of the song was not played, your computer may not meet the system requirements to play this song. Move the playhead to the beginning and try again. If you still get a warning message, read "Strategies for Minimizing Processor Load" (Bonus Exercises > **Minimizing_Processor_Load.pdf**) on the accompanying DVD.

For more information on system requirements and performance, see the introduction to this book, "Getting Started."

3   Click the Play button again to stop playback.

Now you'll do the same thing using keyboard shortcuts.

4   Press the Return, Home, or Z key to move the playhead to the beginning of the song.

> **TIP** ▸ If you're working on a laptop, use the Return or Z key to get to the beginning of the Timeline. On a laptop, the Home key is also the left arrow, so you need to hold down the function key first. The function key for Mac PowerBooks and MacBook Pro laptops is located in the lower-left corner of the keyboard and is labeled "fn."

5   Press the spacebar to begin playback.

6   Press the spacebar again to stop the playhead.

7   Press Z, or click the Go to Beginning button to move the playhead back to the beginning of the Timeline.

I composed and recorded the original version of this song for a project I edited and scored in 1988 during the wildfires in Yellowstone Park. At the time the song was called "Splendor" and was inspired by the incredible wildlife and scenery, despite the charred ground and smoky surroundings. That was two decades ago, using what now seems like ancient recording technology, an audio engineer, and a studio full of equipment. If someone told me back then that I would be able to record and mix music with a simple program on my home computer, I probably would have laughed and said something skeptical like, "We'll have flying cars and robot maids before that happens!" Of course that was before GarageBand. (I'm still waiting for the flying cars and robot maids.)

I rerecorded and arranged the song after a trip to Alaska in 2002 where I was once again inspired by the scenery and wildlife. This book includes a portion of the song recorded and arranged using GarageBand.

Exploring the Timeline

Now that you've played the project, let's take a closer look at the Timeline. The Timeline is the largest portion of the GarageBand window. It contains tracks where you can record both Software Instruments and Real Instruments. You can also add loops of prerecorded musical parts and arrange the different regions to create a finished song, score, or podcast.

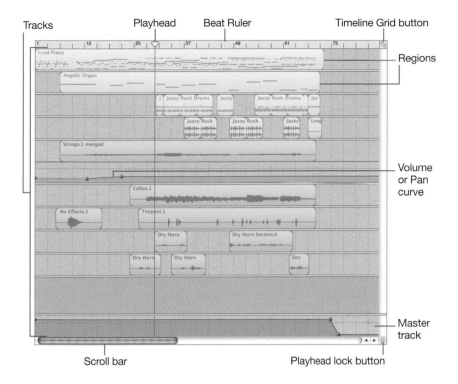

The Timeline includes the following controls:

► Playhead—Shows exactly what part of the song is currently playing. The playhead is a triangle (with a red vertical line underneath) on the Beat Ruler. You also use the playhead to determine where to cut, copy, and paste music regions within the Timeline.

► Beat Ruler—Shows musical time in beats and measures. Click anywhere in the Beat Ruler to move the playhead to that position.

► Tracks—Contain recordings of the Real Instrument or Software Instrument parts. They can also contain loops of prerecorded musical parts from the Loop Browser called Apple Loops.

► Timeline Grid button—Lets you choose the note value of the Timeline grid, or you can choose Automatic so the value will change as you zoom in to and out of the Timeline.

▶ Regions—Display the individual musical parts that are either prerecorded loops or parts that you record using Real Instruments and Software Instruments. Each region is color-coded according to type. Regions can be moved, copied, cut, and pasted, as well as extended or looped, in the Timeline. You can use the editor to edit or transpose both Software Instrument regions and Real Instrument regions made from loops or recordings.

▶ Volume curves—Graphically represent the volume within a track. You can dynamically change the volume of a track for different parts of a song using control points along the Volume curve.

▶ Pan curves—Graphically represent the left-to-right panning of a track within the stereo field. You can dynamically change panning for different parts of a song using control points along the Pan curve.

▶ Master track—Lets you change the volume, pitch, and effects for the overall song. You can dynamically adjust the Volume curve in the Master track just as you can for individual tracks, but adjustments to the Master track's Volume curve affect all of the tracks in the Timeline. You can also dynamically adjust the Master pitch to transpose (change the key of) the project.

▶ Playhead Lock button—Locks (gangs) the playheads in the Timeline and editor together, or unlocks them to show different sections of the song at the same time.

▶ Scroll bars—Let you see a different part of the song in the Timeline. Click and drag the horizontal scroll bar to move horizontally in the Timeline. Use the vertical scroll bar to move vertically.

Exploring Tracks and Regions

Let's take a moment to examine what makes up the song in the Timeline. The song **1-1 Alaska Sunrise** contains nine tracks.

Each track, in turn, contains individual musical parts—regions—from a particular instrument. An instrument track may contain only one region, or it may contain many smaller regions—individual takes and retakes, often called *overdubs*—which, when arranged in a track, are the basic building blocks of an entire instrument's part for a song.

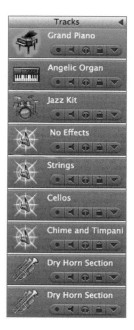

Regions come in a variety of colors (by type) and sizes. A track may have one region that lasts the entire duration of the song, or different regions representing different musical parts played by the same instrument at different times in the song.

Take a look at your Timeline. The Lead Piano region is one long region that lasts for the entire duration of the song, which indicates that the performance was recorded all in one take from start to finish. The Dry Horn Section tracks have five separate Dry Horn regions located at the middle and end of the song. These regions were recorded one at a time with the same instrument. The No Effects.1 region is only at the beginning of the Chime and Timpani track because that's the only place where the musical part was needed. (You'll change the name of that region from No Effects.1 to Chime later in this lesson.) There are three Jazzy Rock regions on the No Effects track. The first two Jazzy Rock regions include notches (rounded corners), to show that they were each created by extending a single loop to repeat multiple times. The notches indicate the end of one repetition and the beginning of another.

One long Lead Piano region   Two Jazzy Rock regions with notches

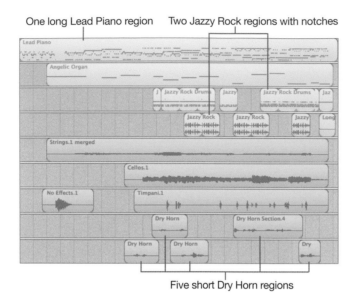

Five short Dry Horn regions

Real Instruments

Purple, blue, and orange regions represent Real Instrument parts recorded from Real Instruments.

You can record Real Instrument parts into GarageBand through a microphone, guitar, or keyboard that is plugged into the microphone jack on your computer. You can also record Real Instrument parts through other input devices that you connect to your computer. You will learn more about recording Real Instruments and about orange (imported) regions later in this book.

For the **1-1 Alaska Sunrise** song, I recorded five Real Instrument parts using a synthesizer as the instrument (Strings, Cellos, Wind Chime, Timpani, and Dry Horns).

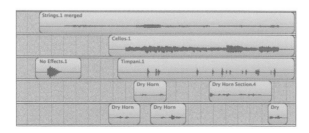

Real Instrument regions are placed in the Timeline as is. Once a Real Instrument region has been recorded into the Timeline, you can enhance the tuning, timing, and pitch. However, in contrast to Software Instruments, Real Instrument regions do not include individual notes, so you can't change the content of a Real Instrument region once it is recorded.

Software Instruments

Software Instruments are recorded performances that are more flexible than Real Instruments because they are recordings of MIDI note events, rather than sounds. Software Instruments utilize some of the same powerful music editing tools found in Apple's professional recording software, Logic.

> **NOTE ▸** MIDI stands for Musical Instrument Digital Interface. It's an industry standard that allows all devices, such as synthesizers and computers, to communicate with each other.

Software Instrument regions are green and are recorded using a USB music keyboard, a MIDI synthesizer–type keyboard, the GarageBand onscreen keyboard, or Musical Typing using the GarageBand software and your computer's keyboard as the MIDI instrument. Because Software Instrument regions don't contain sounds from actual musical instruments, they do not display the sounds, or notes, as waveforms, as do Real Instrument regions (purple or blue). Software Instrument regions represent individual notes as "note events" that look like a series of bars, lines, or dashes, which can be assigned to any Software Instrument, before or after it is recorded.

Once the notes for the Software Instrument region are recorded, you can change the sound of the instrument that plays the notes, fix the timing, notation, and velocity, or change the pitch of the region to a different key.

For this song, I recorded two Software Instruments located in the top two tracks in the Timeline.

Apple Loops

GarageBand also comes with over 1,000 prerecorded Apple Loops. These loops are regions that contain either digital recordings of real instruments or editable MIDI notes. Real Instrument Apple Loops are colored blue, and Software Instrument Apple Loops are green. Prerecorded loops can be used to accompany the other instrument tracks and are incredibly useful for adding tracks with instruments you can't play and record yourself. These loops are like your backup band.

For the **1-1 Alaska Sunrise** song, I used prerecorded Apple Loops for the percussion section. The Jazzy Rock Drum regions in the Jazz Kit track are green, which means the individual notes are editable, like a Software Instrument.

The Jazzy Rock Drum regions on the No Effects track are blue, which means they are a digital recording with notes that can't be edited. Many Apple Loops can be used as either Real Instrument or Software Instrument recordings, depending on the type of track in which they are placed. You'll learn more about specific tracks in the next lesson.

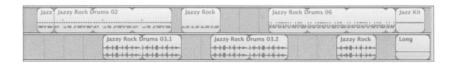

Zooming In to and Out of the Timeline

Now that you have identified the different regions and tracks, let's zoom in for a closer look.

You can zoom in to and out of the Timeline by using the Zoom slider, located in the lower-left corner of the window, or by using a keyboard shortcut.

GarageBand zooms in to your current playhead position in the Timeline. For this exercise, let's start by zooming in to the beginning of the song.

1   Press the Z key to move the playhead to the beginning of the Timeline (if it is not there already).

2   Locate the Zoom slider in the lower-left corner of the window.

3   Drag the slider to the right to zoom in to the Timeline at the playhead position. As you zoom in, the tracks in the Timeline get longer, and you can see more detail within a track.

No Effects region before zooming in to the Timeline

No Effects region after zooming in to the Timeline

4   Drag the slider to the left to zoom out of the Timeline.

5   Drag to the middle position on the slider.

> **NOTE ▶** You can also zoom in and out with keyboard shortcuts. Pressing Ctrl-right arrow (press the Control key and the right arrow key together) zooms in; Ctrl-left arrow zooms out.

Exploring the Editor

Now that you're zoomed in to the Timeline, look at the green and purple regions visible in the Timeline.

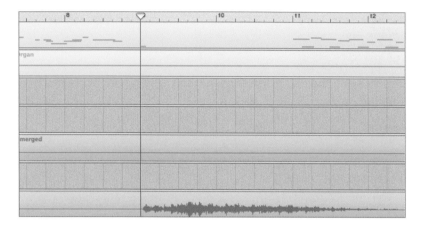

Notice that the green regions have a series of dashes and lines to represent the musical note events. The purple regions, on the other hand, show a waveform that illustrates the digital recording.

The editor is a tool that lets you magnify and edit a particular region or track.

Opening the Editor

The editor can be used to edit an entire track or a specific region within that track.

The editor differs depending on whether you're working with a Software Instrument or a Real Instrument. You can have only one editor open at a time because they occupy the same space in the lower third of the GarageBand window.

Let's start with the editor for Software Instruments. Remember that the green regions are created by Software Instruments and can be edited in the editor.

There are four ways to open the editor:

▶ Double-click the region you wish to edit in the editor.

▶ Click the editor button, located in the lower-left corner of the window.

▶ Go to the Control menu at the top of the screen and choose Show Editor.

▶ Press Cmd-E (the Command key and the E key at the same time).

Since we haven't used any of the menus in this lesson, this is a good time to try out the menus at the top of the screen. First, you need to select the track that you wish to open in the editor.

1 On the top track of the Timeline, click the Grand Piano track header to select it (if it is not already selected).

The track header turns green to indicate it has been selected. Note that the green color of the track header also shows that the regions within that track are Software Instrument regions. A track can either be a Software Instrument track and contain Software Instrument regions, or a Real Instrument Track that contains Real Instrument regions. You can't mix the types of regions within a track. Selecting a track also selects all of the regions within that track and turns on that track's Record Enable button.

NOTE ▶ Double-clicking a track header opens the Track Info pane at the right side of the GarageBand window. If you double-clicked the track header, press Cmd-I to close the Track Info pane. You'll work more with the Track Info pane later.

2   Choose Control > Show Editor.

NOTE ▶ In this book, the shorthand for steps that involve menus is written as "Choose Control > Show Editor." In other words, Control is the title of the menu, and Show Editor is the selection within that menu.

The editor appears in the lower third of the GarageBand window. The gray bars in the editor represent the individual note events displayed in Graphic view.

3   Press Return or the Z key to move the playhead to the beginning of the Timeline and the editor.

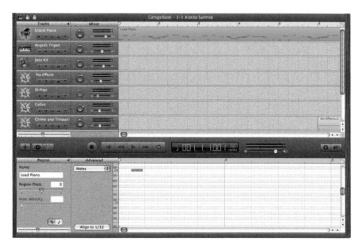

TIP ▸ If you don't see many note events (bars) in the editor, you can drag the scroller on the right side of the editor to reveal additional notes. Dragging upward reveals notes played in higher octaves, and dragging downward reveals notes played in lower octaves.

4 Drag the vertical scroller at the right of the editor upward to reveal additional note events (bars).

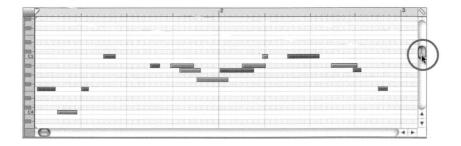

As described earlier, Software Regions display individual notes as note events. While in the editor, you can view and edit the MIDI note events in either Graphic view (bars) or Notation view (musical notes).

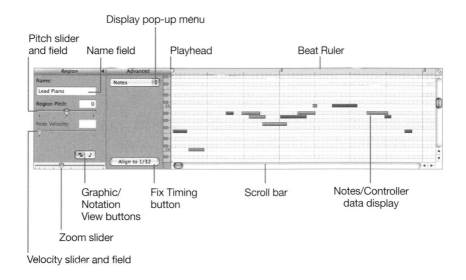

Using the Editor for Software Instruments

Let's take the editor out for a test drive. In this exercise, you'll work in Notation view to delete the last piano note in the song, then switch to Graphic view to extend another note within the Grand Piano track.

1   Drag the Timeline Zoom slider to the left so that you can view the entire song in the Timeline.

2   To view the Lead Piano notes in the Grand Piano track in Notation view, click the Notation View button, which looks like a musical note.

Graphic View button ────  ──── Notation View button

The Notation View button turns blue when it is selected, and the note events in the editor change to musical notation.

3   Press the spacebar to play the song in the Timeline.

You can see the playhead move along the Notation view in the editor as it slides across the same notes in the Timeline.

4   In the transport controls, click and hold the Fast Forward button to move the playhead through the song to the end.

You can use the left or right arrow keys to move the playhead one measure at a time toward the left or right.

5   Click the left arrow key three times to move the playhead three measures earlier in the Timeline and play the ending of the song.

The last piano note sounds like it is continuing the melody and the song rather than ending.

6 In the editor, locate the last note in the Lead Piano region. The last note is at the beginning of the 69th measure (bar 69).

7 Click the last note to hear and select it.

The note turns green when it is selected. To change a note, you simply drag it up or down to a different location on the musical staff, or select the note and press the up or down arrow keys.

8 Drag the note down to a different position on the musical staff.

You can hear the key of the note change as it moves to a different position. Now that you've demonstrated how to change a note's position and key, it's time to delete it from the song. This extra note isn't working in the song.

9 Press the Delete key to delete the selected note.

The note is deleted from the song in both the editor and the Lead Piano region in the Timeline. Let's listen to the last two measures of the song to hear the revised ending.

10 Press the left arrow key several times to move the playhead to the beginning of the 67th measure (bar 67).

The time display shows that the current playhead position in the Timeline is the 1st beat of the 67th measure.

Measures Beats Ticks (fractions of a beat)

11 Play the last two measures and listen to the ending.

It sounds fine, but it might work even better if the last note was held a little longer instead of ending abruptly.

Extending the final note is a good example of editing notes in Graphic view.

1 Click the last piano note to select it.

2 Click the Graphic View button to change the editor back to Graphic view.

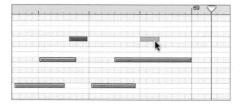

The selected note is green in Graphic view, just as it was in Notation view.

Notes in Graphic view appear as gray bars that vary in length and position. You'll work more with the editor in Graphic view in Lesson 3. For now, you'll focus on simply extending the last note.

3   Drag the right edge of the selected note toward the right and extend it to the 2nd beat of the 69th measure (as shown in the screen shot).

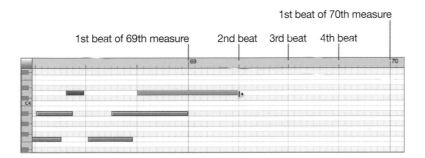

4   Click the Notation View button to see the change in the last note reflected in musical notation.

5   Click the empty white space in the editor to deselect the last note.

Before extending note   After extending note

6   Press the left arrow key three times to move the playhead back three measures, then play the end of the song.

Nice work. The last note sounds much better now that it holds longer at the end.

NOTE ▶ You'll work more with the Region Pitch slider, Velocity slider, and Fix Timing button in a later lesson.

Using the Editor for Real Instruments

The editor is different when you're working with Real Instrument tracks.
Let's look at the Real Instrument track that was used to record the Chime
and Timpani regions in the Chime and Timpani track.

1   Locate the Chime and Timpani track in the Timeline.

2   Double-click the Timpani.1 region in the Chime and Timpani track to
    select the region and open it in the editor.

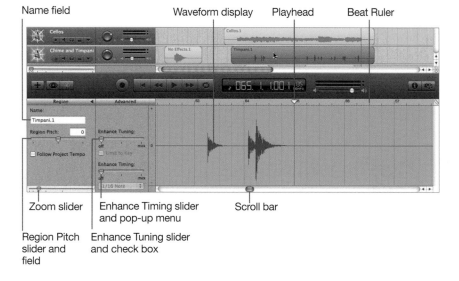

Name field   Waveform display   Playhead   Beat Ruler

Zoom slider   Enhance Timing slider   Scroll bar
              and pop-up menu

Region Pitch   Enhance Tuning slider
slider and   and check box
field

The purple color of the track means this track is a digital recording of a
Real Instrument through either a microphone or other input device. The
good news is that you can record live musicians and their instruments
directly into the Timeline. The bad news is that this recording method
maintains the integrity of the recorded performance. In other words, you
can't edit the individual notes and change them to a different note the same
way that you edit Software Instrument regions. However, you can select
parts of the waveform and cut, copy, paste, move, or delete the selection.

Your goal in this exercise is to fix the timing for one of the timpani drum
hits by selecting it in the editor and moving it in the track.

The timpani hit in question is in the 45th measure of the song. One easy way to get to a specific measure is to double-click the measures portion of the time display and type a new number.

3   Press Z to move the playhead to the beginning of the Timeline and editor.

4   Double-click the first three digits (001) in the time display; these numbers represent measures.

The selected numbers will flash after you select them.

5   Type *43*, then press Return.

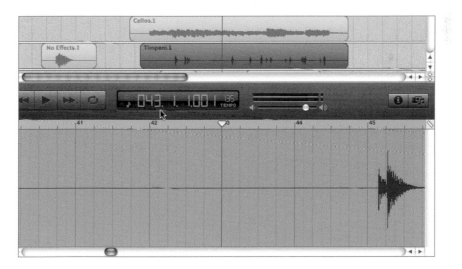

The playheads in both the Timeline and editor move to the beginning of the 43rd measure. Why move to the 43rd measure when we want to hear the 45th? Because you'll hear and understand the timing problem with the timpani hit if you hear it in context with the rest of the song. In other words, give yourself a measure or two to get your acoustic bearings.

TIP ▶ You can also change numbers within the time display by click-dragging the mouse up or down over the desired number.

6 Play the song from the 43rd measure through the 47th measure.

Did you notice that the timpani drum hit sounds a little late, or early, or just doesn't quite feel like it belongs where it is? If you didn't notice, play the same section again. If you still don't hear it out of place, don't worry about it. My ear may be more sensitive to such things. The point is that if you want to move the drum hit a little later or earlier, you can, using the editor.

7 Use the left arrow key to move the playhead to the beginning of the 45th measure.

8 Drag the editor Zoom slider toward the right to about the one-third position to zoom in closer to the waveform in the editor.

To select a portion of the waveform in the editor, drag the pointer over the section you want to select. The pointer automatically becomes a crosshair-shaped selection tool over a Real Instrument region in the editor.

9 Move the pointer (crosshair) to the beginning of the drum hit waveform in the 45th measure.

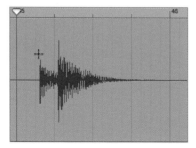

10 Click and drag the pointer from the beginning to the end of the waveform in the 45th measure.

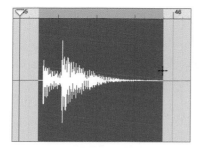

The selection turns blue in the editor.

11 Click the selection in the editor.

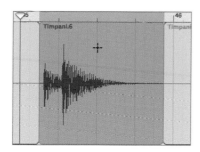

The selection becomes a separate Real Instrument region that can now be moved, copied, pasted, or deleted.

12 Drag the scroller at the bottom of the editor toward the right until you can see the entire 46th measure in the editor.

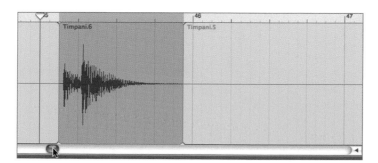

Next you'll move the playhead between the 2nd and 3rd beats of the 46th measure. This is where you'll move the new Timpani region.

13 Click the Beat Ruler between the 2nd and 3rd beats of the 46th measure.

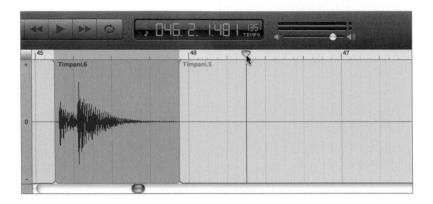

14 Move the crosshair pointer near the top of the selected Timpani region in the editor to change the crosshair pointer to the move pointer. The move pointer looks like a line with arrows pointing left and right.

15 With the move pointer, drag the new Timpani region right until it starts at the playhead position (between the 2nd and 3rd beats of bar 46).

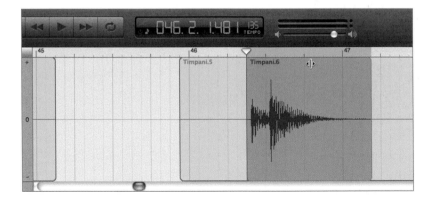

16 Use the left arrow key to move back a few measures and listen to the edited Timpani region. (Play through the 50th measure to hear your edited timpani in context with the next timpani hit in the 49th measure.)

There you have it. A nice improvement on the timing, and you've successfully demonstrated editing a Real Instrument region in the editor.

NOTE ▶ You'll work more with the Region Pitch slider and the Enhance Tuning and Enhance Timing sliders in a later lesson.

Renaming Tracks and Regions in the Editor

While you're in the editor, this is a good time to change the name of the Wind Chime recording from No Effects.1 to Chime. Keep in mind that regions don't have to be named after the track and vice versa. They often share the name of the track because GarageBand automatically names regions after the track when you record. The No Effects region was originally recorded in a track named No Effects.

1 In the Chime and Timpani track of the Timeline, double-click the No Effects.1 region to open it in the editor.

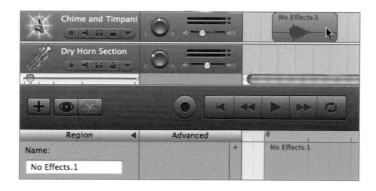

The No Effects.1 region appears in the editor.

2   Type *Chime* in the Name field and press Return.

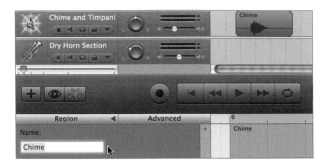

The region's name changes to Chime in the Timeline and editor.

You can also use the same technique to change the name of a track in the editor.

3   In the Timeline, click the No Effects track header.

The No Effects track and all of its regions are selected.

4   Click the empty gray track space to the right of the No Effects track header and mixer to deselect the regions within the track.

The editor now shows that you're working on the full track instead of just a region. Notice that the header on the left side of the editor now reads Track instead of Region.

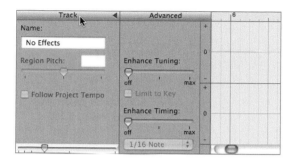

5 Type *Jazz Kit 2* in the Name field to change the name of the track. Press Return.

The track header for the selected track changes to Jazz Kit 2.

TIP ▶ You can also change the name of a track header by double-clicking the name in the header and typing the new track name.

Your editor work is complete for this lesson.

6 Click the editor button, or press Cmd-E, to hide the editor.

Exploring the Loop Browser

The Jazzy Rock Drums regions came from a library of over 1,000 prerecorded Apple Loops that are included with the GarageBand software. Loops are musical parts that can be repeated (looped) over and over seamlessly. These loops can be accessed through the Loop Browser. The Loop Browser organizes the loops by categories and helps you search for loops using the Musical Button, Column, or Podcast Sounds views.

There are three ways to open the Loop Browser:

▶   Click the Loop Browser button.

▶   Choose Control > Show Loop Browser.

▶   Press Cmd-L.

Let's open the Loop Browser now.

1   Click the Loop Browser button to open the Loop Browser.

The Loop Browser and the editor occupy the same space in the GarageBand window. You cannot open both at once.

Keyword buttons   Loop library pop-up menu

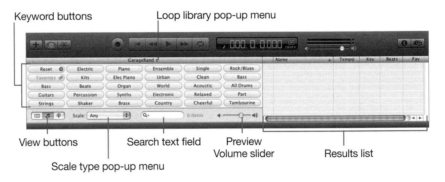

View buttons   Search text field   Preview
                                                 Volume slider   Results list

Scale type pop-up menu

Imagine if you had to listen to hundreds of loops just to find the sound you want. Luckily, the Loop Browser sorts and organizes the loops for you—all you need to do is narrow the search. The Loop Browser has the following controls:

▶   Keyword buttons or columns—Click the keywords to display the matching loops. Click additional keywords to narrow the search.

▶   View buttons—Changes the layout of the Loop Browser to Column view, Musical Button view, or Podcast Sounds view.

▶   Scale type pop-up menu—Narrows your search to a specific scale type.

▶ Search text field—Type the name of the loop or the kind of loops you want to find.

▶ Preview Volume slider—Adjusts the volume of the loops as you preview them.

▶ Results list—Shows the results that match whatever keywords you have selected or text you have entered in the Search field. Once you have used keywords or buttons to narrow or refine your search, the results are listed in this pane. You can sort the results by columns, including by name, tempo, and key.

▶ Loop library pop-up menu—Click to choose the loops you want to show in the Loop Browser.

Using the Loop Browser in Podcast Sounds View

You'll be using the Loop Browser extensively throughout this book. Rather than search for music loops at this time, let's try something new to GarageBand 3 and browse the Podcast Sounds.

1   Click the Podcast Sounds View button to change the Loop Browser to the Podcast Sounds view.

The podcast sounds in the Loop Browser are neatly organized by Jingles, Stingers, Sound Effects, and Favorites. The Jingles and Stingers are prerecorded musical pieces you can use for your podcasts or videos. The Sound Effects can also come in handy for all types of projects including songs. Since this project was inspired by nature, adding some nature ambience to the piece would be nice.

2   In the first column of the Browser, click Sound Effects.

The Sound Effects column appears to the right, listing different sound effect categories.

The song **1-1 Alaska Sunrise** could use some forest ambience with cheerful chirping birds to go with the mood of the music.

3   Select Ambience from the Sound Effects column.

The results list shows 14 different ambience sound effects.

NOTE ▶ The blue icon next to each of the sound effects indicates that it is a Real Instrument loop.

4   Click any of the sound effects in the results list to preview (listen to) the sound.

When previewing a Real Instrument file in the Loop Browser, the entire duration of the file will play and stop automatically at the end. You can stop the preview any time by clicking the file again or selecting another file to preview.

5   Press the up or down arrow keys to move up or down through the results list.

6   Select the Forest sound effect.

This sound effect should work well with the song, but the only way to be sure is to audition it with the music.

Auditioning Loops with a Song

Now that you have found a sound effect for the song, you can audition it to make sure it works before adding it to the project.

1   Press Return to move the playhead to the beginning of the song.

2   Press the spacebar, or click the Play button, to start playback.

3   In the search results, select the Forest sound effect to hear it with the song.

Sounds great. A little loud, but the volume can easily be adjusted once the loop is added to the project.

4   Audition a few more ambience effects with the music just for fun.

5   Press the spacebar to stop playback of both the sound effect loop and the song.

Once you have auditioned your loops and selected one that works, you can add it to the Timeline and make it part of the song, which will be the first thing we do in the next lesson.

6   Click the Loop Browser button to close the Loop Browser.

Adding Movies to the Media Browser and Timeline

There is one last thing to do in this tour-de-interface: see the exciting new Media Browser, where you can access the music, photos, and movies on your computer to add to your GarageBand projects.

To add a video clip to your project, you first need to show the video track in the Timeline.

1   Choose Track > Show Video Track.

The Video track appears at the top of the Timeline and the Track Info pane opens on the right side of the window.

2   In the lower-right corner of the GarageBand window, click the Media Browser button.

You can also open the Media Browser by choosing Control > Show Media Browser or by pressing Cmd-R.

The Media Browser appears on the right side of the GarageBand window.

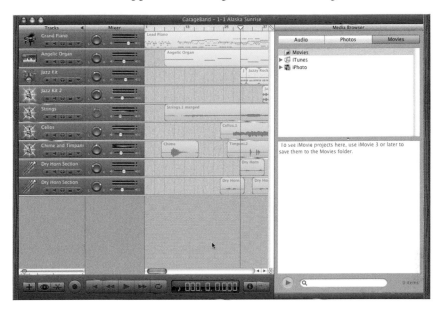

The Media Browser lets you browse through the Movies, Photos, or Music (Audio) folders already on the computer. You can also access additional folders of audio, photos, or movies by simply dragging them from their current location on the computer to the appropriate pane of the Media Browser.

Adding a folder of media to the Media Browser creates a reference to that media in its current location on your computer and does not actually move the media.

The GarageBand 3 Lessons folder includes a Movies for GarageBand folder containing all of the movies you'll use for this book. Let's take a moment and add that folder to the Media Browser.

First, you'll need to move or resize the GarageBand window so that you can see the GarageBand 3 Lessons folder on the Desktop.

3 Drag the GarageBand window by the title bar at the top, or by the wooden side panels, toward the left to reveal the right half of your computer's Desktop.

NOTE ▶ If your GarageBand 3 Lessons folder is on the left side of the Desktop, drag the GarageBand window downward to reveal the folder. The important thing is to drag the GarageBand window so that you can still see the Media Browser onscreen.

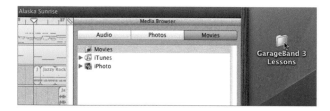

4 Double-click the GarageBand 3 Lessons folder.

5 In the Media Browser, click the Movies button.

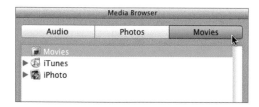

Now you'll add the Movies for GarageBand folder.

6   Drag the Movies for GarageBand folder from the GarageBand 3 Lessons
     folder to the Media Browser.

The Movies for GarageBand folder and its contents are now added to the
GarageBand Media Browser.

7   In the Media Browser, click the Movies for GarageBand folder to see the
     contents, which are displayed in the lower pane of the Media Browser.

8   Move the GarageBand window back to its normal position on the screen.

     Now that you've added the content to the Media Browser, you can add one
     of the movies to the project.

9   Drag the **Alaska** movie from the Media Browser to the Video Track in the
     GarageBand window.

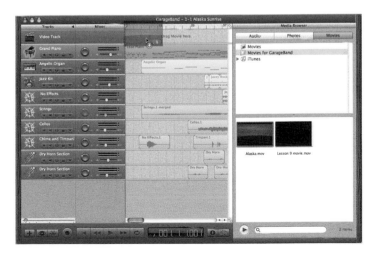

An alert appears, warning you that there is no audio that can be used (because the video clip you are importing does not contain audio).

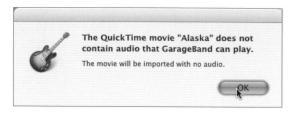

10 Click OK.

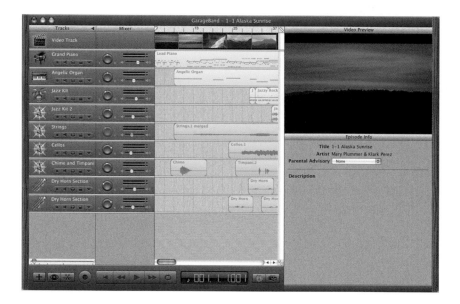

The Video Preview pane appears so that you can see the video as you play the project.

11 Play the project from the beginning to see and hear it with the video track.

NOTE ▶ This video is home movie footage from a trip to Alaska with my family, and isn't part of any documentary or professional production.

Saving and Closing Your Project

The last step is to save your finished project. For this exercise, you'll do a basic save. In the later lessons, you'll learn about the other GarageBand save features. To save the project, first you'll open the Save As window, then you'll create a new folder to save all of your GarageBand book projects.

1   Choose File > Save As.

An alert appears asking if you'd like to save your project with an iLife preview.

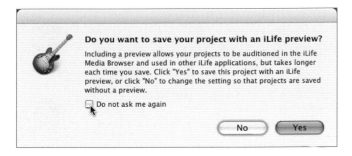

This saving method is great for finished projects, but takes longer to save, and is not necessary until you are ready to share the project with other iLife applications. You'll save files with iLife Preview in Lesson 10.

2   Click the Do not ask me again box on the Alert. Then click No.

The Save As dialog opens.

NOTE ▶ To expand the Save As dialog, click the downward pointing arrow at the right side of the Save As field.

3   Click the Desktop icon on the Sidebar (left side) of the Save As window.

You've now selected the Desktop as the location to save your project.

4 Click the New Folder button, located in the lower-left corner of the window.

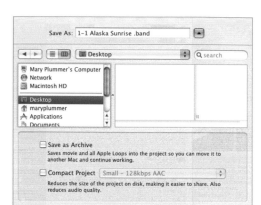

A New Folder dialog opens.

5 Type *My GarageBand Projects* in the "Name of new folder" field. Click Create.

The new folder is created on your Desktop.

6 In the Save As window, click Save.

7 Press Cmd-W or choose File > Close Project.

Your project has been successfully saved to the folder you created on your Desktop and closed.

Congratulations! You completed the first lesson in the book, and have a good working knowledge of the GarageBand basic interface.

Now you're ready to move on to the next lesson.

Lesson Review

1. What are three ways that you can launch Garageband?

2. How can you move or resize the GarageBand window?

3. Where in the interface can you see the current playhead position?

4. Which keys on the computer keyboard are shortcuts to move the playhead one measure at a time?

5. What are the four different colored musical regions in the Timeline?

6. Where can you find and preview the over 1,000 audio files that come with GarageBand?

7. What is the difference between Software Instrument regions and Real Instrument regions?

Answers

1. Double-click the application icon in the Finder, click once on the Garage-Band icon in the Dock, or double-click any GarageBand song file.

2. To move the GarageBand window, click and drag any edge of the window. To resize the window, drag the resize control in the lower-right corner of the window.

3. You can see the playhead position in the time display or the Beat Ruler.

4. You can move the playhead one measure at a time left or right with the left and right arrow keys.

5. The four different colored regions are: purple Real Instrument recordings, blue Real Instrument Apple Loops, green Software Instrument recordings and Apple Loops, and orange imported Real instrument regions.

6. You can find and preview the different loops in the Loop Browser.

7. Software Instrument regions include MIDI information, and each note can be edited or modified. Real Instrument regions are digital recordings of audio waveforms, and the individual notes cannot be edited.

2

Lesson Files	GarageBand 3 Lessons > Lesson_02 > 2-1 Alaska Sunrise
Time	This lesson takes approximately 1 hour to complete.
Goals	Understand tracks
	Work with the Track Info pane
	Use the time display as a reference
	Add and extend a loop region in the Timeline
	Use the onscreen keyboard
	Add a Software Instrument track
	Record a basic Software Instrument part
	Create a cycle region
	Delete a region from the Timeline
	Change a track's icon and instrument
	Save a project

Working with Tracks in the Timeline

In this lesson, you'll learn how to work with tracks. Sure, that doesn't sound like much fun—until you get a better perspective on the power of tracks. Have you ever heard of a 4-track recorder? In its time, the 4-track revolutionized the music industry as much as the mouse revolutionized computers. The 4-track recorder made it possible to record four different instrument tracks one at a time, and play them back all mixed together. Eventually, 4-track recorders were replaced by 8-track recorders, and finally by digital recording.

What does that mean to you? For one thing, you don't have to limit your songs to four tracks. In fact, you can have up to 255 Real Instrument tracks or 64 Software Instrument tracks, depending on the speed of your computer. Chances are, most of your songs can be arranged in 10 or fewer tracks, but it's nice to know that if you need more tracks, they're there for you.

This lesson focuses on the different types of tracks. You'll learn to add, delete, and change tracks, as well as evaluate tracks to determine how well they fit with the song.

Understanding Tracks

Think of the tracks in your Timeline as the different musicians in your band. Each musician plays a different instrument and is represented by a separate track. As the leader of your band, you can decide which instruments are used in a song and how you want to record them. If you don't like an instrument part, you can always fire the musician—or in this case, just delete the track. If you really like the way a part sounds, you can clone the musician, or just double that track in the Timeline.

The best way to understand tracks is to work with them, so let's get started.

Preparing the Project

Open project **2-1 Alaska Sunrise** from the Lesson_02 folder. This is the same project you were working on in the previous lesson. You may continue working with **1-1 Alaska Sunrise** if you prefer.

Showing and Hiding the Track Info Pane

At the end of Lesson 1 you dragged the Movies for GarageBand folder to the Media Browser, then added the **Alaska** movie to the Video Track in your project. Now that you know how to add a video file and play it in the Video Preview pane, you're probably wondering how to close it when you don't need it. The Video Preview pane is directly above the Track Info pane (labeled Episode Info when a video track is selected). Anytime the Track Info pane is showing, you'll also see the video preview of your project.

The Track Info pane shows information for any selected track. There are three primary ways you can show or hide the Track Info pane:

▶   Choose Track > Show Info (or Track > Hide Info if it is already showing).

▶   Click the Track Info button.

▶   Press Cmd-I.

Before we hide the Track Info pane, let's select a music track to see its details.

1   Select the Video Track, if it is not already selected. If the Track Info pane is not showing on the right side of the window, press Cmd-I.

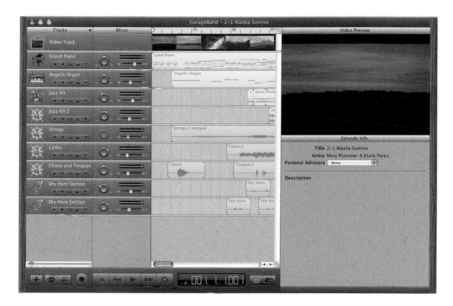

2   Select the Grand Piano track to show the track info for that track.

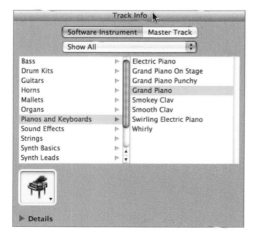

The Track Info pane shows that you have selected a track that is a Software Instrument track, Pianos and Keyboards instrument category, Grand Piano instrument.

The lower-left corner of the Track Info pane also shows the track's icon, which in this case is a Grand Piano.

3 Select one of the Dry Horn Section tracks.

The Track Info pane now shows that you've selected a Real Instrument track, Band Instruments category, Dry Horn Section as the instrument. Even the track's icon illustrates that the track includes horns.

NOTE ▶ The Real Instrument Track Info pane also includes recording information for the track, including Input, Volume, and Monitor. You'll work more with Real Instrument recording in Lesson 6.

4 Press Cmd-I, or click the Track Info button, to hide the Track Info pane.

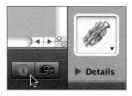

TIP ▶ To maximize the workspace in the Timeline, close the Track Info pane when you don't need it. You can always open it when needed to see the Video Preview or change a track's icon or instrument.

Selecting Prerecorded Loops and Sound Effects

Remember the Forest sound effect loop you auditioned in the last lesson? Well, it's time to add it to the project **2-1 Alaska Sunrise**. First, you'll need to find it again in the Loop Browser and make room for it at the beginning of the song.

1   Click the Loop Browser button, or press Cmd-L, to open the Loop Browser.

2   If the Loop Browser displays a view other than Podcast Sounds, click the Podcast Sounds View button to list the Podcast Sounds.

NOTE ▶ The Loop Browser opens in the last view you used. In the previous lesson, you used the Podcast Sounds view, so it should open that way.

3   Select Sound Effects > Ambience > Forest to hear the Forest sound effect loop.

In the last lesson, you auditioned (listened to) the Forest sound effect with the project. Now that we are ready to add the loop to the project, let's audition it one more time to be sure.

4   Press Return or Z to move the playhead to the beginning of the Timeline.

5   Press the spacebar to begin playback of the project.

6   Click the Forest sound effect to play it along with the project.

The birds seem a bit loud, but you can always turn down the sound effect once you add it to the Timeline. You can also use the Preview Volume slider to turn down the volume of the loops as you listen to them in the Loop Browser.

7   Drag the Preview Volume slider toward the left to lower the preview volume of the Forest sound effect.

8   Press the spacebar to pause playback when the song ends.

NOTE ▶ You won't be able to see the Video Preview/Track Info pane and the Loop Browser at the same time. So if you want to audition a loop, you'll need to do so without looking at the video preview. However, once you've added a loop to the project, you can play it and watch the video at the same time.

The sound effect is cheerful, and it definitely adds a natural and relaxing feel to this New Age instrumental song. Trouble is, the music starts at the very beginning of the project, and it would be better if the project started with the forest sounds to set the mood, then had the music join in. No problem, you'll just move the existing song over a measure or two.

Selecting and Moving All Regions in the Timeline

Normally, you might move one or two regions at a time. In this case, to move them all, you'll select all the regions at once and move them toward the right. Keep in mind, the video clip will not be moved, and it always starts at the beginning of the project, regardless of where the first audio region starts in the Timeline.

1   Press Cmd-L, or click the Loop Browser button, to hide the Loop Browser.

You won't lose the selection when you close the Loop Browser. Instead, the Loop Browser remembers the last selection as long as you don't close the project.

2   Press Ctrl-left arrow several times to zoom out of the Timeline until you can see the beginning and end of the project in the Timeline.

3   Choose Edit > Select All, or press Cmd-A, to select all of the regions in the project.

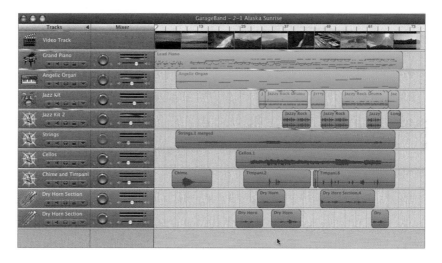

The selected regions become darker in color in the Timeline.

NOTE ▶ If the Video Track is selected in the Timeline, the Edit > Select All function will be dimmed. However, the shortcut Cmd-A will always work to select all of the project's audio regions, even if the Video Track is selected.

4   Move the playhead to the beginning of the Timeline (001.1.1.001 in the time display).

5   Press the right arrow key two times to move the playhead two measures to the right (003.1.1.001).

This is the new starting position for the song.

6   Click any of the selected regions and drag toward the right until the Lead Piano region begins at the playhead position.

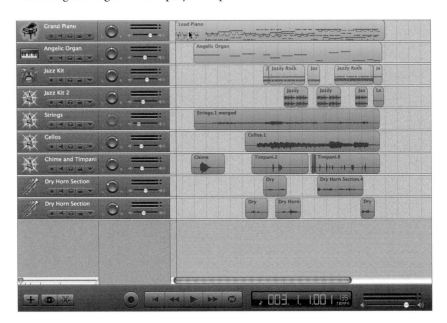

7   Click any empty gray space in the Timeline to deselect all of the regions.

Now that you've selected and moved everything over so the song starts at the beginning of the 3rd measure, it's time to add the sound effect to the project.

Adding a Track

Since you're working with prerecorded Apple Loops, you don't have to add a track to the Timeline first. A track will be created automatically when you add the loop to the Timeline.

The easiest way to add a prerecorded loop to the Timeline is to drag it there.

1   Press Cmd-L to reopen the Loop Browser.

The Forest sound effect should still be showing in the Loop Browser. If for some reason it's not showing, select Sound Effects, Ambience, Forest before moving on to the next step.

You'll add the loop to the empty gray space below the lowest track in the Timeline.

2   Drag down the vertical blue scroller until you can see below the lowest Timeline track.

3   Drag the Forest loop from the results list in the Loop Browser to the
Timeline and release it at the beginning of the Timeline below the
bottom track.

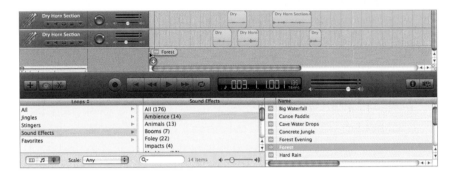

The green circle with the plus sign in it shows that you're adding a loop to
the Timeline.

A new track appears at the bottom of the Timeline with the Forest region
starting at the beginning of the track. Notice that the track color is blue,
indicating that you added a Real Instrument loop, and therefore created a
Real Instrument track.

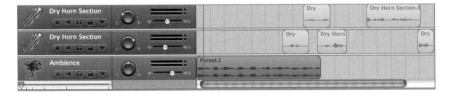

The new track is named after the loop's category, Ambience, and the loop
maintains its original name, Forest.1.

As you can see, adding a prerecorded loop to the Timeline is as easy as
select, drag, and release.

NOTE ▶ The *.1* after the region's name in the Timeline indicates that this
is the first instance of the Forest loop in the project. If you add a second
Forest loop, or copy and paste the current loop to a different position in
the Timeline, the number will change to reflect which numbered copy it
is within the project.

4   Close the Loop Browser.

5   Press the spacebar to listen to a few measures of the Ambience track with the rest of the song. Press the spacebar again to stop playback.

It works, but as expected, the volume level of the Ambience track is way too high for this project. It sounds more like musicians trying to perform in a bird sanctuary than a subtle touch of nature added to an existing song.

Fortunately, each track includes a mixer with a Volume slider, Pan wheel, and level meters. You can click the disclosure triangle above the Timeline track headers to show or hide the mixer.

Level meters

Pan wheel   Volume slider

6   Drag the Ambience track's Volume slider toward the left to around –32.

A handy yellow tooltip appears to show you the Volume level as you adjust the slider. The lowest Volume level in GarageBand is –144.0 dB (silence); the highest level is +6. You'll work more with volume and panning controls in Lesson 7 later in this book.

7   Play the beginning of the song again to hear it with the lowered ambient sound. While the song is playing, press Cmd-I to open the Track Info pane to see the video while you preview the first part of the song.

So, what did you think of the Ambience track? I think it really complements the song's light and down-to-nature feel, especially when you see it with the video clip. Music is extremely subjective, and everyone has different tastes in what they like. If the forest ambience doesn't work for you, feel free to delete that track after you finish this lesson.

Extending a Loop Region

Now all you need to do is extend the Forest loop to make it last until the end of the song. The whole process is incredibly easy. Loop regions are designed to repeat (loop) over and over seamlessly. To extend a loop region, all you have to do is click the upper-right corner and pull.

First, let's close the Track Info pane to maximize your workspace. Then, you'll move the playhead so you can use it as a guide for extending the loop region.

1   Close the Track Info pane.

2   Drag the playhead through the Beat Ruler to the beginning of the 73rd measure. (This is also the end of the Lead Piano region.)

Check the time display to make sure your playhead is in the right location.

3   Move your pointer over the upper-right corner of the Forest loop region.

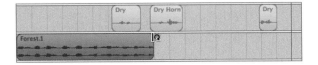

The pointer becomes a loop pointer, a vertical line next to a curved arrow, which indicates the pointer is in the correct position to drag the loop to repeat.

4   Drag the upper-right corner of the Forest loop region and extend it to the playhead position (the beginning of the 73rd measure).

You don't have to extend a loop for the full length of the original region. If you make the looped section shorter than the original, you will only hear the notes included in the new loop segment.

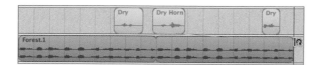

Notice that as the loop repeats, you can see notches that show the beginning and end of the original loop within the new region.

The project is really coming together. However, I'm beginning to have second thoughts about the intensity of the chime sound at the beginning of the song. The other instrumentation is very delicate—even the birds in the Forest ambience are light—yet the chime seems overly dramatic. The whole piece is supposed to start delicately to go with the whole sunrise and nature theme. I still like the idea of a chime here, just not this particular recording. Looks like we'll have to record a new wind chime, and delete the old one.

Recording a Basic Software Instrument

You can record Software Instruments in GarageBand using a USB music keyboard or a MIDI synthesizer-type keyboard. You can also use Musical Typing, which allows you to use the keys on your computer keyboard to play music. You'll learn more about recording with external devices and Musical Typing in the next lesson.

For this exercise, you'll work with the handy built-in onscreen keyboard that comes with GarageBand.

Using the Onscreen Keyboard

There are two ways to open the built-in onscreen keyboard:

▶   Press Cmd-K.

▶   Choose Window > Keyboard.

Let's use the menu method so you'll know where to find the keyboard in the future.

1   Choose Window > Keyboard.

A small window opens that looks like a music keyboard.

You can move the onscreen keyboard by dragging the gray space in the upper half of the window.

2   Drag the onscreen keyboard to a different location on the Timeline. Placing it under the green Software Instrument tracks offers easy access to the tracks and the keyboard.

NOTE ▶ The onscreen keyboard works only with Software Instrument tracks. If the blue (Real Instrument) Ambience track is selected in the Timeline, the onscreen keyboard will appear, but it will be disabled until you select or create a Software Instrument track.

For some of you, this may be your first fully functional MIDI keyboard controller. What is a MIDI keyboard controller? MIDI is an acronym that stands for Musical Instrument Digital Interface. MIDI is a standard protocol that is used by computers to communicate with electronic musical instruments and vice versa.

The instruments you play using a MIDI keyboard are either synthesized or professional samples. Each note you press on the keyboard triggers a synthesized sound, or a sampled digital recording.

What's the difference between sampled and synthesized sounds? Sampled instruments are made from actual recordings of real musical instruments, while synthesized instruments are generated mathematically by the computer. Just like some processed foods contain pieces (samples) of actual fruit along with other ingredients, others use artificial (synthesized) fruit flavors created in a lab and contain no actual fruit. Both examples may taste like fruit, but only one actually came from fruit somewhere along the way.

Selecting a Software Instrument Track

Now that you have your onscreen keyboard open, let's test it out. The onscreen keyboard works only with Software Instruments, so you will need to select a Software Instrument track.

1 Select the Grand Piano track.

   The instrument name changes at the top of the onscreen keyboard to match the selected Software Instrument track.

2 Click any of the keys with your mouse to trigger the sampled Grand Piano notes.

   The keys turn blue as you select them.

   There are only 12 different musical notes (white and black keys on the keyboard) before the same note repeats either higher or lower. If you move 12 notes to the right, you will be moving an octave higher. If you move 12 notes to the left, you will be moving an octave lower.

3 Click the small arrow at the left of the keyboard to move an octave lower.

4 Click several keys on the keyboard to hear the change in octave.

5   Drag your pointer across several keys to play them one after another.

6   Select the Angelic Organ track to switch to a different Software Instrument.

7   Click several notes to trigger the Angelic Organ synthesized notes.

8   Click and hold one note.

The note will keep playing (sustain) until you release the mouse.

9   Release the mouse to stop the note.

10 Select the Chime and Timpani track.

The onscreen keyboard becomes disabled because the Chime and Timpani track is a Real Instrument track instead of a Software Instrument track.

Remember, the onscreen keyboard works only for Software Instrument tracks. Real Instrument tracks (blue and purple) are recorded instrument tracks.

11 Select the Jazz Kit track to trigger the drum samples.

12 Play several notes using the drum samples.

Each white or black key represents a different sampled drum or percussion instrument. The drum samples are packaged with additional percussion instruments that usually accompany a drum kit.

MIDI drum and percussion samples are assigned to the same notes, so the cymbals, bass drum, kick, snare, whistle, and even cowbell sounds are always the same key on any MIDI keyboard.

NOTE ▶ If you're not familiar with the MIDI drum and percussion mapping (which key plays which percussion instrument), there are many resources on the Internet that supply more specifics.

Exploring Additional Onscreen Keyboard Features

You've had a chance to test out the onscreen keyboard's basic click-and-play functionality. However, it also comes with other, less obvious but very cool features. Did you know that you can also change the size of the keys, quickly change the range of notes that the keys play, and control the velocity (loudness) of the note events? Really. All that in a little keyboard window.

1 Drag the lower-right corner of the onscreen keyboard (resize control) downward to increase the size of the keys. You can choose either the larger (middle) key size, or the full (largest) size.

Original key size

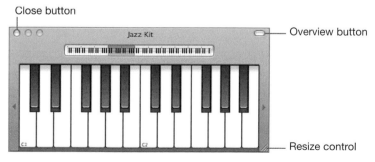

Larger key size

Full key size

By default, the onscreen keyboard displays four octaves of keys at the original (smallest) key size. You can resize the keyboard to display up to 10 and a half octaves.

2 Drag the resize control toward the right to extend the length of the keyboard.

3 Click the Overview button to show the overview (if it is not already showing).

The overview looks like a miniature keyboard, illustrating a global view of all the keys from the lowest to the highest notes. The blue region illustrates the range of keys currently selected on your keyboard. You can drag the blue region toward the right or left to quickly change the range of notes the keys play.

4 Drag the blue region of the overview toward the right or left to change the range of notes on the keyboard.

5 Drag the blue region of the overview to the middle to select the middle range.

OK, so you know how to resize the keys and change the range of notes. There is something else to know about the keyboard: The keys are sensitive to the touch so that you can modify the velocity (loudness) of a MIDI note event as it is played. In the real world, keyboard sensitivity is gauged by how hard you depress a key as you play it. With the GarageBand onscreen keyboard, you play the keys by clicking the mouse, and the computer can't tell how hard you click. Instead, the velocity is determined by *where* you click on the note.

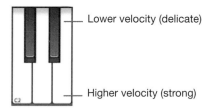

So, let's experiment with the velocity of the notes as you click the keys.

1 Click one of the onscreen keyboard's keys on the bottom (highest velocity) portion of the key.

A percussion instrument plays in response to selecting the key.

2 Click the same key on the top (lowest velocity).

The percussion instrument plays at a much lower volume.

If you start at the top and continue clicking toward the bottom of the key, you can clearly hear the difference in velocity. The changes are most prominent toward the upper half of each key. The larger keys' size makes it easier to select the desired note and gives you a greater range of velocity as you play (click) the notes with the mouse.

TIP If you're not sure how loudly to play a note, it works well to just record everything at the highest velocity. You can always change the velocity of the notes in the editor later.

Project Tasks

Now that you've adjusted the keyboard, take a moment to familiarize yourself with the various percussion samples. Click each of the onscreen keyboard keys to hear the different drum and percussion sounds.

You can change octaves by either clicking the right and left arrows on either side of the onscreen keyboard, or by using the keyboard overview. When the octaves get too high or too low, you will no longer hear percussion samples. That's because MIDI samples are only assigned to keys within a certain range of the keyboard.

Your overall goal is to eventually record a new wind chime sound, so while you're experimenting try to locate the key that triggers the wind chime sound. (Hint: It's somewhere in the upper middle range of keys.)

Adding a New Software Instrument Track

To record the new wind chime part, you'll need to create a new Software Instrument track in the Timeline.

There are three ways to add a new Software Instrument track:

▶   Choose Track > New Track.

▶   Press Option-Cmd-N.

▶   Click the Add Track button.

For this exercise, you'll use the Add Track button.

1   Click the Add Track button. (It looks like a plus sign [+].)

The New Track dialog appears.

The New Track dialog lets you choose either a Real Instrument track or a Software Instrument track. The default setting is a Grand Piano Software Instrument track.

2 Select Software Instrument, if it is not already selected, and click Create.

A new Grand Piano Software Instrument track appears at the bottom of the Timeline, and the Track Info pane opens so you can assign a new instrument to the track.

Since your goal is to record a wind chime sound, the drum kits would be a good place to start.

3   In the Track Info pane, select Drum Kits from the list of Software Instruments.

A list of different drum kits appears in the column on the right.

NOTE ► If you have installed any of the Jam Pack expansions with additional loops and instruments, your list will be more extensive than the one shown below.

4   Select Jazz Kit from the list.

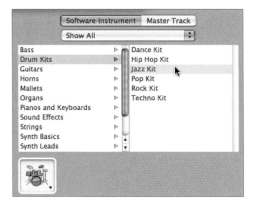

5   Press Cmd-I to close the Track Info pane.

The onscreen keyboard name changes to Jazz Kit, and the new track at the bottom of the Timeline changes to Jazz Kit.

6   Click the octave change arrows on the onscreen keyboard, or change the range in the keyboard overview until you see the key labeled C5.

7   Click the C5 key to play the wind chime sample on the keyboard.

C5 is the note that triggers the wind chime sound.

NOTE ▸ C5 will trigger the wind chime sound on any of the Software Instrument drum kits. The sound will vary slightly between kits, just as it will for any drum sound.

Next, to record the wind chime sound, you need to move the playhead to the position on the Timeline where you want to start recording. This is not always where you want the first recorded note to appear in the Timeline.

8   Move the playhead to the beginning of the 11th measure.

This is where the chime waveform in the Chime and Timpani track starts.

9 Press the left arrow twice to move the playhead to the beginning of the 9th measure in the Beat Ruler. Check your playhead position in the time display.

Why the 9th measure if we actually want the wind chime to start later in the song? Because the final recorded region will start whenever you click the first note. If you back your playhead up a few measures and then click Record, it's like giving yourself time to count in and prepare—one, two, three, go. If you click Record exactly where you need to record the first note, you start on go! The finished recorded region will resize to start with the first played note event, regardless of the playhead position when you started recording.

It's always a good idea to start your recording a measure or two before the point at which you actually need to record a part. That gives you a chance to follow along with the music and get into the groove of the song before you have to perform.

10 Click the C5 note again to practice clicking and holding the wind chime sound.

Practice is always a good idea, even if it is only a wind chime. Also, to avoid confusion, you should also mute the Chime and Timpani track so you won't hear the existing chime while you're recording.

11 In the Chime and Timpani track, click the Mute button.

The regions within the muted track turn light gray, indicating that they have been muted.

12 Select the Jazz Kit track, if it is not already selected.

NOTE ▶ Before you can actually record, make sure the Record Enable button is on (red). Selecting the track automatically turns on Record Enable. The Record Enable button doesn't start recording, it only enables a track for the possibility of recording. To actually record to a track, you need to click the Record button in the transport controls.

TIP ▶ Move the onscreen keyboard so it is above the track you want to record. This way, you can see the keyboard, the new track, and the time display without having to look away from what you're doing.

Understand the part you're about to record. Your goal is to record a new wind chime sound that starts around the beginning of the 11th measure and stops when the piano part starts again in the 13th measure. Watch the time display for your cue, and when you get to the 11th measure, click the C5 note. Release the note when you get to the beginning of the 13th measure.

The Record button is the red button at the left end of the transport controls.

13 Click the Record button to start recording.

14 Select and hold the C5 note at the beginning of the 11th measure.

15 Release the mouse to stop the note when you reach the beginning of the 13th measure.

16 Press the spacebar to stop recording and playback.

Your finished recording should look something like the following picture:

Don't let the look of the recorded region fool you. The note, albeit only a single bar in the Software Instrument region, includes the entire performance.

Using Undo to Delete a Recording

Fortunately, GarageBand—like most software—has an Undo feature. Undo allows you to move back one step in your project to the way it was before the last thing you did.

In this case, we recorded a part. Undo will reset the project to the way it was before that recording. Not that there is anything wrong with your recording. This is just a good time to show you the Undo feature.

If you undo a recording immediately, before you save the song file, you delete the recording from memory. If you keep a recorded region in the Timeline, it can be saved with your project file data and remains part of the project.

There are two ways to undo the last step:

▶   Press Cmd-Z.

▶   Choose Edit > Undo Recording.

Since you will be using the Undo feature frequently throughout your recording career, Cmd-Z is a good keyboard shortcut to memorize.

1 Press Cmd-Z to undo the last recording.

2 Move your playhead back to the beginning of the 9th measure.

3   Repeat steps 13 through 16 from the previous exercise to rerecord the wind chime part. Make sure the Jazz Kit track is selected before you click the Record button.

4   Listen to the song with your new recording. If you're satisfied with your recording, move on to the next task. If you want to try again, press Cmd-Z to undo and repeat the process to record again.

5   Press Cmd-K, or click the Close button, to close the onscreen keyboard.

Saving Your Song

Now that you have successfully recorded a Software Instrument region, it's a good idea to save the changes you've made to the song.

You can also Save As to save a new version of the song with a different name. Let's try that for this exercise.

To Save As, you can either press Shift-Cmd-S, or choose File > Save As.

1   Choose File > Save As.

A Save As window appears so you can change the song name and location.

2   Change the name to *Alaska Sunrise* (delete the *2-1*) in the Name field.

If you have been working with **1-1 Alaska Sunrise** from Lesson 1, change the name to *Alaska Sunrise* also.

3   Click the blue downward-pointing arrow to the right of the Save As field for an expanded view of the Save As window (if it is not already expanded).

The window extends to show the expanded view. If you were already looking at the expanded view, clicking the upward-pointing arrow takes you back to the minimized view. Click the downward-pointing arrow again to see the full window.

4 Select the My GarageBand Projects folder on your computer's Desktop as the destination for your files.

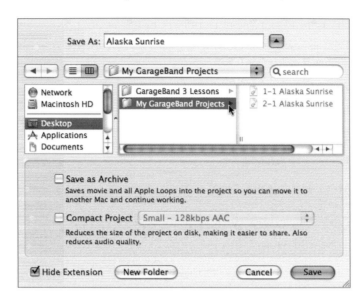

NOTE ▶ Creating the My GarageBand Projects folder was part of the last exercise in Lesson 1. If you didn't complete Lesson 1 and don't have a My GarageBand Projects folder, click the Desktop in the sidebar, then click the New Folder button at the bottom of the Save As window and create the folder.

GarageBand offers several additional save options. The first save option is to Save as Archive, which saves all of the media for a project into the project, including the movie and all loops, so that you can move it to another Mac and continue working. Saving a file as an archive is only necessary at the end of a project, or if you're moving it. So you can leave this option deselected until needed.

The Compact Project option, new in GarageBand 3, lets you reduce the size of a project to make it easy for sharing. You'll work with this feature in Lesson 10. For now, leave this option deselected as well.

5   Make sure the Hide Extension option is selected. If it isn't, select it now.

Now the .band extension will be hidden from your saved project.

NOTE ▶ The .band extension is useful if you are copying your projects to a computer or server that may not have the application installed. The .band extension makes it easier for the new computer to recognize or maintain the GarageBand file format. However, since you will be using one computer for the lessons in this book, let's leave the Hide Extension option selected to hide the extension on all the files you save as GarageBand projects. (Note that the default setting for GarageBand is to hide the .band extension.) Hiding the extension is not the same as deleting the extension. You never want to delete a file extension from a filename because then applications won't recognize or open the file.

6   Click Save to save the song into the My GarageBand Projects folder.

Creating a Cycle Region

You've finished recording and saving a new wind chime region. Next, you'll need to decide if it is an improvement for the song. If so, you can delete the Chime region that was originally recorded in the Chime and Timpani track. To make the process easier, we'll set up a cycle region in the Timeline.

A *cycle region* is a specific portion of the Timeline that you want to repeat (cycle) over and over. Cycle regions are very useful for tasks such as auditioning, or evaluating parts so you don't have to keep stopping and resetting the playhead every time the song ends.

1   In the transport controls, click the Cycle button.

The Beat Ruler extends to reveal the Cycle Region Ruler.

Cycle region — | GarageBand – Alaska Sunrise | — Cycle Region Ruler

To select a specific part of the Timeline to cycle, click and drag in the Cycle Region Ruler below the Beat Ruler. The cycle region appears as a yellow bar. You can move a cycle region by clicking in the middle of the yellow bar and dragging forward or backward in the Cycle Region Ruler. You can extend or shorten the cycle region by dragging the left or right edge of the yellow bar.

2   Press the spacebar to begin playback of the cycle region.

Notice that only the (yellow) cycle region plays and repeats (cycles).

Now let's create a new cycle region. First, let's zoom in to the Timeline for a clear view of the 9th through the 14th measures and the chime regions. This is the area of the Timeline where you'll create the cycle region.

3   Move the playhead to the beginning of the 9th measure (bar 9).

4   Press Ctrl-right arrow to zoom in until you clearly see the 9th through the 14th measures in the middle of the Beat Ruler.

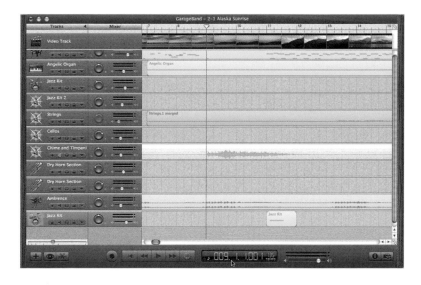

5   Click and hold the cycle area below the Beat Ruler at the beginning of the 9th measure. Don't release the mouse.

This is two measures before the break in the piano part of the song.

6   While holding down the mouse button, drag through the Cycle Region Ruler to the 14th measure. Release the mouse.

A new yellow cycle region appears from the 9th to the 14th measures.

You can only have one cycle region at at time. By creating a new cycle region later in the Timeline, the original cycle region at the beginning of the Timeline disappears.

7   Play the new cycle region.

The playhead will play only the portion of the song marked by the yellow cycle region. The cycle region is played over and over until you stop playback.

8   Stop playback.

9   Click the Mute button on the Jazz Kit track with your recording, and unmute the Chime and Timpani track.

10   Play the cycle region, and listen to the original chime part with the song.

What do you think of the first recording now? It's a nice chime recording, but it feels more like rain than a delicate chime, and I still think it's too intense for the beginning of this song.

11   Unmute the Jazz Kit track, and mute the Chime and Timpani track.

NOTE ▶ If the volume level of the Jazz Kit with your recorded chime is too low, feel free to adjust the track's Volume slider.

12 Repeat the muting and unmuting steps until you have successfully evaluated both chime recordings. Then pause playback. What do you think of the new chime recording?

13 Click the Cycle button to close the cycle region, then turn off all Mute buttons.

Deleting a Region from the Timeline

Now that you have recorded a new wind chime region and evaluated it against the original recording, you no longer need the original Chime region.

There are two ways to delete a selected region from the Timeline:

▶   Press the Delete key.

▶   Choose Edit > Delete.

1   Zoom out until you can see the entire Chime region in the Chime and Timpani track (if it is not already fully in view).

2   In the Chime and Timpani track, click the Chime region to select it.

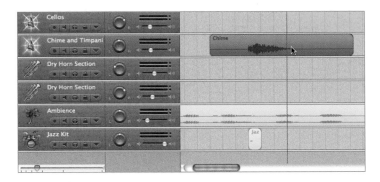

NOTE ▶ When you press Delete, all selected regions will be deleted. Make sure you have selected only the regions you want to delete. If you selected the Chime and Timpani track, all regions within that track become selected as well. Click the empty track area to the left of the Chime region to deselect all regions in the track. Then click only the Chime region to select it.

3   Press Delete on your keyboard to delete the selected region.

4   Press Z or the Home key to move the playhead to the beginning of the song.

5   Play your new and improved version of the finished song.

Nice job on the wind chime recording! It sounds a lot better than the original wind chime I recorded from my synthesizer.

Changing a Track Name and Icon

There's one last thing to do to this song before we move on to another lesson. Let's change the icon for the Jazz Kit track to reflect the instrument you actually recorded in that track. The track icon is the picture of an instrument on the left side of the track header.

To change a track's icon, you first need to open the Track Info pane. An easy way to open the Track Info pane is to double-click a track's header.

1   Double-click the track header for the Jazz Kit track that contains your chime recording.

The Track Info pane for the Jazz Kit track opens.

2   In the Track Info pane, click the track icon to reveal the Track Icon menu.

3   Drag the vertical scroller to locate the Wind Chime icon.

The Wind Chime icon is located in the upper-right corner of the Track Icon menu.

4   Click the Wind Chime icon to select it for the track. Close the Track Info pane.

Now let's change the name of the track itself from Jazz Kit to Wind Chime.

5   Click the Jazz Kit track header to select the entire track, if it is not already selected.

6   On the Jazz Kit track header, click the track name to select it. Hold the pointer over the name momentarily.

When the name appears highlighted, you can type a new name in the name field.

7   Type *Wind Chime* in the track's name field, then press Return.

The track has now been renamed.

8   Press Cmd-I to hide the Track Info pane.

Project Tasks

Now it's your turn to change another track name and several track icons. In this exercise, you'll change the name of the Chime and Timpani track to Timpani. Then change the track icons for the Timpani, Jazz Kit 2, Strings, and Cellos tracks. Feel free to try these changes on your own. If you need assistance, refer to the following steps. Keep in mind a track's icon doesn't have to exactly match the instrument in the track, it's just something to help you visually recognize the instrument type in a track.

1   Click and pause over the Chime and Timpani track name. Then change the track's name to *Timpani*.

2   Double-click the Timpani track header to see it in the Track Info pane, then open the Track Icon menu and select the icon that looks like two padded mallets (drum sticks) used to play timpani drums.

3   In the Timeline, select the Jazz Kit 2 track header and select a new icon from the Track Icon menu.

4   Repeat step 3 for the Strings and Cellos tracks.

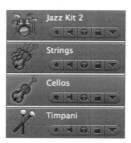

Saving Your Finished Project

You're now finished with the song Alaska Sunrise. Let's save the project one last time.

1   Close the Track Info pane (if it is still open).

2   Press Cmd-S to save the current project.

That's it. You're ready to move on to the next lesson where you'll work extensively with Software Instruments to create the theme song to use for the opening of a show or podcast.

Lesson Review

1. How can you add a new track in the Timeline automatically with a loop from the Loop Browser?

2. Name three of the four ways to show the Track Info pane.

3. What track information is shown in the Track Info pane?

4. How do you change a track's name in the Timeline?

5. Which one of these three is the first step to delete a region from the Timeline: click the track header for the track containing the region, click the empty space within the track, or click the region itself?

6. What is a cycle region, and how do you access it?

7. When you mute a track, what happens to the regions within the track?

8. What steps are necessary to record a Software Instrument region in a new track?

9. Name two features found on the onscreen keyboard.

10. The onscreen keyboard changes its MIDI instrument to match what selection in the Timeline?

Answers

1. Drag the loop from the Loop Browser below the bottom track of the Timeline and release the mouse.

2. Click the Track Info button, press Cmd-I, choose Track > Show Track Info, or double-click a track's header.

3. The type of track, track's instrument category and instrument, icon, and, if it is a Real Instrument track, the track's recording settings. The Track Info pane will also show a Video Preview if the project includes a Video Track.

4. Click and pause over the track's name, then type a new name in the highlighted name field.

5. To delete a region, click and select only that region. Then press Delete. Selecting the track will select all regions within that track.

6. A cycle region plays a selected portion of the Timeline over and over; turn it on by clicking the Cycle button in the transport controls.

7. The regions in a muted track turn gray to indicate they have been silenced.

8. To record a Software Instrument region in a new track, you first create a new track. Then in the Track Info pane, you choose Software Instrument as the track type and choose the track's instrument category and instrument. You also need to make sure the track's Record Enable button is turned on and the playhead is in position. Finally, you click the Record button to begin.

9. You can resize the keyboard, use the overview to quickly change the range of notes, and control the velocity of the played notes depending on where you click.

10. The selected Software Instrument track.

3

Lesson Files	GarageBand 3 Lessons > Lesson 3 > 3-1 Edit Recording
Time	This lesson takes approximately 1 hour to complete.
Goals	Monitor and minimize processor load
	Split, trim, and join a Software Instrument region in the Timeline
	Change a track's instrument
	Work with project tempo
	Start a new song and set its properties
	Use the metronome to record a basic drum part
	Record a multipass drum region using a cycle region

Editing and Recording Software Instruments

You already have a basic understanding of the GarageBand window, and you have some experience working with tracks. Now it's time to dive in and start filling those tracks with custom music that you create with Software Instruments.

In this lesson, you are going to learn editing and recording techniques for building music with Software Instrument regions. You'll also learn how to change the tempo, record your own beats, and split, join, and change instruments for Software Instrument tracks in the Timeline.

Preparing the Project

Let's take a moment to open and save the first project for this lesson before moving on to the main exercises.

1   Locate Lesson_03 in your GarageBand 3 Lessons folder and open the project **3-1 Edit Recording.**

The song **3-1 Edit Recording** opens in the GarageBand window.

2   Choose File > Save As and save the project to your My GarageBand Projects folder on the Desktop.

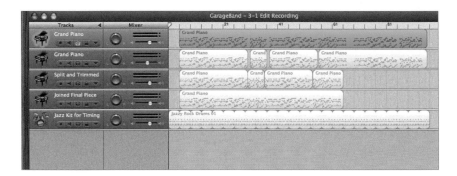

This project shows the complete workflow of a recorded Software Instrument region starting with the original recording in the top track. The Joined Final Piece track shows the finished edited version of the recording. You'll work on editing this project shortly. But first, this is a good time to learn how to monitor the processor with the playhead because this project may be demanding on your computer.

Monitoring the Processor with the Playhead

Did you know that the playhead changes color to indicate the level of demand on your computer's processor? The playhead turns from white to yellow to orange to red to indicate how processor-intensive the song is. White indicates the lowest processor load, red the highest.

When the playhead turns dark orange to red, you are pushing the maximum load on the computer processor, and you could be overloading it. When the processor overloads, playback will be interrupted by a dialog warning that you are using too many tracks, effects, and notes.

Software Instrument tracks and regions are more demanding on the processor than Real Instrument regions, especially if they contain a lot of notes played simultaneously.

To see how the playhead helps you gauge the load on your processor, let's play the project **3-1 Edit Recording** in the Timeline.

1   Press the Home key to move the playhead to the beginning of the project, if it is not there already.

    Notice that only the upper Grand Piano track is active. The track has been *soloed*; in other words, the Solo button in the track header is on.

    Soloing a track means that the sound of that track will be isolated, and all of the other unsoloed tracks will be mute.

2   Play the first half of the project.

3   Watch the playhead change colors when you get to a part of the song with more notes played simultaneously.

The number of Software Instrument notes that are played simultaneously include notes within the same region, and notes in other Software Instrument regions on different tracks that play at the same time.

You will likely see the playhead change color several times as the project plays, depending on the speed of your computer processor and available RAM. If you don't see any color change at all, smile because you are working with a really fast computer.

NOTE ▶ If you see an alert dialog that you can't play the project because of high demands on the processor, click the Lock button on the top track to lock the track. Then play the project. The locked track will be rendered first before playing, which should free up some of the processor demands. If you still can't play the project after locking and rendering the top track, see "Strategies for Minimizing Processor Load" (Bonus Exercises > **Minimizing_Processor_Load.pdf**) on the accompanying DVD for more options.

Now you know how to identify changes in the processor load by the color of the playhead.

Working with a Software Instrument Recording in the Timeline

When you played the first part of the project in the previous exercise, you probably noticed the pauses between certain parts of the song. These pauses were added intentionally during the recording process. Even if I thought I could record a song straight through, I'd still leave pauses between sections to give myself more options later.

For example, if I make a mistake, it's easier to rerecord that section than to start over. Also, I may not know exactly how I want to arrange the song with other instrumentation. Maybe I'll leave a pause at a particular point in the song for a cymbal swell, strings, or some other instrument highlight. Maybe I won't want a pause at all. The good thing about pauses is that they are easy to remove if I decide not to use them. Keep in mind, there's nothing wrong with recording a long piece in one take. However, you may find that with some songs it's easier in the long run to give yourself more options.

When you're recording long takes, such as the one in this project, consider creating edit-friendly moments within the take by inserting a brief pause and releasing the sustain pedal if you're using one. This will produce a clean break between notes for editing. (Obviously you wouldn't do this in a live performance.) Note that this technique works not just for piano but for all the other instruments as well, including vocals, and it is not limited to Software Instrument recordings.

Let's work with this edit-friendly Software Instrument piano recording in the top track. The first pause is at the 30th measure, so you'll move the playhead a few measures before that to hear the pause in context. One of the easiest ways to get to a specific measure is to use the time display.

1   Press Z or Return to move the playhead to the beginning of the Timeline.

2   Click and hold the measures portion of the time display, then drag the mouse upward until the display shows the 25th measure (025).

The playhead is now at the beginning of the 25th measure.

3   Play the project from the 25th measure through the first pause.

Any thoughts on the pause? I think it feels more like a big pause or hesitation than a light break in the song. I say we get rid of it by splitting the region and deleting the pause.

NOTE ▶ This project is part of a song called *A Perfect Day*, about a day with my family and dog at a park with no watches, phones, pagers, deadlines, or interruptions. This was a few years ago when I lived in Los Angeles and I was juggling several major projects at once. At times like that, you can really appreciate a day off to recharge the ol' creative batteries.

Splitting a Region

Splitting a region means that you physically slice the region at the playhead position, creating two regions, one on either side of the split. To split a region within a track, first select the region, then place the playhead at the point where you want to divide the regions, then press Cmd-T or choose Edit > Split.

The trick in splitting a track is finding the right spot to create the split.

1   Select the Grand Piano region in the top track of the Timeline, if it is not already selected. Make sure the region itself is selected and not just the track header.

2   Press the left arrow key until the playhead is at the beginning of the 30th measure, which is also the beginning of the pause.

3   Press Ctrl-right arrow several times to zoom in for a closer look at the selected region in the Timeline.

NOTE ▶ The Zoom command zooms in to or out from the playhead position in the Timeline.

4   Press Cmd-T, or choose Edit > Split, to split the selected region at the playhead position.

The region splits at the playhead position into two separate regions.

5   Press the right arrow once to move to the beginning of the 31st measure, which is also the end of the pause.

6   Press Cmd-T to split the region at the 31st measure.

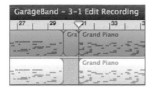

That was easy. Now you can simply select the small region containing the pause and delete it from the project. Right now all of the regions in the top track are selected. Before deleting, you'll need to be sure that only the region you want to delete is selected.

7   Click the empty gray space below the Timeline tracks to deselect all regions in the Timeline.

8   On the top track in the Timeline, select the short region containing the pause.

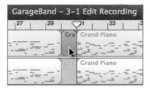

9   Press Delete.

All that's left to do is close the gap where the pause used to be in the track.

10   Drag the second region in the top track to the left until it starts at the beginning of the 30th measure.

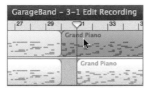

11 Play the song from the 25th measure to around the 33rd measure and listen to the section without the pause.

12 Press Cmd-S to save your progress.

Voila! No pause, and the piano part continues seamlessly without the gap as if it was originally recorded that way. The best part is, if you decide to add a little bit of a pause back in, you can always separate the regions a beat or so as needed.

Project Tasks

It's your turn to find the second pause in the song, split the region, and delete the pause. Feel free to work on your own, or use the following steps. Closing the gap on this edit will be a little trickier because, in this case, the song will sound better if you leave a one-beat gap between regions. When you're ready to close the gap, move the playhead to the 2nd beat of the measure, then drag the edited region to the playhead. Use the time display to move the playhead to the 2nd beat of the measure (036.2.1.001).

1 Play the project from the 33rd measure and listen for the gap.

   The gap is between the 36th and 37th measures.

2 Select the region and move the playhead to the beginning of the 36th measure.

3 Press Cmd-T to split the region.

4 Press the right arrow to move one measure to the right. Then press Cmd-T to split the region again at the 37th measure.

5 Deselect all regions, then select the region containing only the gap.

6 Press Delete.

7 Press Ctrl-right arrow to zoom in to the Timeline until you can see the beat marks between the measures in the Beat Ruler.

8 Change the the time display to show the 2nd beat of the 36th measure, which will move the playhead to that position (036.2.1.001).

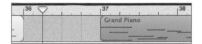

9 Drag the last region to the playhead position so that it begins on the 2nd beat of the 36th measure.

10 Press Cmd-S to save your progress.

11 Play the project from the 33rd to 38th measures.

Nice work! Sounds very natural, yet still includes a slight pause between sections of the song.

Trimming a Region

There are two ways to extend or shorten a Software Instrument region. You can extend it as a new looped segment by dragging the *upper-right* corner to the right in the Timeline, or you can trim it by dragging the *lower-right* corner toward the left. You can only extend or trim a region from the right side. This is to maintain the original integrity of the piece. If you want to remove part of the beginning of a region, you can always split it and delete the segment before the split.

In this exercise, you'll trim the excess notes from the end of the last region. These were backup sections I recorded at the end of the song in case I wanted to use them instead of the first take.

1 Play the song from the 60th measure.

You should hear a clear ending of the song, before it starts to repeat. The repeated notes, starting around the 67th measure, are a second take of the recording.

2   Move the playhead to the beginning of the 65th measure. This is where the region will end after you trim it.

TIP ▶ You can trim or move regions with or without using the playhead. However, using the playhead as a guide while editing in the Timeline is useful to see exactly where you are moving or trimming.

3   Adjust the zoom level in the Timeline if needed for a clear view of the region from the 65th measure to the end of the song.

4   Move the pointer over the lower-right corner of the last region in the top track to see the resize pointer.

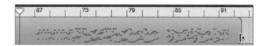

5   Drag the lower-right corner of the region to the left until you reach the playhead position (65th measure).

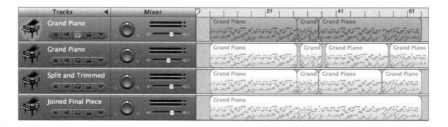

The region has been trimmed so that it now ends at bar 65.

6   Press Ctrl-left arrow to zoom out of the Timeline until you can see the entire project.

The second Grand Piano track in the Timeline shows the recording before all of the gaps were split and deleted. The Split and Trimmed track shows the final timing with all of the gaps removed and adjusted and the excess trimmed off. You'll notice that there is an extra split section at the end, which was created to remove a slight gap between the last two parts of the song. Feel free to experiment in removing the last gap after this lesson.

Joining Regions in the Timeline

Once you've split and positioned all of the regions in a track, you can join the parts together to create one long region. Although joining isn't necessary, it can come in handy sometimes if you want to move the entire finished piano parts around in the track, or copy and paste them, or even modify their timing or velocity.

You can join any recorded regions together, or regions from loops that came from the same original loop. The Joined Final Piece track shows all of the separated regions joined into one finished region.

To join regions, you first select them, then press Cmd-J or choose Edit > Join. Let's try it.

1   Click the top track's header to select all three regions in the track.

2   Press Cmd-J or choose Edit > Join.

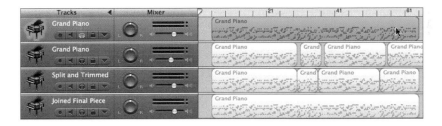

The separate regions become one joined region.

Now you know how to split, delete, move, and join regions to edit a Software Instrument recording in the Timeline.

Changing a Track's Instrument

I originally composed this piece on my baby grand piano, then recorded the piano part into GarageBand using a MIDI keyboard and the Grand Piano Software Instrument. However, in the back of my mind I was always torn between recording it as a piano or as an acoustic guitar part. Fortunately, it's a Software Instrument region.

Not only can you edit Software Instrument regions, but you can also change the instrument itself. Imagine recording a music part like this one using a piano sample, then deciding that you would rather have a guitar play that part—or vice versa. No problem. All you have to do is open the Track Info pane and change the instrument for the track. Really!

1   Double-click the top Grand Piano track header.

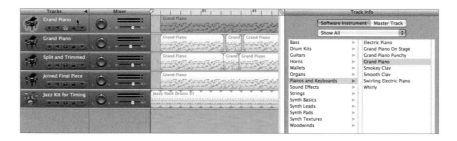

The Track Info pane opens for the selected track.

2   Select Guitars as the Software Instrument, and Steel String Acoustic for the specific guitar.

3 Press Cmd-I to close the Track Info pane.

The first track in the Timeline is now called Steel String Acoustic, and the track icon is a guitar.

> **NOTE** ▶ Notice that the actual Software Instrument region is still called Grand Piano because that was its original name. You can always change the name of a region in the editor. At this time, it's fine to leave the original name as a reminder of how it was recorded.

4 Play the Grand Piano region in the Steel String Acoustic track to hear how it sounds with the guitar as the lead instrument.

5 Press Cmd-S to save your progress.

Fantastic! You'd never know it was originally recorded as a piano part.

Now you see how easy it is to change one Software Instrument to another. This is incredibly useful if you play keyboards but not guitar, for example, or the other way around.

I like the guitar as the lead for part of this song, but I miss the piano for other parts. Later on, when we work on song arrangement in Lesson 4, you'll learn how to break up a lead instrument part into different regions on different tracks. For now, let's stick with one instrument for the lead.

> **TIP** ▶ Changing the instrument of a Software Instrument track is a very handy technique for varying a piece of music, such as the theme music for movie, TV show, or even podcast episode. Theme music is often repetitive, yet by simply changing the instrument, you can change the feel to better fit a particular scene. For example, a song like this with a guitar lead could be used as the opening credits music, and the same song using the piano as a lead could be used later for a more emotional scene.

Changing Project Tempo

Tempo is pacing—the pulse or speed of the song—and it affects how the song sounds and feels. Software Instruments and Apple Loops automatically change tempo to match the project. A project's tempo is always visible on the right side of the time display.

1   Locate the time display at the bottom of the window.

The time display shows the tempo as 100 bpm (beats per minute).

Before changing the project's tempo, let's solo the Jazz Kit for Timing track to hear it along with the Steel String Acoustic track.

2   On the Jazz Kit for Timing track, click the Solo button (looks like headphones).

Now both soloed tracks will be audible, and the unsoloed tracks will remain silent.

3   Play the song from the beginning to hear the Jazzy Rock Drums 01 region along with the guitar (Grand Piano) region.

4   While the song is playing, click the Tempo portion of the time display and drag the Tempo slider upward to the highest position.

Whoa! This tempo is wide awake and in a serious musical hurry.

I couldn't play the song that fast on a piano or guitar if I wanted to. Chances are you won't build a lot of projects at the tempo of 240 bpm, which is the fastest setting.

TIP If a part needs to be played faster than you can physically play it, record the part at a slower tempo, then speed up the project's tempo after you're done recording.

Now let's try the opposite end of the Tempo slider.

5   Continue playing the song, or start again from the beginning if needed.

6   Drag the Tempo slider to the lowest, slowest level of 40 bpm.

How does it sound? Slow? Relaxed? Comatose? 40 bpm is slow even for a really slow song. It also sounds like someone learning how to play a part one…note…at…a…time.

7   Change the Tempo slider back to 100 bpm and listen to the first measure or two from the beginning.

This is the speed the song was intended to be. Clearly there are many variations in tempo you can choose for your projects. The default tempo for a new song is 120 bpm.

NOTE ▶ The drum part works OK with the guitar, but it was never intended to be part of the song. Chances are I'll never use it in the final song arrangement. I just prefer to record a part with *feeling* to a drum track rather than a basic metronome click track to keep the recording in musical time.

8   Pause playback.

9   Press Cmd-S to save the final changes to the project.

Now that you've had a chance to work with a Software Instrument recording, it's time to record a region of your own.

Starting a New Song

Let's create a new project, which will replace the current project in the window.

There are three ways to open a new song:

▶   Click the New Project button on the GarageBand 3 welcome screen when first opening GarageBand.

▶   Press Cmd-N.

▶   Choose File > New.

1   Choose File > New.

The current project closes, and the GarageBand 3 welcome screen appears.

2   Click the New Music Project button to create a new music project.

3   The New Project window opens.

4   Type *Soft Inst Test* in the Save As field.

NOTE ▶ If the Save As field includes a .band file extension, that is because the last time you performed a Save As on the computer, you had the Hide File Extension box deselected. If you do not see a .band extension, there is no reason to add one. The .band extension is already there; it is just currently hidden from view. You can change the setting to hide, or not hide, the extension the next time you perform a Save As in GarageBand.

5   Click the pop-up menu (below the Save As text field) to browse for a location on your computer to save your song.

The Recent Places pane at the bottom of the menu is a fast and easy way to navigate to recently visited folders on your computer.

6   In the Recent Places pane, choose your My GarageBand Projects folder from the Desktop.

If your My GarageBand Projects folder does not appear in Recent Places, choose the Desktop icon, then choose your folder from the Desktop.

Setting Project Properties

Your next step is to set the properties for the project. The lower part of the New Project window shows the project properties.

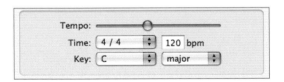

▶ Tempo is the pacing of the song, measured by bpm (beats per minute).

▶ Time is the musical time signature used to count beats within a measure of the song and is displayed as a fraction. A song using 4/4 time means there are four beats per measure. A song using 3/4 time has only three beats per measure.

▶ Key is the musical key for the entire project. Once you set the key, all of the prerecorded loops will automatically match the project key. There are 12 different notes or keys you can set for your project.

The current settings are the default settings for each new GarageBand project.

1   Locate the Tempo slider in the middle of the New Project window.

The current tempo is 120 bpm, as you can see in the bpm field.

2   Click the Time pop-up to see the various time signature choices.

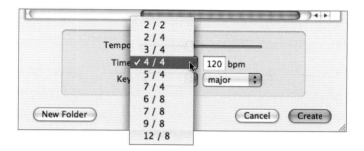

Different types of music use different time signatures. A pop or rock song uses 4/4 time. If you count the beats out loud, they would be one-two-three-four, one-two-three-four. A waltz, on the other hand, uses a slower 3/4 time. The count sounds like one-two-three, one-two-three.

Let's leave the time signature at 4/4 for the new song.

3   Click the Key pop-up menu.

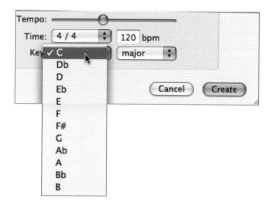

There are 12 different keys from which to choose. The default is a good key to work with, so let's leave it set to C.

> **NOTE ▶** GarageBand also includes a Major/Minor pop-up menu. You'll learn more about major and minor keys in Lesson 7.

4   Click Create to create your new project.

Your new project, titled Soft Inst Test, opens with all of the properties you set in the New Project window.

By default, every new song opens with the Grand Piano Software Instrument track in the Timeline, and the onscreen keyboard showing for that track.

Previewing Drum Loops

In a few minutes, you'll be recording your own Software Instrument drum loops. First, it's a good idea to listen to a few of the prerecorded drum-based Apple Loops for inspiration.

1   Close the onscreen keyboard, if it is open.

2   Press Cmd-L, or click the Loop Browser button, to open the Loop Browser.

The Loop Browser opens to whatever view you used previously. If you've been following along in this book, it will open to the Podcast Sounds view.

3   Click the Musical Button View button (looks like musical notes).

The Loop Browser view changes to show musical keyword buttons.

4   Click the All Drums button.

A list of over 280 drum loops appears in the results list.

	Name ▲	Tempo	Key	Beats	Fav
♪	70s Ballad Drums 01	80	–	8	⊟
♪	80s Pop Beat 07	110	–	8	⊟
♪	80s Pop Beat 08	110	–	16	⊟
♪	80s Pop Beat 09	110	–	16	⊟
♪	80s Pop Beat 10	110	–	16	⊟
♪	Ambient Beat 01	100	–	16	⊟
♪	Classic Rock Beat 01	140	–	16	⊟
♪	Classic Rock Beat 02	140	–	16	⊟

Filter buttons: Single / Ensemble, Clean / Distorted, Acoustic / Electric, Relaxed / Intense, Cheerful / Dark. 283 Items.

NOTE ► The number of drum loops available in the list may be greater than the default number if you have installed additional loops from the Jam Packs or other sources.

Each loop was originally recorded at a specific tempo and key. This information is part of the data that can be used to sort loops and can be seen in different columns in the results list of the Loop Browser.

A loop will always conform to the open project's key and tempo.

5   Click the 80s Pop Beat 07 loop to hear it at 120 bpm.

6   Click the same loop again to stop previewing it.

Locate the Tempo column to the right of the Name column in the Loop Browser results list.

Notice that the native tempo for the 80s Pop Beat 07 loop is 110.

	Name ▲	Tempo	Key	Beats
♪	70s Ballad Drums 01	80	–	8
♪	80s Pop Beat 07	110	–	8
♪	80s Pop Beat 08	110	–	16

Now let's add the loop to the Timeline below the Grand Piano track.

7   Drag the 80s Pop Beat 07 loop to the beginning of the Timeline below the first track. Release the mouse.

A Kits track appears in the Timeline with the 80s Pop Beat 07 region at the beginning of the track.

8   In the Drum Kit track, play the 80s Pop Beat 07 region at 120 bpm.

9   Change the project's tempo to the loop's native tempo of 110 bpm. Play the region again.

The loop sounds good at its native tempo, but it would have worked fine at the original 120 bpm. Let's keep the project at 110 bpm.

10   In the Kits track, select the 80s Pop Beat 07 loop and press Delete to clear the track for your recording.

11   Close the Loop Browser.

In the next series of exercises, you'll record your own drum loops.

Recording a Simple Drum Part

You have listened to the drum and percussion loops used in the **Alaska Sunrise** song from Lessons 1 and 2, and the 80s Pop Beat 07 in the previous exercise. Now it's your turn to create a drum region of your own. This exercise will be challenging, especially if rhythm isn't one of your specialties. Fortunately, GarageBand comes with a built-in metronome to help you.

Turning On the Metronome

A metronome is a device used by musicians to keep time. The metronome clicks at a steady beat based on the tempo of the project. You can use the clicks as a guide for "practicing" instrument parts during playback and for recording them.

To hear the metronome during playback, you need to change a setting in the General Preferences.

1   Choose GarageBand > Preferences, or press Cmd-, (comma).

The Preferences dialog opens. If the General pane is not already visible, click the General button.

2   Locate the Metronome settings near the middle of the window.

There are two settings for the metronome: "During recording" or "During playback and recording."

3   Select the "During playback and recording" setting.

The metronome will now play during playback (as you practice) and while you record.

4   Press Cmd-W, or click the Close button (red X) on the General Preferences window, to close the window.

5   Press Return to move the playhead to the beginning of the Timeline.

6   Locate the time display at the bottom of the GarageBand window.

The time display shows you are at the first beat of the first measure. Remember, this project is in 4/4 time, so there will be four steady beats in each measure. The metronome will count off the beats (4) to the project tempo (110).

7   Press the spacebar to hear the metronome. Watch the beats count 1 through 4 in the time display for each measure.

Notice that the measure counter advances one for every four beats.

The beat changes with each click of the metronome. The first beat of every measure is of a slightly higher pitch.

8   Press the spacebar again to stop playback.

Practicing with the Metronome

Before you record the actual drum part, it's a good idea to practice a few times. For this exercise, you will use the onscreen keyboard to play a drum part and practice using the metronome.

1   Press Cmd-K to open the onscreen keyboard.

   Make sure that the Kits track is selected and that the onscreen keyboard shows that you are working with the Kits instrument.

2   On the left edge of the onscreen keyboard, click the octave change arrow until the first note on the keyboard is C1.

NOTE ▶ If your keyboard starts lower than C1, click the octave change arrow on the right edge of the keyboard until the first note is C1.

To keep this exercise simple, you will only be working with the first five notes (white and black keys), which are C1, C1#, D1, D1#, and E1. Each note triggers a different sampled drum sound from the drum kit.

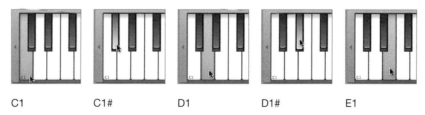

C1   C1#   D1   D1#   E1

3   Click each of the five notes with your pointer to hear what each one sounds like.

   Feel free to drag the lower-right corner of the onscreen keyboard to resize the keys.

4   Select one of the five sounds to practice your timing.

If you can't decide on a sound for the recording, try C1. It's a nice kick drum sample and will work well for this recording.

5   Press the spacebar to start the metronome.

6   Click the drum sound—the note you've selected on the keyboard—on each beat of the metronome.

OK, so that's kind of boring. Let's make it a little more interesting.

7   Play every other beat with the metronome.

8   Play between metronome beats.

9   Press the spacebar to stop playback.

Now that you are warmed up, you can try recording a simple drum beat. Notice that the emphasis is on *simple* at the moment. You'll get to try a more complex beat in a few minutes.

Recording a Single Take

Here is the plan: you are going to record a simple drum part that is four measures long. You will click the same instrument key as before, only this time you'll record it to the Timeline. Watch the time display so you'll know to stop when you have finished recording four measures.

1   Move the playhead to the beginning of the Timeline.

Let the first measure pass (four metronome clicks) before you start playing. That will give you a chance to get in the groove.

Try whatever pattern you want. If you are not sure what to record, try this: hit once on the first beat, skip a beat, then twice on the third beat, and skip the fourth beat. Then repeat the pattern.

2   Make sure the Kits track's Record Enable button is on. By default, the Record Enable button turns on when you select the track.

When you are ready to try, you'll click the Record button or press R to begin recording. Remember, skip the first measure to get your timing. Then begin recording.

3   Press R, or click the Record button, and record your part.

4   When you finish, press the spacebar to stop recording.

Your finished recording will look something like the following picture.

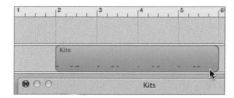

5   If you are unhappy with your recording, press Cmd-Z to undo the recording and try again. Make sure that your finished recording ends at bar 6. If it is longer or shorter than four measures, trim the region from the lower right corner until it ends on bar 6.

6   Press Cmd-S to save your finished recording.

Don't worry if it isn't perfect. The idea of this exercise is to learn how to record a single take in the Timeline, not how to record perfect drums.

Did you notice that although you started your recording at the beginning of the first measure, the recorded region actually begins wherever you played the first note event?

This is a great feature because it means you can click the Record button *before* you need to start recording to get into the groove of the song. The recorded region will begin wherever you record the first event.

Extending Your Recorded Region

One of the best things about recording Software Instruments is that you don't have to record the same part over and over. You only have to get it right once. Let's assume the drum part you recorded is perfect. Now you can loop the region by extending it.

1   Drag the upper-right corner of your recorded region and extend it to the right to repeat four more measures.

The extended region will have a notch in the middle to show where the original region ends and the extension begins.

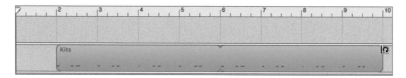

2   Play your looped region to hear how it sounds.

OK, it's still a little boring. But at least you know how to record a single take. The piano parts in the earlier projects were recorded the same way. The only difference is that I used a drum loop to play along with instead of the metronome. Let's go ahead and mute this recording and try another recording.

3   On the Kits track, click the Mute button to silence the track before we move on to the next recording.

You just recorded a drum loop in GarageBand. Now let's move on to creating some more complicated beats.

Multipass Recording

In the last exercise, you just recorded a simple drum part in one take. To create a mixed drum part, you may wish to try multipass recording. With multipass recording, you can record into the same region over and over, adding different sounds with each pass.

Your goal in this exercise is to record a drum region that has different drum sounds. You'll then use that region as a drum loop.

Creating a Recording Cycle Region

The first step in multipass recording is to create a cycle region for the number of measures you wish to record. For this exercise, you will set a cycle region that is two measures in length.

1   In the transport controls, click the Cycle button to show the cycle region.

The cycle region appears beneath the Beat Ruler at the top of the Timeline.

2   Drag the yellow cycle region to the beginning of the 2nd measure.

NOTE ▶ If you don't have a yellow cycle region within the Cycle Region Ruler, click and drag the Cycle Region Ruler to create a region between the 2nd and 4th measures.

Next you'll resize the cycle region so that it ends at bar 4.

3   Drag the right edge of the cycle region to the beginning of the 4th measure.

The cycle region should now start at bar 2 and end at bar 4.

Creating a New Software Instrument Track

Before you record, you'll need to create a new Software Instrument track.

1   Choose Track > New Track to open the New Track window.

2   Select Software Instrument for the type of track, if it is not already selected and click Create.

3   In the Track Info pane, select Drum Kits > Hip Hop Kit from the Software Instrument choices.

4   Press Cmd-I to close the Track Info pane.

A new Hip Hop Kit track appears in the Timeline.

5   Click the first five keys (C1–E1) of the onscreen keyboard to hear the drum samples.

The Hip Hop Kit samples are the same drums for each key you had in the Kits track, but they are now Hip Hop versions so they'll sound a little different.

Recording a Rough Draft

Brace yourself—the first time you try multipass recording will likely be rough. Don't worry—with the Undo command, you can always do it again.

Select one drum sound, perhaps the kick drum (C1) or the snare (E1), and play only that drum part for the first pass. Choose a second drum part for the next pass. Each time you finish recording a drum part, switch to a different sampled drum sound (a different key on the keyboard) to add a new part.

Experiment with the different drum parts to come up with one that you like. If you are having trouble coming up with a pattern, start with the pattern I describe for the kick drum and snare. Keep in mind that your drum pattern will be two measures in length, making it a total of eight beats, four per measure.

Try playing the kick drum (C1) once on the second beat and twice on the fourth beat. Then again in the next measure, record once on the second beat and twice on the fourth beat.

Now try the snare (E1) twice on the first beat, once on the second beat, twice on the third beat, and once on the fourth beat for both measures.

Keep the recording going until you have recorded a pass with all five of the different sounds.

The key (pun intended) to making this work is that you *can't* stop recording. If you stop recording, the multi-take option is over. If you try to record in that region again, you'll erase the previous recording.

One more thing: let's slow things down a bit for this first version. Remember, if you slow down the tempo for a Software Instrument, you can always speed it up again after you record.

1   Change the project tempo to 90 bpm.

90 bpm is a common tempo for Hip Hop music. The metronome will change to match the new project tempo.

TIP ▸ Let the metronome count off a few measures first to get a feel for the tempo before you start recording.

2   Select the Hip Hop Kit track, if it is not already selected, and make sure the Record Enable button for that track is on.

3   Press R, or click the Record button, to start the multipass recording.

4   Record each instrument one at a time through each pass.

5   When you finish, press the spacebar to stop recording.

NOTE ▸ If you hold a note at the end of the loop region, it may cause the finished loop to extend longer than two measures. If your loop is longer than two measures, use the split feature to trim the front of the loop, or drag the lower-right corner to resize the end of the loop.

6   Change the project tempo to 120 to hear your recorded loop at a faster tempo.

So, how did it go? Recording drum loops takes a lot of practice and patience. Fortunately, you can always press Cmd-Z to undo the recording and start over.

If you had a rough time creating your own drum tracks, there's good news. GarageBand includes hundreds of prerecorded drum loops from which to choose. For those of you who like creating your own beats, you now have the tools to do it.

Project Tasks

It's time to practice your skills by recording another multipass drum loop at full tempo. If you feel like creating a really fat beat, feel free to try some of the other drum sounds (keys) within the Hip Hop Kit.

1   Create a new Software Instrument track and select Drum Kit > Hip Hop Kit for the instrument.

2   Select the new track and make sure the Record Enable button is on.

3   Mute the previously recorded tracks.

4   Turn the cycle region on and record a new drum loop using multiple drum sounds.

5   Extend your finished region so that it loops three times in the Timeline.

Deleting a Track and Saving Your Project

Now that you've created three different drum loops, let's save your work so you can come back and listen to it another time for pleasure—or torture, depending on the quality of your recordings. Also, this is a good time to delete the Grand Piano track, since it was never used in this project. To delete a track, you select the track and press Cmd-Delete, or choose Track > Delete Track.

1   Select the Grand Piano track, then press Cmd-Delete.

The Grand Piano track no longer exists at the top of the Timeline.

2   Unmute the first two tracks to turn them back on.

3   Click the Cycle button to turn off the cycle region in the Timeline.

4   Close the onscreen keyboard.

5   Press Cmd-S to save the project into the My GarageBand Projects folder on the Desktop.

Lesson Review

1. How do you split a region in the Timeline?

2. What types of regions can be joined in the Timeline?

3. Which corner do you drag on a region to trim (resize)?

4. Which corner do you drag to extend a region as a loop segment?

5. Which project properties can you set when creating a new song?

6. What are the default time signature, project key, and tempo?

7. How can you change a project's tempo in the time display?

8. What determines the length of a single-take Software Instrument recording?

9. What determines the length of a multipass Software Instrument recording?

10. Where do you change the GarageBand settings so the metronome plays during both recording and playback?

Answers

1. Select the region, move the playhead to the position where you'd like to split, and press Cmd-T, or choose Edit > Split.

2. You can join any recorded regions together, or join loop regions that come from the same original loop.

3. Drag the lower-right corner to trim (resize) a region.

4. Drag the upper-right corner to extend a region as a loop segment.

5. Tempo, Time (time signature), and Key.

6. The default time signature is 4/4 (four beats per measure), project key is C, and tempo is 120.

7. You can change a project tempo by clicking the Tempo portion of the time display and adjusting the Tempo slider.

8. A single-take Software Instrument recording starts when the first note event is pressed during recording, and ends when you stop recording.

9. Multipass recordings use a cycle region to determine the length of the recording.

10. You can change the metronome settings in the GarageBand General Preferences.

4

Lesson Files	GarageBand 3 Lessons > Lesson_04 > 4-1 SpaceBass start; 4-4 SpaceBass final
Time	This lesson takes approximately 1 hour to complete.
Goals	Differentiate between rhythm and melody tracks
	Build a rhythm track with Software Instruments
	Save a song in stages
	Build a melody track with Software Instruments
	Connect a MIDI or USB keyboard to the computer
	Record a Software Instrument keyboard part
	Work with Musical Typing
	Edit a note in a Software Instrument region
	Double tracks, and offset, duplicate, and transpose regions
	View actual time in the time display

Arranging a Song with Software Instruments

Now that you know the basics of working with Software Instruments, it's time to move on to more advanced recording and arranging techniques. In this lesson, you'll record an additional Software Instrument track using the Musical Typing feature and edit it in the editor. Along the way, you'll learn some new keyboard shortcuts, recording tricks, and advanced music arrangement techniques to double parts, mix instruments, offset regions, transpose key, and *fatten* the melody tracks as you build the intro score for a podcast or radio show from the rhythm tracks up.

Previewing the Finished Song

Let's take a sneak preview of the finished song, so that you'll have an idea what you're going to build. I've called this song **SpaceBass,** because the inspiration came from the combination of several strong bass loops with a spacey keyboard part. This is the sort of thing I would score for the intro music to a cool podcast show.

1 Choose File > Open to open an existing song file.

2 Select GarageBand 3 Lessons > Lesson_04 > **4-4 SpaceBass final**.

3 Double-click **4-4 SpaceBass final** to open the song.

The song opens in the GarageBand window.

4 Press the Home key to move the playhead to the beginning of the song.

Before you play the song, it's a good idea to turn off the metronome if it is on.

You've successfully worked with the metronome turned on while recording and have probably noticed that it is still on during playback. That might get a little annoying after a while. You have two choices to turn off the metronome during playback. You could go back to the General Preferences window and change the metronome settings to "During recording" only. Or you can go to the Control menu and toggle off the metronome. The shortcut to toggle the metronome on and off is Cmd-U.

5   Choose Control > Metronome, or press Cmd-U, to turn off the metronome if it is turned on.

6   Play the project.

There you have it. Let's get started.

Preparing the Project

The next series of exercises will walk you through the steps of building a song using Software Instruments. Most of the song will be arranged using prerecorded Apple Loops that are Software Instruments. You'll also add a recording of your own using the Musical Typing feature. Once the parts are in place, you will apply some advanced arranging techniques to edit, transpose, and finish the piece.

First, you need to open the starting version of the song. This version contains three bass loops that will act as the foundation to the entire song.

1   Open the project **4-1 SpaceBass start** from the Lesson_04 folder.

2   Choose File > Save As and save the project as *SpaceBass* into your My GarageBand Projects folder.

3   Play the project to hear the combined bass loops.

Sounds interesting. Not much of a song yet, but these bass parts inspired the entire piece. There's just one thing to take care of before moving on with building the song. The metronome! As soon as you opened another song, the metronome was right back on, clicking away during playback. Rather than turn it off every time you open a project, it's easier to just change the preferences. The metronome may not be playing on your system depending on your most recent metronome settings.

4   Choose GarageBand > Preferences.

The General Preferences window opens.

5   Select "During recording" from the Metronome controls.

6   Close the General Preferences window.

Understanding Melody and Rhythm

What's the difference between melody and rhythm?

Melody is the plot, or story, of a song. It's the memorable part that you hum to yourself when you think of the song, and it's the part other people will remember as well. If you think of the theme song to your favorite movie, you are thinking of the melody. Melody is usually played by the lead instrument, or lead vocal, just as the lead storyline of a movie is played by the lead characters.

In a melody-driven song, you write the melody first, then add other tracks that work well with the melody. Songs with lyrics usually use the vocals as the melody line. Most of today's popular music is melody-driven.

The songs "Alaska Sunrise" and "A Perfect Day," which you worked on previously, were melody-based. I wrote and recorded the piano melody first, then added the other instrument parts.

Rhythm is the pulse or heartbeat of the song. Rhythm can be played by one instrument or many different instruments. Rhythm is felt as much as it is heard, and it dictates the pacing of the different instrument parts. Rhythm is usually set by the drums and followed by the other rhythm instruments, such as bass, rhythm guitar, and keyboards. The rhythm of a song may be faster or slower depending on the song's tempo. A slow tempo song might be a ballad with a slow and easy rhythm. A fast tempo song might be a rock song with a driving beat.

In a rhythm-driven song, you create the beats, percussion, or rhythm parts first, then add other instrument parts that fit well with the rhythm. Rhythm-driven songs are often used to score movie trailers (previews), and fast-paced promos or commercials. Rap music is often rhythm-based, but it depends on the song.

The song **SpaceBass**, which you are building for this lesson, is rhythm-driven. For this piece, I built the rhythm tracks first, and then came up with a melody to fit.

Building Rhythm Tracks

With the **SpaceBass** song, it will be much easier to add the melody if we already have the rhythm tracks in place.

Rhythm tracks can consist of a bass line, a steady rhythm guitar, or drums—whatever the song uses to convey the rhythm. For this song, the bass and drums will carry the rhythm.

Instead of recording the bass and drum parts, you'll use some prerecorded Apple Loops.

Arranging Loops in the Timeline

Placing and adding different instrumental parts to build a song is also referred to as *arranging* a song. The bass loops for this project are already in the Timeline. The trick now is to arrange them in a way that creates an interesting rhythm pattern for the song. Using the same loop or loops over might start off sounding cool, but eventually it becomes monotonous and sounds very repetitive. Your goal in this section is to spread the loops around a bit in the Timeline to give each one a chance to be heard, and create natural changes in the song's overall rhythm pattern.

Let's start by spreading them out one after another in the Timeline.

1   Drag the Synthbass Sequence 01 region on the middle Syn Bass track to the right so that it starts on the 5th measure.

2   Drag the Synthbass region on the lowest track to the 9th measure.

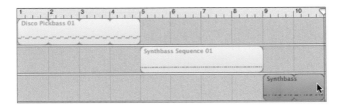

Now each bass part takes a turn one at a time.

3   Play the project to hear the bass parts.

What do you think? Each one by itself is interesting, but they seem to go on a bit long. Also, there is no feel of a song or rhythm track coming from this particular arrangement. Often, combining parts will not only provide much needed change, but also create a different feel altogether.

4   Drag the Synthbass Sequence 01 region in the middle track to the left until
it starts at the 3rd measure.

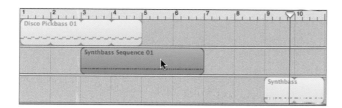

5   Drag the Synthbass region on the lowest track to the 6th measure so it
overlaps the bass part in the middle track.

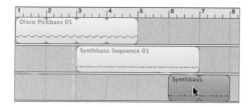

6   Play the new bass arrangement to hear how it sounds.

Much more interesting, plus you can use the changes between parts to
drive changes in the other musical parts you'll add later.

7   Press Cmd-S to save your progress.

Duplicating Regions in the Timeline

The bass parts are working, they're just a little short. Since most songs are
repetitive, it would be great if you could just duplicate the entire section so it
will repeat.

To duplicate selected regions in the Timeline, you can simply hold the Option key while dragging the regions. This method is also referred to as Option-dragging to duplicate When using this method, it is very important to click the selected regions first before you press the Option key.

1   Choose Edit > Select All, or press Cmd-A, to select all of the regions in the Timeline.

2   Press and hold Option, click any of the selected regions, and drag toward the right.

3   Release the duplicate regions so that the upper region begins at the 7th measure.

Done. You could also use copy and paste to duplicate parts, but Option-dragging is the most efficient technique in this case.

Auditioning Software Instrument Drum Loops

Many songs start with the drum parts to build the song's rhythm tracks, then add bass and other instruments. Let's look for a few drum parts that work well with the rhythm you've already established in the bass tracks.

1   Open the Loop Browser.

2   Click the All Drums button to narrow the search results to drums only.

3   Drag the vertical scroller to the right of the results to scroll through the various choices.

4   Locate the far-left column in the search results.

There are two symbols in this column: a green note, which indicates a Software Instrument loop, or a blue waveform, which indicates a Real Instrument loop.

You can sort the search results by clicking the top of any of the different columns. Usually you sort by name and look at the results in alphabetical order. For this exercise, you want to look at only Software Instrument loops, so let's click the top of the Loop Type (left) column.

5   Click the top of the Loop Type column to sort the loops by type.

The loops are now sorted by type. If the list shows blue Real Instrument loops at the top of the list, click the Loop Type column head again to reverse the sort so that the Software Instruments show at the top of the results list.

NOTE ▶ If you want to reverse the sort order of any column, just click the column header.

6   Scroll to locate the Software Instrument loops called Simple Funk Drums 01 and Simple Funk Drums 02.

7   Click the Simple Funk Drums 01 loop to preview it.

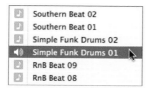

It is definitely simple, and in this case simple is good. Remember, you're looking for a subtle drum part that works well with the bass loops rather than distracts from them. There's only one way to find out. You can audition it with the bass tracks.

8   Press Z or Return to move the playhead to the beginning of the Timeline, then press the spacebar to begin playback.

9   Click the Simple Funk Drums 01 loop to hear it with the bass tracks.

> **NOTE ▶** Make sure that you select the Simple Funk Drums 01 loop and not the Simple Funk Drums 02 loop. They may be in reverse numeric order because you are sorting by loop type rather than alphanumerically.

When you audition loops, they will start playing at the next full measure. The loops you audition will always match the project's tempo.

It starts out cool, and it is. However, if you listen to that same beat over and over, it's going to lose its coolness real fast. The song needs an additional drum part.

10   Repeat the audition process from the beginning of the project, this time auditioning the Simple Funk Drums 02 loop. When you're finished, pause playback.

Both drum loops work with the bass tracks. Now it's just a matter of arranging them in the Timeline.

> **TIP ▶** Apple Loops often come in numeric groups with the same name and different numbers to indicate variations. Generally, these loops with matching names will sound good together if used in the same song.

Building the Drum Track

Now that you've selected two drum loops to use in the project, you need to add them to the Timeline. Let's start with the Simple Funk Drums 01 loop.

1 Drag the Simple Funk Drums 01 loop from the browser to the beginning of the Timeline below the lowest Syn Bass track.

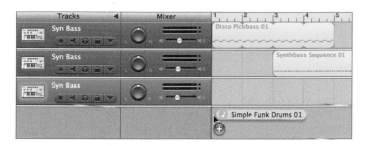

A new Kits track appears in the Timeline with the Simple Funk Drums 01 region inside.

Instead of having the song start with the drums in the first measure, let's give the bass parts a chance to establish the rhythm before bringing in the drums.

2 In the Kits track, drag the drum region to the right so it starts at the 4th measure.

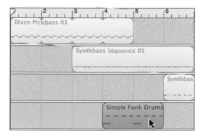

3 Play the beginning of the project to hear the drums come in at the 4th measure.

Good stuff! It really adds a nice grooving accent to the bass without taking away from it. All you need to do now is extend the drum loop so that it repeats three times.

4   Drag the upper-right corner of the Simple Funk Drums 01 region to
extend it until it loops three times.

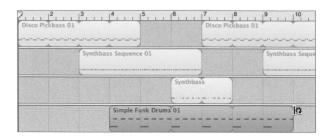

The first drum part is in place, and now you can add the second drum
part to finish out the end of the song.

5   Drag the Simple Funk Drums 02 loop from the browser to the Kits track so
that it starts at the 10th measure. This is also where the first drum part ends.

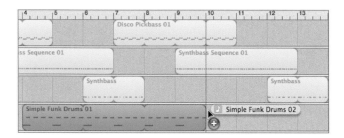

When you add loops to the Timeline, a dark gray vertical line appears as a
position indicator from the Beat Ruler to the bottom of the Timeline.

6   Extend the new drum region so that it repeats once and ends at bar 14.

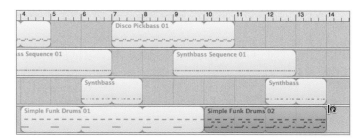

7   Listen to the bass and drum parts together, then save your progress.

> **NOTE** ▸ If you use only one drum loop for an entire song, no matter how good the loop is, eventually it becomes nothing more than a complex metronome. Try to mix it up and add some variety to your drum tracks to keep them from sounding so "loopy."

You're off to a good start. It's time to dive into the Loop Browser and find a few more Software Instrument loops that will complement your **Space-Bass** song.

Backing Up a Song File in Stages

It's a good idea to save your song with different names as you build it. That way, you can go back to an earlier stage of the song to change the outcome or to create different versions. Up to this point, you have only created the rhythm tracks for this song. Let's save the project and identify it as rhythm tracks only, so later you can go back to the song at this level and arrange or record different parts to the beats.

1   Choose File > Save As, or press Shift-Cmd-S, to open the Save As dialog.

2   Change the name to *SpaceBassRhythm* and save it to the My GarageBand Projects folder.

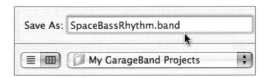

Now that the Rhythm version of the song is saved, let's create another version that includes the melody tracks. You'll rename and save it now so that you can just save as you go while following the next series of exercises.

3 Choose File > Save As or press Shift-Cmd-S to open the Save As dialog.

4 Change the name to *SpaceBassMelody* and save it to the My GarageBand Projects folder.

Building the Melody Tracks

For the melody tracks, you'll use many of the skills you've already learned in this lesson to add some keys and synthesizer parts. You could audition loops to find parts that work. For these exercises, you'll find and add specific Software Instrument loops to the project.

1 Open the Loop Browser, if it is not already open.

2 In the upper-left corner of the Loop Browser, click the Reset button to clear the results list, and deselect all of the keyword buttons.

Since the song is called SpaceBass, let's narrow the search of all 1,000+ loops to sounds with *Space* in the title.

3 Type *space* in the search field, then press Return.

Eight items with *Space* in the name appear in the results list. Remember, you're focusing on the Software Instruments in this lesson, so scroll down to see only the four Spacey Electric Piano loops.

4 Listen to each of the four Spacey Electric Piano loops.

As you play each loop, try to focus on the melody of the loop. The melody is the memorable part that you could hum, after you stop playing the loop.

They are all pretty cool and would work together to make a nice spacey song. However, for this project you need just one, specifically the first one (Spacey Electronic Piano 01).

5   Drag the Spacey Electric Piano 01 loop from the Loop Browser to the space below the Kits track and release it at the beginning of the 2nd measure.

Next you'll duplicate the new region so that it repeats again at the 7th and 12th measures.

6   Option-drag the Spacey Electric Piano 01 region, and move the duplicate to the beginning of the 7th measure.

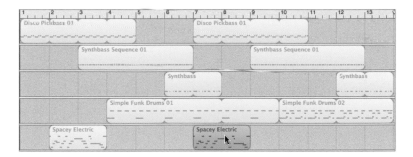

7   Option-drag the Spacey Electric Piano 01 region at the 7th measure, and move the duplicate to the beginning of the 12th measure.

The loops are in place; all you need to do is extend the first two so that they repeat one full loop segment.

8 Drag the upper-right corner of the first electric piano region and extend it one full segment so it ends at bar 6.

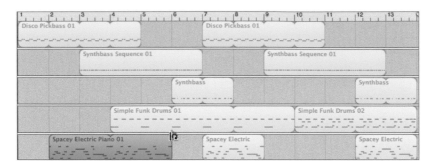

9 Extend the second electric piano region so it ends at bar 11.

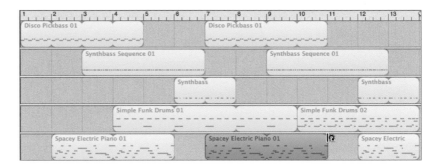

10 Press Cmd-S to save your progress.

Now you'll just need to find a good loop to fill the space between the electric piano regions. Of course, you won't literally place the new loop on the same track as the electric piano parts. But musically, it will fill in the spaces.

11 In the Loop Browser, click the Reset button to reset the search parameters.

Project Tasks

It's your turn to find, add, resize and duplicate the last loop to fill the gaps between the electric piano parts. The loop you're searching for is called Funky Pop Synth 01. Feel free to search for it on your own in the Loop Browser. One strategy might be to select the Synths keyword button to narrow the search, then type *funky* in the search field.

Once you've located the loop, add it to the Timeline below the Synths track. Place the loop so it starts at the beginning of the 6th measure (bar 6). Resize the loop by dragging the lower-right corner until it is only one measure in length. Option-drag the new loop and place the duplicate between the 11th and 12th measures. When you are finished, listen to the project, and save your progress.

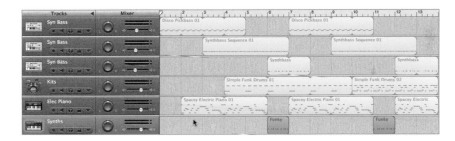

Nice work! The melody version is nearly finished. Of course, it could really use a low synth pad to add some spacey dimension to the overall project. You could search for a loop that might fit, or just record your own part.

Recording a New Software Instrument Part

Now that the rhythm and melody tracks are in place, it's time to start recording an additional part. Another terrific feature about Software Instruments in GarageBand is that you can edit them once they have been recorded.

In this next exercise, you'll record a synth part for the song. The part is very simple to play, so let's try the Musical Typing feature to record the part.

> **NOTE ▶** If you wish to use a different musical keyboard (such as the GarageBand onscreen keyboard) for this recording, you're welcome to do so.

Connecting a MIDI Instrument to the Computer

If you prefer to use an external music keyboard, guitar, or other MIDI controller instead of Musical Typing for this exercise, you can connect a MIDI-compatible controller through a USB connection or MIDI interface.

A USB MIDI keyboard or other MIDI controller connects directly to the computer and to the keyboard with a USB cable.

To connect a standard MIDI controller such as a keyboard, you will need a USB-to-MIDI interface. Connect the keyboard to the MIDI interface device using standard MIDI cables. Then connect the interface to your computer using the USB cable. Carefully read the instructions that come with the keyboard and MIDI interface, and be sure to install all of the necessary drivers.

> **MORE INFO ▶** For more information about GarageBand accessories, including MIDI keyboards, USB keyboards, or MIDI interfaces, visit Apple's Web site: www.apple.com/ilife/garageband/accessories.html.

Working with Musical Typing

Musical Typing is a GarageBand alternative for recording Software Instrument tracks. Instead of using the onscreen keyboard or external MIDI musical instrument, you use your computer's keyboard. Let's try it.

First, you'll need to create a new Software Instrument track for the recorded region.

1   Choose Track > New Track, or press Option-Cmd-N.

The New Track window opens.

2   For the type of track, select Software Instrument, then click Create.

3   In the Track Info window, select Synth Pads from the left column as the Software Instrument category.

4   For the specific Synth instrument, select Falling Star.

The new Falling Star track appears in the Timeline.

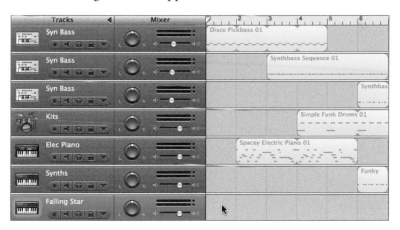

5   Press Cmd-I to close the Track Info pane, then press Cmd-S to save the project with the new track.

Now that the track is in the Timeline, you can test it out with the Musical Typing window.

6   Choose Window > Musical Typing or press Cmd-Shift-K.

The Musical Typing window opens and turns your computer keyboard into a fully functional MIDI keyboard.

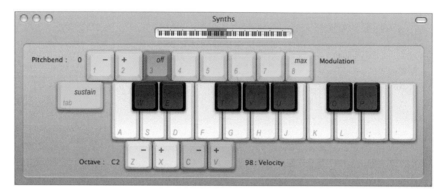

The Musical Typing window illustrates how different keys on your computer keyboard correspond to different musical notes.

NOTE ▶ If you are using an external music keyboard, you don't need to open the Musical Typing window. Whenever I refer to pressing specific keys on the onscreen keyboard, locate the corresponding keys on your external keyboard to play along. Also, if you prefer clicking the mouse to typing, you can click the keys on the Musical Typing window, just as you would the onscreen keyboard to record this part. I'll give instructions for both types of recording.

7   Press different letter keys (A–') on your computer keyboard to hear the corresponding notes.

Whenever you press a key on the computer keyboard, the corresponding key is selected in the Musical Typing window. Because you currently have the Falling Star track selected, you are playing that instrument.

The Musical Typing window includes keys for sustain (Tab) and changing octaves (Z, X), velocity or volume (C, V), pitchbend (1, 2), and modulation (3–8).

8   Press several keys and watch the time display carefully.

A small blue dot flashes near the bpm number (120). That flashing dot is the MIDI status light that indicates that GarageBand is receiving a MIDI signal. This reacts to any MIDI signal, whether it comes from an external MIDI device, your computer keyboard in Musical Typing mode, or the onscreen keyboard.

NOTE ▶ If you have another external MIDI device active when you open the Musical Typing window, you may see a steady blue dot rather than a flashing blue dot until you play notes on the device.

Practicing the Part Before You Record It

Now that the Musical Typing window is active, you have selected the Software Instrument track, and you have a MIDI signal, it's time to practice the part you will be recording.

The part you are about to record uses only three long notes played sequentially. I made this part simple for those of you who are beginners. Feel free to record a more elaborate part after you finish this lesson.

There are a total of 12 notes (black and white keys) in an octave. The keys are: A, A#, B, C, C#, D, D#, E, F, F#, G, and G#. The sharp (#) keys are the black keys. If I ask you to move two white keys to the right, I will say "move two steps to the right." Moving to a black key from the nearest white key would be considered a half a step.

To indicate specific notes, I'll give the computer keyboard key, plus for anyone using the onscreen keyboard or interested in learning musical notation, I'll include the musical note and the octave number. For example, A (C2) would be the A key on the computer keyboard, which plays the musical C note in the second octave. Musical notes run consecutively from A through G, then they repeat. If you move toward the right on the keyboard, you are moving toward a higher octave, and the notes get higher in pitch. If you move toward the left on the keyboard, you are moving toward a lower octave and lower pitch.

If you work with an external keyboard, C1 is usually the first key on the left side of the keyboard, and C2 is one octave higher (12 notes/keys) to the right. The Musical Typing window opens with the C2 note as the first note by default.

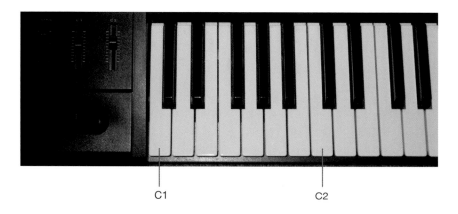

1   Press the A key on your computer keyboard to play the C2 note.

This is the 1st note of the synth pad part you will be recording.

Move three steps (three white keys) to the right to find F (F2).

2   Press F (F2) on your computer keyboard.

This is the second note you'll play in the recording.

Move four steps (four white keys) to the right to find K (C3).

3   Press K (C3) on your computer keyboard.

K (C3) is the third and final note you will play.

You'll notice that the 1st and 3rd notes are the same note, one octave apart.

4   Press each of the notes again in order: A (C2), F (F2), K (C3).

OK, you have the notes down. Now all you need to do is practice pressing and holding them with the song.

The first note starts at the 3rd measure and lasts until the beginning of the 6th measure. The second note starts at the 7th measure and lasts until the 9th measure. The third and final note starts at the 11th measure and lasts until the 13th measure.

NOTE ▶ Normally, pressing the Home, Return, or Z keys will move the playhead to the beginning of the Timeline. However, when the Musical Typing window is open, pressing the Z key will lower the octave of the note you're playing. If you pressed Z, you'll need to press X to raise the octave again before recording or playing along. The Home key will not move the playhead either. You'll need to either press Return or click the Go to Beginning button in the transport controls to move the playhead to the beginning of the project while the Musical Typing window is active.

5   Play the project from the beginning and try playing along all three notes for the corresponding measures. A (C2) from bar 3 to bar 6, F (F2) from bar 7 to bar 9, and K (C3) from bar 11 to bar 13.

So, how did it go? Any thoughts on the part before you record it? My only thought is I'd like the Falling Star notes to be lower for a more ominous bassy sound. That's easy enough—all you need to do is lower the octave. You'll press the same keys, they'll just play the notes C1, F1, and C2 now instead of C2, F2, and C3.

6   Press Z, or click the Z key on the Musical Typing window, to lower the octave to C1 for the first note. If you are using another keyboard, lower the octave accordingly.

7   Play the project once more and practice the part using the new lower octave. A (C1) from bar 3 to bar 6, F (F1) from bar 7 to bar 9, and K (C2) from bar 11 to bar 13.

Recording a Single-Take Synth Part

Let's put your practice to the test and try recording this part into the Timeline. You will use the single-take method to record the Falling Star synth part. Make sure the Cycle button is turned off (so that the cycle region is not showing) before you begin.

The Falling Star part you will record starts at the beginning of the 3rd measure and ends at the beginning of the 13th measure. The Musical Typing window is fairly large. Move it below the track you'll be recording so you'll be able to clearly see the track, the Beat Ruler, and time display at the bottom of the Timeline.

1   Press Return, or click the Go to Beginning button, to move the playhead to the beginning of the Timeline.

2   Make sure that the Falling Star track header is selected and the Record Enable button is on.

3   Click the Record button and try recording a take.

Remember: The keys to type are A-F-K, and you'll record from the 3rd to the 13th measure.

Press the spacebar to stop recording when you finish.

4   Listen to your recording. If it sounds good, skip down to the next exercise.

TIP ▸ If your recorded region extends beyond the beginning of the 13th measure, you'll need to trim the right edge before you continue. Drag the lower-right corner of your recorded region toward the left until it ends at bar 13.

5   If you want to try the recording again, press Cmd-Z to undo the recording. Repeat steps 2 through 4 a few more times.

NOTE ▶ If you are totally frustrated and want to move on, choose File > Open and select **4-2 SpaceBass recorded** from the Lesson_04 folder to open a version of the song with the part already recorded for you.

6   Press Shift-Cmd-K to close the Musical Typing window.

7   Press Shift-Cmd-S to save the new version of your song.

8   Change the name to *SpaceBass draft* to show that it is the first draft of your song with the rhythm, melody, and recorded synth pad. Save the song to your folder on the Desktop.

9   Play the project one last time and listen to your recorded region with the other parts.

Good recording. The synth pad you recorded really adds a spacey presence to the piece. There's just one thing. In hindsight, I think the last note would sound better if it was lower (C1) like the first note, rather than an octave higher. Luckily, this is a Software Instrument recording so you're free to edit the notes any way you see fit, from copying, cutting, and pasting, to making them longer, shorter, or simply a different note.

Changing a Note in the Editor

Let's take a moment and change the last note in the recorded Falling Star region.

1   Double-click the Falling Star region to open it in the editor.

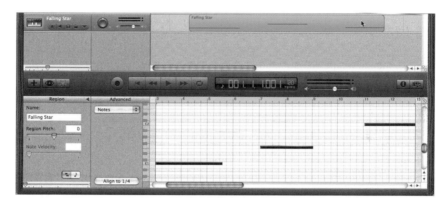

2   Drag the horizontal scroller to the right until the last note in the Falling Star region is close to the Graphic view's vertical keyboard.

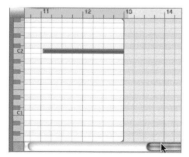

The vertical keyboard shows that the note is currently C2.

3   Locate C1 on the vertical keyboard. It's one octave lower than C2.

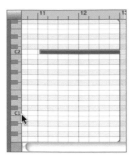

4   Drag the note (bar) straight downward in the editor. Stop when it is at the C1 line in the vertical keyboard.

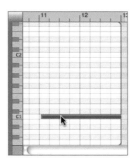

You just changed the last note to C1.

NOTE ▶ You can also transpose (move) a note up or down one semitone at a time in Notation view by selecting the note and pressing the up or down arrow keys. (See Lesson 1 for more on Notation view.)

5   Press Cmd-S to save your progress.

6   Press Cmd-E to hide the editor.

7   Play the project with the edited version of the recording.

Great. I like the lower octave version of the last note much better. The song is coming together nicely. But like all works of art, you need to keep refining it to craft the finished piece.

Working with Advanced Music Arrangement Techniques

Now that you understand working with Software Instruments and basic arrangement, let's take this project to the next level by using some advanced techniques as you finish the song.

Doubling a Track with Mixed Instruments

One easy method to enhance the melody arrangement in a song is to double (duplicate) the melody track, then change the instrument on the duplicate track to reinforce the original track. As you know, with Software Instruments, changing a track's instrument is very easy. All you have to do is figure out what instrument you'd like to change to. In this case, let's double the Elec Piano track containing the electric piano regions, and change the duplicate to a nylon guitar. In the previous lesson you turned a piano recording into a guitar, so you already know that those types of instruments are pretty interchangeable.

There are four ways to double the Elec Piano track to create a Nylon Guitar track that reinforces the electric piano part:

► Select the Elec Piano track, then choose Track > Duplicate Track, or press Cmd-D. Change the duplicate track's instrument. Then Option-drag, or copy and paste, the regions from the original track to the duplicate.

► Create a new Software Instrument track, make the track instrument Nylon Guitar, and duplicate the regions from the Elec Piano track into the new track.

► Create a new Software Instrument track, make the new track Synths > Electric Piano, duplicate the region from the original Synths track to the new track, and change the original track to Nylon Guitar.

► Drag the Spacey Electric Piano 01 loop from the browser to the empty space below the lowest track to create a new Software Instrument Synths track. Change one of the two Synths tracks to Nylon Guitar.

Since you've been working with Option-drag in this lesson, let's try the first method and put your new skills to use.

1   Select the Elec Piano track containing the electric piano regions.

2   Press Cmd-D to duplicate the selected track.

A new Elec Piano track appears below the original Elec Piano track in the Timeline.

3   Click the track header on the original Elec Piano track to select all of the regions inside the track. Then Option-drag the selected regions from the original Elec Piano track to the new duplicate track below.

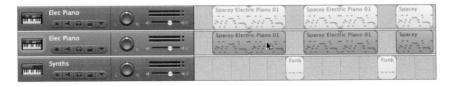

4   Double-click the duplicate Elec Piano track header to open the Track Info pane.

5   Select Guitars > Nylon Shimmer as the track instrument.

An alert appears, telling you that you have made changes to the current instrument setting.

You can choose to save the current track settings before changing them to the new instrument, or discard the changes and use the new instrument sound in the track without saving the original first.

6   Click Discard to discard the Elec Piano settings, and change the track directly to the Nylon Shimmer instrument.

The track name changes to Nylon Shimmer.

7   Press Cmd-I to close the Track Info pane.

8   Play the first half of the project to hear the doubled tracks.

9   Press Cmd-S to save your progress.

Doubling a track is an advanced arranging technique that is used to make a musical part stronger. Doubling is also called *fattening* a track.

Offsetting Parts in the Timeline

Now that you've doubled the melody parts, you can apply another advanced arranging technique to offset the parts to create an overlap or "call and answer" effect. Offsetting the different parts within the Elec Piano and Nylon Shimmer tracks at the beginning and end of the song will really separate the parts, enhance the fact that they are two different instruments, and make the song a bit more interesting.

Offsetting just means trimming or moving the regions so they don't always start and end at exactly the same time. What really makes the difference is if one region starts, then a similar region begins after an interval. For this exercise, you'll apply some of the editing and arranging techniques that you've learned to adjust the part.

To start, let's shorten the first electric piano region in the Elec Piano track and move it so it starts a little earlier.

1   Shorten the first region in the Elec Piano track (drag from the right edge) until it is only one loop segment in length.

2   Zoom in one level to the Timeline if needed until you can see the beat ticks in the Beat Ruler between measures.

3   Drag the first region in the Elec Piano track to the left until it starts at the 3rd beat of the 1st measure (halfway between bar 1 and bar 2).

4   Shorten the first region in the Nylon Shimmer track so it is only one loop segment in length, then move it to the right so that it begins at the 3rd measure.

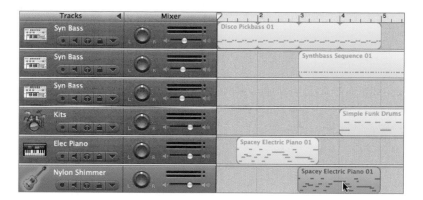

5   Play the beginning of the project to hear the offset regions.

This technique can really make a big difference in the overall sound of a piece. Not to mention it is much more interesting than just hearing the same old loop over and over.

6   Press Cmd-S to save your progress.

Project Tasks

It's your turn once again to put your new skills to work and finish arranging the melody tracks of the song. First, shorten the middle region on the Elec Piano track so it is only one loop segment in length. Then move the region to the right so it starts at bar 9. (You can either shorten it and move it, or split the region in the middle and simply delete the first half.) Shorten the Nylon Shimmer track's middle region so it is only one and one-half loop segments in length. There's no need to change its position, just its length. It should start at bar 7 and end at bar 10.

Be sure to save your progress once you finish the steps.

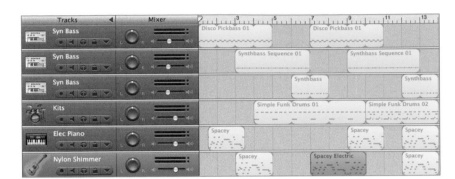

Splitting Multiple Regions

Your goal for the electric piano regions at the end of the melody tracks is to split them both in half, simultaneously, then offset the last halves of the regions. Why split instead of resize? Because you can only resize from the right side of a loop. If the right side (end) of the loop is the part you want to keep, you'll need to cut off (split) the first part that you don't want and delete it.

1   Move the playhead to bar 13 (13th measure).

2   Click the last region in the Elec Piano track to select it.

3   Shift-click the last region in the Nylon Shimmer track to select it also.

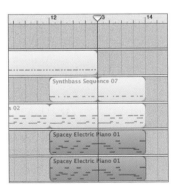

4   Press Cmd-T to split the selected regions at the playhead position.

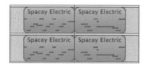

5   Delete the first half of the split section on both tracks.

6   Drag the last region in the Elec Piano track to the left so it starts at bar 12.

7   Drag the last region in the Nylon Shimmer track so it starts at the 3rd beat of the 12th measure (halfway between the 12th and 13th measures).

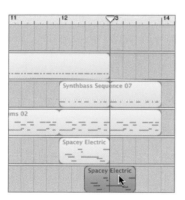

8   Play the end of the song to hear the ending arrangement.

9   Save your progress.

Moving Regions Between Tracks

The new arrangement sounds good. Of course, now there's something new that bothers me. The Funky Pop regions in the lower Synths track stand out a bit too much, probably because they are an entirely different instrument. If only you could make them sound like the Spacey Electric Piano parts in the Elec Piano track. Because these are Software Instrument tracks, it is easy to drag the Funky Pop regions from their original track to the same position on the Elec Piano track. That instantly changes their instrument to the electric piano sound, but keeps intact the notation that is already in the region.

1   Select the first Funky Pop region in the Elec Piano track, then Shift-click the second region to select them both.

2   Drag the selected regions upward to the same position on the Elec Piano track.

3 Select the empty Synths track near the bottom of the Timeline and press Cmd-Delete.

The empty track is deleted.

4 Play the entire piece to hear the full arrangement.

5 Press Shift-Cmd-S and rename the project *SpaceBass arranged.*

> **NOTE ►** If you didn't complete any of the previous exercises, feel free to open the project **4-3 SpaceBass arranged** to catch up. Once you open the catch-up project, resave it to the My GarageBand Projects folder on your Desktop.

Transposing a Region in the Editor

You know how to change a single note by clicking it and dragging it up or down in the editor. You can change all of the notes in the region at once by changing the pitch of the region. The musical term for changing the pitch or key is *transposing*. Remember, there are only 12 different keys (black and white) before a note repeats an octave higher or lower. Each key represents a semitone. To transpose a region by –12 semitones would be to lower the entire thing one full octave. To transpose a region by 12 would be to raise the entire region to a higher octave. Anything other than a full octave will change each note in the region to a different key, either higher or lower. Software Instrument regions can be transposed up to 36 semitones (three full octaves) higher or lower.

Let's transpose some of the doubled parts to add even more depth to the piece. Transposing is also a great advanced technique for making parts less repetitive. For this exercise, you'll transpose two of the regions in the Nylon Shimmer track.

1   Double-click the middle region in the Nylon Shimmer track to open it in
the editor.

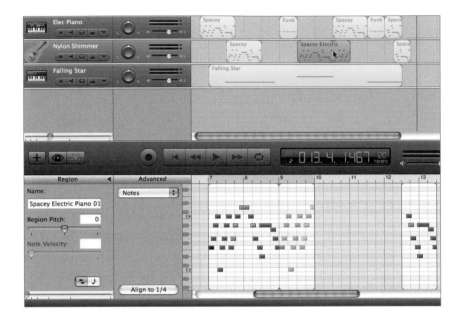

A green shaded area appears above the selected region in the editor's
Beat Ruler.

2   Locate the Region Pitch slider at the left side of the editor.

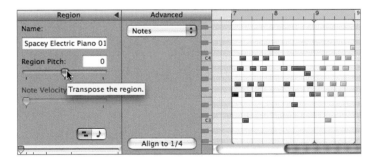

The current Transpose setting is 0, which indicates the region is in the
original recorded key.

3   Type *12* in the Transpose field and press Return to raise the entire part by one octave.

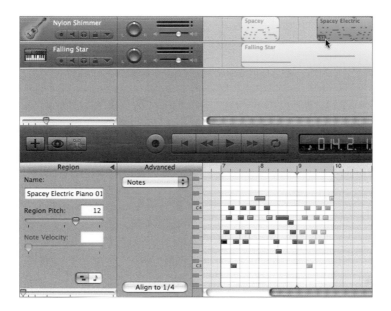

Notice that the selected region in the Timeline has a small +*12* in the lower-left corner to indicate that it has been transposed by +12 semitones.

4   Play the region in the editor to hear it at the higher octave.

5   Type *5* in the Transpose field and press Return, or drag the Region Pitch slider to transpose the region by five semitones higher than the original recording.

The transposed region has a small +5 in the lower-left corner to show that the pitch has been raised by 5 keys.

6   Play the transposed region in the Timeline.

Nice. Simply transposing it by 5 semitones makes it feel like a different part even if it looks exactly the same as it did before you transposed it. Transposing changes the sound of a region without changing the note events in the region.

7   Select the last region in the Nylon Shimmer track and transpose it by −12 (one full octave lower).

8   Play the end of the song to hear the transposed region in context with the end of the song.

9   Close the editor and save your progress.

What do you think of the transposed regions? They really add a nice variation to the melody. The only downside is the Nylon Guitar parts seem much quieter than the Synths parts.

Doubling a Track to Fatten the Sound

You've doubled (fattened) the melody tracks to change track instruments, arrange regions, and create an interesting sound. Another reason to double a track is simply to double up the sound of a particular part to make it stronger. You can raise the volume level of a track, but there are limits to how loud you can raise the level. Audio is cumulative, so doubling the same part on two separate tracks will enhance the levels and also make it stand out more.

1   Select the Nylon Shimmer track and press Cmd-D to duplicate the track.

2   Click the original Nylon Shimmer track header to select the regions inside if they are not already selected.

3   Option-drag the selected regions from the original Nylon Shimmer track to the same positions on the duplicate track.

4   Play the song with the fattened Nylon Shimmer tracks.

Can you hear the difference? The guitar sound is much fatter than it was before you doubled it.

5   Save your progress.

Finishing the Project

There are only two things left to do to finish this piece (not counting mixing, which you'll learn in Lesson 7). First, you need to check how long the song is running. Remember it's supposed to be the opening music for a podcast or radio show. Then you'll add a cool stinger to the end to give it a solid finale!

Viewing Absolute Time in the Time Display

Up to this point in the book, you have been using musical time as a reference for the playhead position. The time display also shows absolute time.

The lower-left corner of the time display shows either a musical note or a clock icon. These are buttons that let you select the type of time to be displayed.

1   Locate the Musical Time button in the lower-left corner of the time display. It looks like a blue musical note.

2   Click the Musical Time button, or the empty space to the left of it to change the display to absolute time.

The Absolute Time button, which looks like a clock, appears, and the time in the display changes to absolute time (hours, minutes, seconds, and thousandths of seconds).

3 Move the playhead to the end of the last region in the Timeline to see the length of the song in actual time.

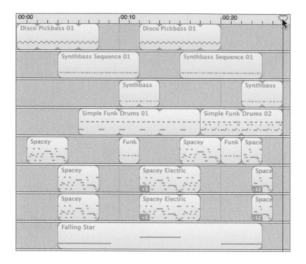

According to the time display, the song is currently 26 seconds long.

Intro music is traditionally 25 to 30 seconds in length, so you're right on target with this project. In fact, you have room to extend it a few seconds if you so desire. For now, you'll just add one more loop to the end.

NOTE ▶ When the time display is in Absolute Time mode, the playhead no longer snaps to beats and measures as you drag it through the Beat Ruler. Moving regions is also more difficult because they won't snap to specific beats or measures either. Just remember, if you're working with sound effects or loops that you are syncing to video, rather than music, change the time display to absolute time. Otherwise, if you're working with musical elements, it's a good idea to keep the time display in musical time.

4 Click the Musical Time button to change back to musical time.

Adding a Musical Stinger

In addition to the sound effects that come with the Podcast Sounds in Garage-Band, there are also a variety of jingles and stingers. Stingers are the short sounds that are added to radio programs and podcasts to accent a moment, or bring the show back from commercial, or just get attention. In this case, you'll add a stinger to the end of the piece as a finale to the intro music and a cue for the talent (announcer) to start talking.

1   Open the Loop Browser.

2   In the lower-left corner of the browser, click the Podcast Sounds button to view the Podcast Sounds.

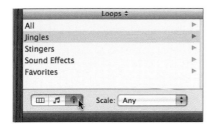

3   Click the Stingers category to see over 50 stingers in the results list.

4   Select any of the stingers in the list to preview (listen to) them.

Most stingers are only a second or two in length.

5   Press the up or down arrow keys to move up or down through the list as you preview them.

6 Preview the stinger called Synth Zap Accent 06.

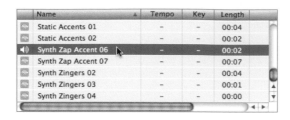

7 Drag the Synth Zap Accent 06 loop from the browser to the space below the last track in the Timeline and release it at the beginning of the 13th measure.

The stinger appears in the Timeline as a blue (Real Instrument) region.

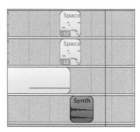

8 Close the Loop Browser.

9 Play the last few measures of the project to hear how it sounds with the stinger.

This stinger is perfect for the project and will lead in nicely to a podcast or radio show. There's just one more thing: the stinger is competing with the last Synthbass and drum regions in the last measure.

10 Shorten both the last Synthbass and drum regions so they end on the 3rd beat of the 13th measure (halfway between the 13th and 14th measures).

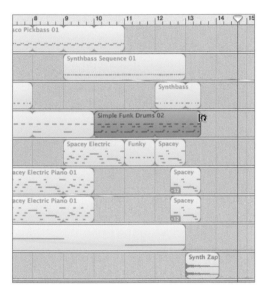

11 Play the last part of the song and listen carefully to the enhanced ending.

Perfect! It's amazing how resizing two loops by only a couple of beats can change the impact of the ending that much. These are the sorts of things that will become instinctual with more practice and scoring experience.

Saving the Finished Project

Congratulations! Not only do you have a much better working knowledge of Software Instruments, you also built a song from the ground up. You even performed advanced music arranging techniques to take the song from a draft to a completed piece. Before you close out the project, it's a good idea to save the final version of the song.

1   Choose File > Save As, and save the project as *SpaceBass final* to the My GarageBand Projects folder.

2   Play the song one last time from start to finish.

>   **NOTE ▶** If you feel like reminiscing on the different stages of building the song, you can open the earlier versions and listen to them one at a time.

Lesson Review

1.   What are common instruments used in the rhythm tracks of a song?

2.   Other than copy and paste, what is another method for duplicating selected regions in the Timeline?

3.   When using the Musical Typing window for recording, what keyboard shortcuts can you use to move the playhead to the beginning of the project?

4.   What does the term doubling mean when referring to an instrument part?

5.   How can you change the pitch of (transpose) an entire Software Instrument region?

6.   How many semitones are in one musical octave?

7.   What is the maximum amount you can transpose a Software Instrument region?

8.   What is a saving method that allows you to go back to an earlier version of the song?

9.   How can you view the actual length of a project in hours, minutes, seconds, and fractions of a second?

Answers

1. Drums, percussion, and bass are common rhythm instruments.

2. The Option-drag method is an easy way to duplicate selected regions in the Timeline.

3. The Return key can be used to move the playhead to the beginning of a song while the Musical Typing window is active. The Z and the Home key methods are disabled during Musical Typing.

4. Doubling refers to duplicating a musical part on a second track to *fatten* the sound.

5. Select the region and open it in the editor, then drag the Region Pitch slider to transpose the region.

6. There are 12 semitones in each octave.

7. You can transpose a Software Instrument up to 36 semitones (three octaves) higher or lower.

8. Save the song in stages with names that indicate what is new in that version.

9. Change the time display to the Absolute Time mode.

5

Lesson Files	GarageBand 3 Lessons > Lesson_05 > 5-1 Loops start; 5-2 IvoryDreams start; 5-3 IvoryDreams melody; 5-4 IvoryDreams draft; 5-5 IvoryDreams final
Time	This lesson takes approximately 1 hour to complete.
Goals	Understand the rules for combining Real Instrument and Software Instrument regions and loops
	Resize the Loop Browser
	Move keyword buttons to a different position in the Loop Browser
	Change the keyword on a keyword button
	Mark favorite loops
	Duplicate, resize, split, and extend loops to build a song
	Draw and edit notes in the editor
	Convert Software Instrument loops to Real Instrument loops
	Reset the Loop Browser to its default settings

Lesson 5

Working with Apple Loops

Apple Loops are prerecorded music files that are designed to repeat (loop) over and over seamlessly as a pattern. Loops are commonly used for drumbeats, rhythm parts, and other repeating musical sections within a song. GarageBand comes with over 1,000 prerecorded Apple Loops.

Apple Loops are incredibly flexible instrument regions that can be cut, copied, pasted, edited, transposed, and repeated to create a song or enhance your recorded tracks.

To extend your loop library, you can add third-party loops, as well as Apple Loops from Soundtrack Pro, Logic, or the Jam Pack expansions for GarageBand. You can also save your own recordings (Software Instruments and Real Instruments) as loops in your loop library.

In this lesson, you will learn how to customize the Loop Browser, mark and find favorite loops, and explore the differences between Software Instrument and Real Instrument loops as you build a song. Along the way you'll also learn more advanced music arranging techniques to turn your GarageBand music into professional-sounding songs.

Preparing the Project

Open **5-1 Loops start** from the Lesson_05 folder in the GarageBand 3 Lessons folder. You will start with a project that has two empty tracks.

Understanding Apple Loops

As you have learned so far, Apple Loops come in different shapes, sizes, instruments, and colors. Before you build a song, let's examine some of the unique characteristics of the prerecorded Apple Loops that come with GarageBand.

In the previous lessons, you discovered that the green loops are Software Instrument loops and can be edited just like any Software Instrument region; you can even edit individual notes. Likewise, the blue loops are Real Instrument loops that can be edited like any Real Instrument region.

What happens if you place a Real Instrument loop into a Software Instrument track, or vice versa? Let's try it and find out. The first track in the current project is a Software Instrument track. The second track is a Real Instrument track.

1   Click the Loop Browser button to open the Loop Browser.

2   In the lower-left corner of the Loop Browser, click the Button View button (if the Browser is not already in Button view).

3   Click the Reset button to clear any current results in the browser.

4   Click the Guitars button to show the Guitars loops in the results list.

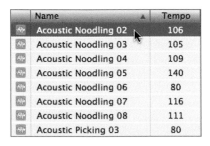

	Name ▲	Tempo
	Acoustic Noodling 02	106
	Acoustic Noodling 03	105
	Acoustic Noodling 04	109
	Acoustic Noodling 05	140
	Acoustic Noodling 06	80
	Acoustic Noodling 07	116
	Acoustic Noodling 08	111
	Acoustic Picking 03	80

The Acoustic Noodling guitar loops should be at the top of your results list. If you've installed the Jam Pack expansions or other additional loops, the Acoustic Noodling loops may be farther down in the results list. Notice that all the Acoustic Noodling loops are blue and have a waveform icon in the Loop Type column, indicating that they are all Real Instrument loops.

5   Drag the Acoustic Noodling 02 loop from the Loop Browser to the Grand Piano track in the Timeline and release the mouse.

The track remains empty after you release the mouse because you can't put a Real Instrument region in a Software Instrument track. Software Instrument tracks can only play regions recorded using MIDI samples and note events.

6   Drag the Acoustic Noodling 02 loop from the Loop Browser to the 1st measure of the No Effects track in the Timeline.

A green circle with a plus (+) sign appears if the track will accept the loop. If you don't see the green plus sign, you will not be able to place the loop in that track.

This time it worked because the Acoustic Noodling 02 loop is a Real Instrument recording, the same as the track.

7   In the results list, click the top of the Loop Type column to move the Software Instrument loops to the top of the list. Drag the vertical scroller to the top of the scroll bar to view the Software Instrument loops at the top of the list.

8   Drag the Southern Rock Guitar 05 loop from the browser to the 1st measure of the top track in the Timeline.

The Southern Rock Guitar 05 loop region appears in the top track as a green Software Instrument region. This is predictable since all you did is put a loop in the appropriate type of track.

OK, so this all seems like old news, right? Well, we're not quite done with our loop experiment.

What if you put a Software Instrument region in a Real Instrument track?

1   Drag the Southern Rock Guitar 05 loop from the browser to the second track, next to the Acoustic Noodling 02 region.

The Software Instrument loop transforms into a Real Instrument region.

As a Real Instrument loop, the Southern Rock Guitar region now shows waveforms in the Timeline instead of MIDI information.

2   Select and delete the Acoustic Noodling 02 region in the second track.

3   Play the Timeline to hear the two Southern Rock Guitar 05 regions.

Were you surprised to hear the Southern Rock Guitar sound like a grand piano?

This is just a reminder that Software Instrument regions will always sound like the track instrument, regardless of the instrument sound used in the original recording. On the other hand, Real Instrument regions will always sound like the instrument that originally recorded the region, regardless of the track instrument. You can add effects to a Real Instrument track, but you can't change the instrument for a region by changing the track instrument, as you can with Software Instruments.

The Southern Rock Guitar region in the Real Instrument track sounds like a guitar because the MIDI data in the file contains instructions to play the notes back using guitar sounds. The fact that the track is named No Effects, implying that there are no effects on the track, has no effect (pun intended) on the instrument sound for the region in that track.

4   Double-click the Grand Piano track header to open the Software Instrument Track Info pane.

5   Select Guitars > Steel String Acoustic for the track instrument, and then close the Track Info pane.

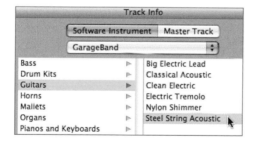

The instrument track header changes to Steel String Acoustic Guitar.

6   Play the region in the top track to hear the instrument change.

7   Double-click the No Effects track header to open the Real Instrument Track Info pane.

8   Select Vocals > Female Basic to change the effects on the track, and then close the Track Info pane.

Before you click Play, see if you can predict the outcome of your actions. Will the Southern Rock Guitar loop sound like a female vocalist? Will it still sound like a guitar? Perhaps it will sound like a southern female rock vocalist?

9   Close the Track Info pane, then play the region to hear the Southern Rock Guitar in the Female Basic track.

You probably guessed it. It still sounds like a guitar (although I have to admit I was curious to hear some of the other alternatives). All you changed was the preset effects or amplifier sounds to enhance Real Instrument recordings. If you are planning to record a basic female vocal part, this might be a terrific choice for your Real Instrument track.

NOTE ▶ GarageBand 3 comes with 30 preset vocal effects. There are basic presets for normal recording, and vocal effects to simulate a live setting. There are also more creative presets, such as Mouse Voice and Helium Breath, which turn normal vocals into high-pitched, comically distorted vocals. These presets can also come in handy with vocal recordings for your podcasts or for narration you record for your movie projects.

So now that you have reviewed these loop basics, let's get ready to compose a new song.

Listening to the Finished Song

Before you start the next series of exercises, it's good to know what you're aiming for. Follow these steps to hear the finished song you will be creating with Apple Loops.

The song you'll create is called **IvoryDreams** and is about a kid suffering though boring piano lessons but always dreaming of being in a band that makes it to the top. I used the creative energy of a live music jam session as a template for the music.

In the many jam sessions I've experienced over the years, somebody in the band has an idea for a riff, and in a matter of seconds, other musicians catch the groove and join in. In **IvoryDreams**, as you'll hear in a moment, something similar happens. The piano comes in, then the strings double-up on the melody, then the basic percussion, bass, and drums come in, and finally the song ends with a cymbal crash.

Keep in mind, a jam session is live musicians joining in to play an unrehearsed piece of music and to see where it goes. In some ways, writing a song in GarageBand is the opposite of a jam session because you have to think and plan each part to add it to the Timeline. On the other hand, since your musical choices in GarageBand are unlimited, the essence of a jam session lives on.

1   Choose File > Open and select **5-5 IvoryDreams final** from the Lesson_05 folder to open the song.

Don't save the changes to the previous project.

The project **5-5 IvoryDreams final** opens in the Timeline. The song is composed of five Software Instrument tracks and six Real Instrument tracks.

2   Play the song from the beginning of the Timeline.

NOTE ▶ If you are running a slower computer and are having trouble playing this song, try locking the Software Instrument tracks by clicking the small Lock button on each track. Not only does this lock the track to prevent unwanted changes, but it also renders the track to the computer's hard drive so it won't need to be processed by GarageBand as it plays.

3   Choose File > Open and open the project **5-2 IvoryDreams start**.

4   Choose File > Save As, and save it to your My GarageBand Projects folder.

Customizing the Loop Browser

The Loop Browser is a complex organizational tool that goes beyond buttons, columns, and podcast sounds. There are many hidden features you can use to customize the Loop Browser. Let's explore some of these features while we build the melody and rhythm tracks for this song using Apple Loops.

Resizing and Rearranging Columns in the Results List

A good place to start customizing your Loop Browser is in the results list. The results list has six different columns.

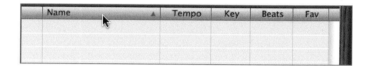

To view additional columns, you can click-drag the horizontal scroller below the results list.

1   Press Cmd-L, or click the Loop Browser button, to open the Loop Browser.

2   Drag the scroller toward the right to see the last columns in the results list, if you don't already see them.

These columns contain information about the individual loops and can be used to sort the loops within the results list.

All the columns can be moved or resized except for the Loop Type column, which always stays on the far left.

To move a column, drag the column header.

3   Locate the favorites column, which is labeled "Fav."

4   Drag the Fav column header toward the left and release it before the
    Name column.

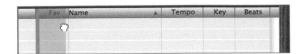

The Fav column does not need to be very wide because it isn't used
for text.

Extending the Name column makes it easier to read the names of the
loops in the results list. You can resize a column by dragging the right
edge of its column header.

5   Move your pointer to the right edge of the Name column header until it
    becomes a resize pointer.

6   Drag the right edge of the Name column to extend the column to the edge
    of the results list.

NOTE ▶ Changes that you make to the columns in the Loop Browser are
saved with the project, rather than the application. New songs that you
create will have the same customized browser settings, but older songs that
were saved prior to the changes will maintain their original settings.

Selecting Favorite Loops

With over 1,000 loops to choose from, sometimes it's a good idea to mark your
favorites or the loops you plan to use for a specific song. That way, when you are
ready to start building the song, you won't have to break your creative flow to go
hunting for loops. Instead, they will all be located in one category—favorites.

Any loop that is marked as a favorite can be located easily with the Favorites button in Button view or in the Favorites column in Column view.

1   Click the Reset button to reset (deselect) any buttons in the Loop Browser.

The song is based around a piano melody, so let's start with the piano.

2   Click the Piano keyword button to select the piano loops.

3   Scroll down through the list of piano loops and select Delicate Piano 01 to preview the loop.

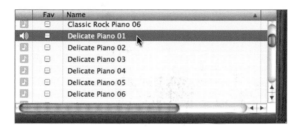

This loop is perfect for the song. All you have to do now is mark it as a favorite so you can look for another piano loop that might go well with this melody.

4   Click the box in the Fav column next to the Delicate Piano 01 loop.

The Favorites button is no longer dimmed, indicating that you now have at least one loop marked as a favorite.

5   Select the Classic Rock Piano 06 loop to preview it. It should be above the Delicate Piano 01 loop in the list.

This melody works well with the delicate piano loop.

6   Mark the Classic Rock Piano 06 loop as a favorite.

7   Click the Piano button to deselect the button and empty the search results list.

8   Click the Favorites button to view the loops you marked as favorites in the list.

9   Click the Column View button to change the Loop Browser to Column view.

Notice the Favorites option in the Loops column.

10 In the Loops column, click Favorites, then in the Favorites column click Piano.

Notice that the Piano descriptors have one or two selections. These descriptors apply to the loops you selected as favorites, and include all the categories you could use to search for them in the Loop Browser. Later in this lesson, you'll see that there are keyword buttons for each of these descriptors that you can use with the Loop Browser in Button view.

11 In the Piano column, click the Acoustic descriptor to see both favorite loops.

12 Click the Button View button again to return to the Button view.

Now that you have searched for a loop, marked it as a favorite, and found it in the Loop Browser using Button view and Column view, it's time to find and mark more loops for the song.

Moving Keyword Buttons

Keyword buttons are not only easy to use, but also easy to move. To move a button, all you have to do is drag the button to a different button location. The button you move will swap places with the button in the current location. The only buttons that cannot be moved are Reset and Favorites.

Why would you want to move a button? Good question. Since you know that you want certain instruments for the song, group all of the instrument buttons together near a common descriptor so you can spend less time searching for buttons and more time searching for loops.

For this song, you'll need piano parts (which you've already marked as favorites), a bass, and some drums and percussion, so let's group them all together with the common descriptor Rock/Blues.

Let's start by moving the Rock/Blues button closer to the results list for easier access.

1   Locate the Rock/Blues button in the Loop Browser.

2   Drag the Rock/Blues button and move it on top of the Ensemble button, located at the top right of the keyword buttons.

The Ensemble button is highlighted when you move the other button over it to show that you are moving the new button to that location.

3   Release the mouse to complete the button move.

The Rock/Blues button is now in the upper-right corner, and the Ensemble button has moved to the old Rock/Blues position.

Let's move the other main instrument keyword buttons we need to the button positions below the Rock/Blues button.

4 Locate the Bass button and move it to the position directly below the Rock/Blues button.

5 Locate the All Drums button and move it to the position below the Bass button.

Now that the buttons are in place, let's hunt for some more loops to use for the song.

1 Click the Rock/Blues button to select it (if it is not already selected).

2 Click the Bass button to narrow the search to Bass loops that are also classified as Rock/Blues loops.

3 Drag the scroller to scroll down through the results list until you locate Muted Rock Bass 01.

4 Click the Muted Rock Bass 01 loop to preview it in the results list.

5 Click again to stop the preview. Then mark Muted Rock Bass 01 as a favorite.

6 Click the Bass keyword button to deselect it.

The Rock/Blues button remains selected.

7   Click the All Drums button to search for Rock/Blues Drums loops.

8   Locate 70s Ballad Drums 01 in the results list and mark it as a favorite.

> **TIP** ▶ When selecting loops for drums, percussion, or melody tracks, select more than one choice for the song. That way you can keep the project from sounding too repetitive, and you can build variation within the tracks.

9   Locate Classic Rock Beat 01 in the results list and mark it as a favorite.

10   Click the All Drums button again to deselect it.

11   Click the Favorites button to view your current favorites.

You now have five loops in your favorites list.

12   Click the Favorites button again to deselect it. Then click the Reset button to deselect all buttons.

Showing More Keyword Buttons

By default, the Loop Browser shows 35 buttons (including the Reset and Favorites buttons). You can easily increase the size of the Loop Browser to show up to 66 buttons.

Why would you want to see that many buttons? If you're just starting a song, you might not know exactly what type of loop you want. Some of the Genre or Mood buttons, like Cinematic, Experimental, Grooving, or Melodic, that are normally hidden from view might inspire you. If 35 buttons are a nice salad-bar-sized selection to choose from, 66 buttons are the full-blown key-word button buffet.

To resize the Loop Browser, you drag upward on the divider between the Timeline and the Loop Browser.

Let's resize the Loop Browser to see more buttons.

1   Move your pointer over the empty gray space to the left of the Record button to change the pointer to a Hand tool.

2   Drag the Loop Browser up until all of the buttons are showing.

Notice all of the new buttons from which to choose. The Part button will be perfect for the shaker and cymbal crash parts.

3   Locate the Part button and swap it with the Intense button.

Having all these buttons at your fingertips is great for browsing through loops and finding favorite loops to use later. Unfortunately, the expanded browser doesn't leave much room in the Timeline for arranging your song.

Now that you've seen the full button spread and have rearranged the buttons you need, it's time to resize the Loop Browser back to the more compact, Timeline-friendly default size.

4   Drag the top of the Loop Browser down to resize it back to the normal size.

Changing a Keyword Button

Now that you have resized the Loop Browser, you have seen some of the additional keyword button choices that are available for you to use.

Instead of dragging buttons to a more convenient location, you can simply change a keyword button to a new keyword.

1   Locate the Dark button.

2   Ctrl-click the Dark button to open a shortcut menu of keyword choices.

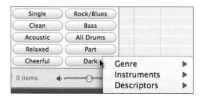

The shortcut menu has three submenus of keyword choices: Genre, Instruments, and Descriptors.

3   Choose Instruments > Percussion > Tambourine from the shortcut menu.

NOTE ▶ Your shortcut menu layout may differ from the picture depending on your screen resolution and the location of the shortcut menu on your screen.

The Dark keyword changes to Tambourine in the Loop Browser.

TIP ▶ You can also use this technique to customize the blank buttons that appear in the expanded Loop Browser view without losing any of the built-in buttons in the process.

Now that you know how to customize your Loop Browser, let's find the rest of the loops for the song.

Project Tasks

It's your turn to find the remaining loops and mark them as favorites. Start with the tambourine parts, then the shakers, and finally the cymbal crash. Use the Keyword buttons and search text field as needed to find and mark the remaining parts. Hint: You should be able to find everything by just clicking the appropriate Keyword buttons.

▶ Tambourine 01

▶ Tambourine 07

▶ Shaker 01

▶ Shaker 06

▶ Shaker 16

▶ Long Crash Cymbal 02

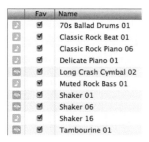

	Fav	Name
♪	☑	70s Ballad Drums 01
♪	☑	Classic Rock Beat 01
♪	☑	Classic Rock Piano 06
♪	☑	Delicate Piano 01
〰	☑	Long Crash Cymbal 02
♪	☑	Muted Rock Bass 01
〰	☑	Shaker 01
〰	☑	Shaker 06
♪	☑	Shaker 16
〰	☑	Tambourine 01

When you are finished, your favorites list should include all the loops shown in the screen shot. Don't forget to click the Reset button and save your work before moving on to the next section.

Building a Song with Apple Loops

Now that you have collected all of the musical parts, it's time to build the song. Along the way you'll learn a few new tricks of the trade, like mirroring the melody with strings, adding or deleting notes, and transposing a region a full octave.

Starting with the Melody

There are different ways to begin a song. In the previous lesson, you started the song **SpaceBass** with the rhythm tracks. For this piece, you will start with the piano melody because it also has a solid rhythm, and all of the other parts work off the piano lead.

1   In the Loop Browser, click the Favorites button to see the favorites that you've selected for this project.

2   Drag the Delicate Piano 01 loop from the Loop Browser to the 1st measure of the Grand Piano track in the Timeline. Then play the region in the Timeline.

When you hear this piano melody, does it make you want to pick up an instrument and play along? Which instrument? Bass? Drums? Guitar? Whichever instrument you imagined, I strongly encourage you to try this exercise again later and record the part you imagine with your instrument of choice. For this exercise, we'll pretend it's another musician who joins in with some strings.

Strings? Don't worry if you didn't select any string parts in your loop favorites. Many string parts mirror the lead instrument. That's exactly what you are going to do here.

An Orchestral Strings Software Instrument track is just below the Grand Piano track in the Timeline. All you need to do is add the piano loop to double the part.

3   Option-drag the Delicate Piano 01 region from the top track to the lower track.

4   Play the doubled piano and strings part in the Timeline to hear how they
    sound together.

    I think they sound pretty good. As I mentioned before, many string parts
    mirror the lead instrument melody. When you are working with Software
    Instruments in GarageBand, it's easy to double your lead part with strings.

Now that you've doubled the piano part with strings, there's a slight problem.
If this song is really supposed to resemble a jam session, the strings can't start
with the piano. The strings have to join in, after a few measures. All you need
to do is split the region and delete the first half.

1   Select the Delicate Piano 01 region in the Orchestral Strings track.

    Make sure that only the region in the lower track is selected.

2   Move the playhead to the middle of the region (bar 3).

3   Press Cmd-T, or choose Edit > Split, to split the region.

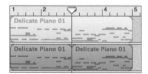

The region splits in two parts. Instead of deleting the first half, let's just
move it down the Timeline a bit. You may wish to use it later in the song.
If not, you can always delete it.

4   Move the first half of the split region down the track to around the 12th
    measure.

5   Extend the 2nd half of the split region from the upper-right corner until it
    loops two more times and ends at the 9th measure.

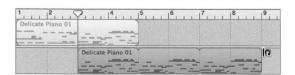

Why is the part that is looped so short? Looping basically clones or duplicates a region in its current state. If the region has been edited, the loops created from the region will match the edited region. If you wanted the original loop back, it is easiest to get it from the Loop Browser and reinsert it in the Timeline.

6   What happens if you extend the piano region in the upper track to go with the newly extended strings part? Chances are it will not sound very good. Let's try it anyway.

Extend the region in the Grand Piano track until it repeats one full looped segment.

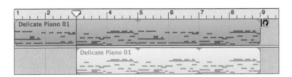

7   Play the song in the Timeline to hear how it sounds.

Yikes. The beginning of the second loop (bar 5) is worse than I expected. Remember, if your strings section is going to mirror the lead instrument, it needs to play the same notes at the same time.

8   Press Cmd-Z (undo) twice to undo the extensions of both regions.

Instead of having the original piano piece repeat again, let's add the other melody part.

9   Drag the Classic Rock Piano 06 loop from the browser to the 5th measure of the Grand Piano track.

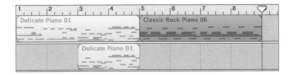

10 Option-drag the new region from the top track to the lower track to place a duplicate in the Orchestral Strings track.

11 Play the song.

The mirrored strings also work well with the rock piano part.

12 Press Cmd-S to save this stage of the song.

Listening to the Completed Tracks

Now that you understand the concept of using two different piano regions and a mirrored strings part to build the melody, let's fast-forward to the final steps to complete the melody tracks.

1 Press Cmd-O, or choose File > Open, and open the project **5-3 IvoryDreams melody** from the Lesson_05 folder in the GarageBand 3 Lessons folder.

2 Choose File > Save As, and save it to your My GarageBand Projects folder.

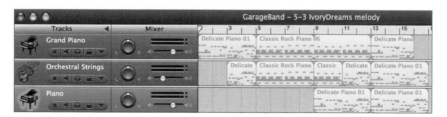

Notice that there are now three tracks, each containing combinations of the same two piano loops. The third track was added to *fatten* the delicate piano part at the end of the song.

3 Play the song to hear the finished melody tracks.

What do you think? It's come a long way since the original two loops. But there are a few things that you could do to make it even better, especially the ending.

Adding Notes to a Loop in the Editor

The ending of the song is okay, but a little abrupt. Instead of settling for a mediocre ending, why not add a final note at the end of the loops? You've already learned how to select and delete Software Instrument notes in the editor. You can also draw new notes, and edit them, just as if they were part of the original recording. Your goal will be to resize the last region of the lower Piano track to make room for an additional note. Then you'll draw a new note at the end of the region. Once the note has been drawn, you'll extend the note, and duplicate it to create two long notes that play at once. Let's try it.

1 Press Ctrl-right arrow several times to zoom in to the last region in the Timeline.

2 Drag the lower-right corner of the region to resize it so it ends at bar 18.

NOTE ▸ Be sure to resize by dragging the lower-right corner, rather than extend it as a loop by dragging the upper-right corner.

3 Move the playhead to the start of the last region in the lowest Piano track (bar 13).

4 Double-click the region to open it in the editor.

The editor opens in either Notation view or Graphic view.

5   Change the editor to Graphic view, if it is not already that way.

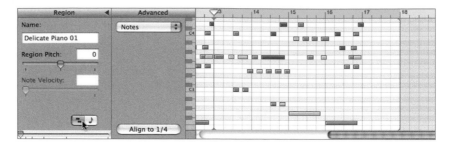

6   Play the last region and pause after the final note.

NOTE ▶ By default, the playhead in the editor will play in sync with the playhead in the Timeline. You can override this feature by unlocking the playhead sync button. You'll learn how to do that in Lesson 9.

Before you draw a note, it's a good idea to decide which note you'd like to draw.

7   In the editor, click different note events at the end of the region to hear them one at a time.

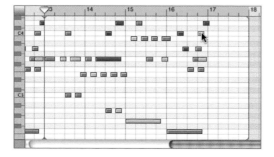

Any of these notes is a potential winner for the note you're going to draw. My vote is for the C4 note (use the vertical keyboard at the left side of the editor to locate a C4 note in the graph).

To draw a note, you hold the Command key, which turns the pointer into a drawing tool. You'll draw a new C4 note at bar 17. Find C4 on the vertical keyboard to make sure you're looking at the right row in the graph.

8 In the editor, Cmd-click the C4 row at bar 17.

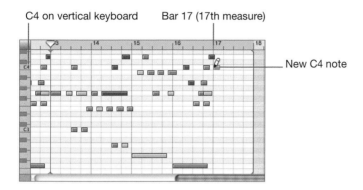

A new green C4 note appears at bar 17 in the editor. If your note is not on the C4 row, or does not start at bar 17, you can simply move it to the right graph position.

9 Drag the right edge of the new note to the end of the region (bar 18) to extend the note.

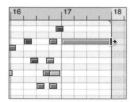

10 Play the end of the region to hear it with the new note.

Nice note! All you need to do now is duplicate it an octave lower to fatten it up a bit. You could draw a new note, or just Option-drag the original note and place the duplicate at C3 (one octave lower).

1   Option-drag the new note and place the duplicate on the C3 row.

As you drag the duplicate down to the C3 row, you'll hear it play at each grid position along the way.

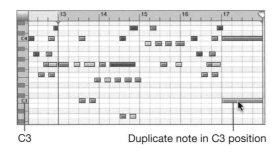

C3   Duplicate note in C3 position

2   Play the end of the region one last time to hear it with the doubled note in two octaves.

Works great. It sounds much more like an ending.

3   Press Cmd-E to close the editor.

The new notes also appear in the region in the Timeline.

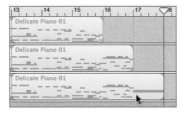

Now that you've added the notes to the Delicate Piano 01 region in the Piano track, you can move the edited version up to the Orchestral Strings track to replace the unedited version in that track. You don't have to delete the strings

region first. That will happen automatically when you cover it up with the duplicate region.

1   Option-drag the last region in the Piano track and place the duplicate in the Orchestral Strings track.

2   Play the song from the 13th measure to hear the new ending.

3   Press Cmd-S to save your progress.

Project Tasks

Now it's your turn to modify the ending a little further using some of the advanced arranging techniques you learned in Lesson 4. First, split the last region in the Orchestral Strings track at bar 15. Then open the second half of the split region in the editor and lower the pitch to –12 (one octave lower). Finally, open the last region in the lower Piano track in the editor and transpose it (change the pitch) one octave lower as well. Close the editor and play the full project to listen to the improved transposed ending. Then save your work.

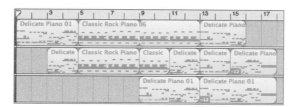

Working with Real Instrument Loops

Now that you've finished the melody, it's time to add the Rhythm tracks. Not only will you start building the Rhythm tracks, but you'll also work with some Real Instrument loops. To continue the jam session theme, the shakers, drums, and bass will join the song.

You'll start by adding the Shaker 16 loop to bar 4.

1   Open the Loop Browser, and drag the Shaker 16 loop from the favorites list to the empty space below the Piano track.

The Shaker 16 region appears in a new Software Instrument track.

2   Move the shaker region to the beginning of bar 4 on the Shaker track.

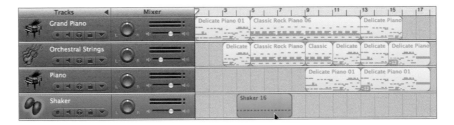

3   Extend the loop (upper-right corner) by one measure so it loops to bar 9. Then Option-drag the region and place the duplicate at bar 13.

Converting Software Instrument Loops to Real Instruments

The melody sections of the song required more intricate editing at the note level, so keeping them all Software Instrument loops was important. The rhythm tracks, on the other hand, don't really need to be Software Instrument regions. In fact, the demands on the processor will be much less if you play them as Real Instruments. All Apple Loops that are Software Instruments can be converted to Real Instruments. You can convert them by dragging them into a Real Instrument track or by changing a setting in the Preferences window. You'll try both methods as you step through the next exercise. Let's start with the bass track.

In the Loop Browser, the Muted Rock Bass 01 loop you marked as a favorite is currently a Software Instrument loop.

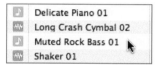

1   Click the New Track button or choose Track > New Track.

2   In the New Track window, select Real Instrument as the type of track, then click Create.

A new real instrument track appears in the Timeline, and the Track Info pane opens.

3   In the Track Info pane, select Bass as the track instrument and Rock Bass as the type of bass.

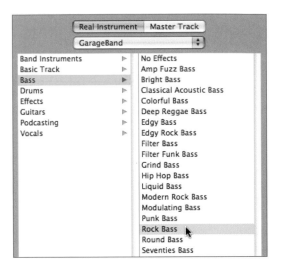

NOTE ▶ GarageBand includes 25 different bass sound presets from which to choose to enhance your bass Real Instrument tracks. These effects are customizable, which you'll learn about in Lesson 7.

The Real Instrument track name changes to Rock Bass in the Timeline.

4   Press Cmd-L to open the Loop Browser.

Opening the Loop Browser will automatically hide the Track Info pane because you can view only one at a time.

5   Drag the Muted Rock Bass 01 loop from the Browser to bar 5 in the Rock Bass track.

6   Extend the region in the Rock Bass track so that it loops continuously until bar 17.

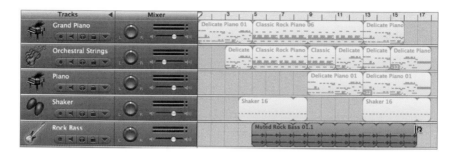

You successfully converted the Software Instrument loop into a Real Instrument loop and extended it in the Timeline.

Next you'll change the project Preferences so that every loop you add to the project is automatically converted to a Real Instrument loop.

1   Choose GarageBand > Preferences to open the Preferences window. Then click the Loops button to view the Loops Preferences.

In the middle of the Loops Preferences, you'll see an option for "Adding Loops to Timeline: Convert to Real Instrument." If the check box is deselected, the loops will maintain their original format unless added to an existing Real Instrument track. If the box is selected, Software Instrument loops will be converted to Real Instrument loops.

2   Select the box to "Convert to Real Instrument." Then close the Preferences window.

Now when you add Software Instrument loops to the Timeline, they will automatically create Real Instrument tracks.

3   Drag the 70s Ballad Drums 01 loop from the browser to the empty space below the Rock Bass track and release it at bar 6.

4   Extend the Real Instrument drum loop so that it repeats four full looped segments and ends at bar 14.

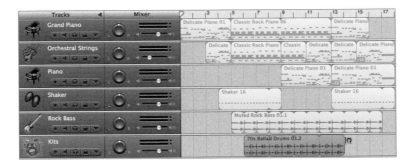

5   Drag the Classic Rock Beat 01 loop from the browser and release it at bar 13 below the Kits track.

The last loop you'll add is the Long Cymbal Crash 02, which is natively a Real Instrument loop, and place it after the Classic Rock Beat 01 loop in the lower Kits track.

6 Drag the Long Crash Cymbal 02 loop from the browser to the lower Kits track and release it at bar 17, right after the Classic Rock Beat loop.

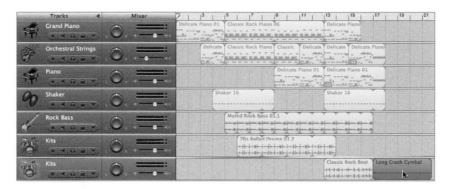

7 Play the project to see how it sounds with the rhythm tracks.

It's coming together. Some of the volume levels are off, but you'll learn to mix those in Lesson 7. The bass track feels very loopy and repetitive. You'll fix that in the next lesson. Also, the shaker seems to go on a few shakes too many at the end, as if the musician with the shaker isn't paying attention.

TIP ▶ It's very cool to lead off the percussion section with a shaker because it feels like a count in, or pre-percussion before the real thing. On the other hand, having the shaker or other hand percussion extend too long at the end of a song usually sounds like a mistake. Endings should be definitive and solid.

8 Resize the Shaker 16 region so it ends on the 2nd beat of the 17th measure (only one shake in the 17th measure).

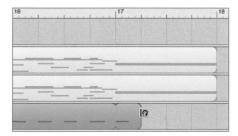

9   Play the ending again.

What a difference it makes to trim off the excess shaker.

10   Choose File > Save As, and save this version of the project as *IvoryDreams Draft* in your My GarageBand Projects folder. Press Cmd-S to save the finished song.

Now that you've finished the draft version of the song, you can reset the Loop Browser and Loops Preferences.

Resetting the Keywords in the Loop Browser

In the GarageBand Preferences window, you can reset the Loop Browser keyword buttons by clicking the Reset button. While you're there, you can also deselect the "Convert to Real Instrument" setting.

1   Choose GarageBand > Preferences to open the Preferences window.

The Preferences window should show the Loops Preferences because that was the last pane you worked with in the Preferences window.

2   Click the Reset button to reset the Loop Browser keyword buttons back to the GarageBand default settings.

A dialog box will ask you if you are sure you want to reset the keyword buttons to the default settings.

3   Click Yes to reset the keyword layout.

The Reset button in the Loop Browser will clear any selected buttons and clear the results list. The Reset button in the General Preferences window resets all of the keyword buttons to their original names and locations in the Loop Browser. However, this does not reset favorites, so your favorite loops will still be marked accordingly.

4   Deselect the "Convert to Real Instrument" box.

5   Close the General Preferences window.

Evaluating the Finished Song

One last thing before you wrap up this lesson. Now that you've finished a draft of the song, I'd like to point out a few tricks that were added to the finished version that you didn't get to in this lesson. At the end of the lesson, feel free to complete the song before moving on to Lesson 6.

1   Choose File > Open Recent > **5-5 IvoryDreams final**.

The Open Recent menu is a convenient way to access recent projects.

Most of the changes to the project are additional percussion tracks, plus the Arena Crowd Cheer at the end. However, there are a few tricks I'd like to draw your attention to.

2   Notice the Big Electric Lead guitar track below the Piano track in the Timeline.

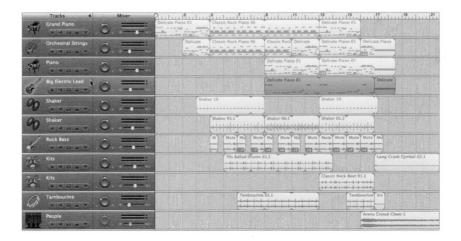

If you look carefully, you'll see that the region within the guitar track is called Delicate Piano 01, but it looks pretty different from the tracks above. What's up with that? Simple. Instead of adding notes to the loop like you did at the end of the song, I deleted most of the notes from the loop so that only some of the melody notes would be played by the guitar. This is just another example of what you can do with Software Instrument loops. This type of note editing wouldn't be possible in a Real Instrument loop.

3 Play the song to hear the addition of the Guitar Lead part. Keep in mind the entire melody was created using two piano loops.

Did you notice the changes in the bass part? Instead of one bass riff that repeats over and over throughout, it was actually edited and transposed. That's right. You can split and transpose Real Instrument regions much the same way you transpose (change pitch) in Software Instrument parts.

4 Play the project one more time focusing this time on the bass part.

Can you hear the changes to the bass riff?

To edit the bass track yourself, and get an introduction to Real Instruments, try the exercise "Editing Real Instrument Loops" (Bonus Exercises > **Edit_Real_Instrument_Loops.pdf**) on the accompanying DVD. Meanwhile, congratulate yourself on learning some new tricks and techniques for working with Apple Loops, including customizing the Loop Browser, editing, and converting loops.

> **TIP** You can add loops to GarageBand 3, even create your own from recordings. Find out how in "Adding Loops to GarageBand" (Bonus Exercises > **Add_Loops.pdf**) on the accompanying DVD.

Lesson Review

1. How can you convert Software Instrument loops to Real Instrument loops?
2. When you extend an edited region by dragging the upper-right corner, does the full length of the original recording or the length of the current region loop?

3. How do you rearrange the columns in the results list of the Loop Browser?

4. How do you resize the columns in the Loop Browser?

5. How do you move a keyword button to a new position in the Loop Browser?

6. Can you change the keyword on a specific button? If so, how?

7. How do you resize the Loop Browser to see all of the available keywords?

8. What happens when you click the Reset button in the Loop Browser?

9. How do you reset all of the Keyword buttons back to the original names and locations?

Answers

1. In the Loops Preferences, select "Adding Loops to Timeline: Convert to Real Instrument," or add Software Instrument loops to Real Instrument tracks to convert them.

2. Extending a region by dragging the upper-right corner will only loop the current region. If you have edited a region in the Timeline, the loop pointer will allow you to loop only the edited portion of the region.

3. You can rearrange the columns in the results list of the Loop Browser by dragging the column header.

4. You can resize columns by dragging the right edge of the column header.

5. You can move a keyword button to a new position in the Loop Browser by dragging the button to the new position.

6. You can change a keyword by Ctrl-clicking a keyword button and choosing a new keyword from the shortcut menu.

7. To resize the Loop Browser, drag upward on the divider between the Timeline and the Loop Browser.

8. All keyword buttons are deselected, and the results list is cleared.

9. To reset the keyword buttons in the Loop Browser to their original names and locations, click the Reset button in the GarageBand Loops Preferences window.

6

Lesson Files	GarageBand 3 Lessons > Lesson_06 > 6-1 Recording Test; 6-2 Tuning; 6-3 Punch-Ins; 6-4 Multitrack
Time	This lesson takes approximately 1 hour and 30 minutes to complete.
Goals	Edit and transpose a Real Instrument track
	Prepare a Real Instrument track for recording
	Record a riff
	Work with the Amp Simulation presets
	Work with the instrument tuner
	Record a punch-in and create a merged region
	Understand multitrack recording
	Find recordings in a project's contents

Working with Real Instruments

GarageBand gives you many choices of instruments, tracks, regions, and methods of recording. In the previous lesson, you worked with flexible, editable Software Instruments. This lesson is dedicated to what GarageBand calls Real Instruments.

Real Instruments are exactly what they sound like: regions recorded from real instruments. With GarageBand, you can record a real instrument such as a guitar, bass, or keyboard directly into the Timeline. You can also use a microphone to record instruments that don't have an output jack, such as a trumpet, violin, grand piano, drum kit, acoustic guitar, or even vocals.

To record a Real Instrument into the Timeline, you have to physically perform or play the part using a real instrument in real time. In contrast to Software Instruments, Real Instrument recordings are "as is"—you can't edit the individual notes or change instruments. However, you can add effects and enhance the tuning and timing of Real Instrument regions once they're recorded.

Why would you record real instruments when you can use Software Instruments? Because they're *real* instruments! Certain instruments can't be simulated very well, so you want to record the real deal.

Suppose you're in a band and you want to record one of your new songs. How do you explain to your drummer that he has to play drums on a MIDI keyboard to get them into the computer? What about the lead vocal, guitar, and bass? Most musicians play best on their chosen instruments, not on a keyboard simulation. (Nothing against keyboards, which happen to be my instrument of choice.)

In this lesson, you'll learn how to work with Real Instruments once they are recorded into the Timeline, and you'll also learn how to record your own Real Instrument regions. Along the way, you'll also learn different recording tricks, techniques, and features.

Connecting Musical Instruments to Your Computer

There are basically two types of musical instruments: electric and acoustic. An electric instrument has a built-in interface for output of its sound, but an acoustic instrument needs a microphone to record its sound.

Electric instruments include electric guitars, keyboards, and electric bass.

You can connect an electric instrument directly to the computer's audio-in port, if your computer has one. The computer audio-in port is a ⅛-inch mini input, so you will need an adapter or cable to convert the ¼-inch output from your instrument to the ⅛-inch audio-in port (mini input) on the computer.

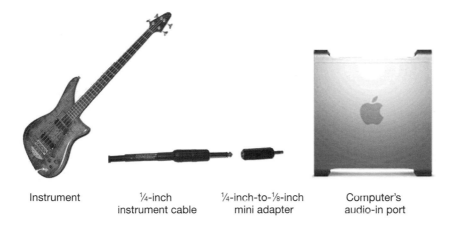

Instrument   ¼-inch   ¼-inch-to-⅛-inch   Computer's
instrument cable   mini adapter   audio-in port

To record an acoustic instrument or vocals, you can connect a microphone to your computer through the audio-in port. G5 computers also include optical digital audio-in/out ports for higher-end audio recording equipment.

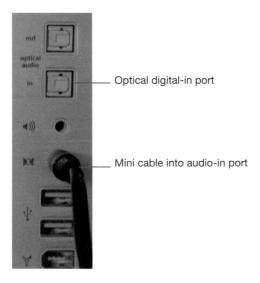

Optical digital-in port

Mini cable into audio-in port

You can also connect an audio interface to your computer and then connect your microphone or instruments to the audio interface. There is a wide range of audio interfaces and compatible formats, including USB, FireWire, PCI, and

PC cards. With the addition of an audio interface, GarageBand allows you to record up to eight Real Instrument tracks and one Software Instrument track simultaneously. So you can record one instrument at a time or the whole band at once. An audio mixer or console will also record more than one instrument or microphone at once, but it will mix all the inputs into only one stereo track. You'll see an example of multitrack recording later in this lesson.

For recording one Real Instrument track at a time, I use the EDIROL PCR-A30 audio interface/MIDI keyboard controller. This interface is both a MIDI controller and an audio interface.

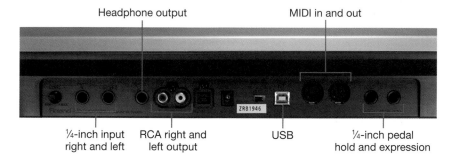

Headphone output   MIDI in and out

¼-inch input   RCA right and   USB   ¼-inch pedal
right and left   left output   hold and expression

Make sure any audio interface is compatible with Mac OS X 10.4 or later (for GarageBand 3) and that your computer supports the format used by the interface.

Also, always follow the manufacturer's instructions, and be sure you install the correct driver on your computer.

Setting Up Sound Input Preferences

If you plan to record through the audio-in port or optical digital-in port on your computer, you will need to set the System Preferences accordingly.

Let's change the preferences to record through your audio-in port. If your computer doesn't have an audio-in port, you won't be able to make the changes, but you'll know how to do it if you ever use GarageBand on a Mac with audio-in.

1   Click the blue apple to open the Apple menu.

This menu is always available, even when you're running an application.

2   Choose System Preferences from the Apple menu.

The System Preferences window opens.

3   Click the Sound button to show the Sound Preferences pane.

4   In the Sound Preferences pane, click the Input button.

The input options on your computer will reflect the current audio devices and hardware you are using. It is very likely your input options will be different from the ones shown in the screen shots.

5   Select the audio interface you will be using for the recording.

If you are using the audio-in port on your computer, select Line In from the sound input list. Likewise, if you are using the optical digital-in port, select that option.

6 Play a riff on your instrument and watch the input level on the Input level meter. Drag the Input Volume slider to raise or lower your input volume levels as needed.

The Input level meter shows the level of your input from left to right. Left is the lowest input level (quietest), and right is the highest (loudest). If your input levels are too high, you will "overdrive" the input, which means the recording is louder than the device can handle, and your music will be distorted.

If the device you select does not have input controls in the Sound Preferences pane, you can raise the output volume on your instrument or device.

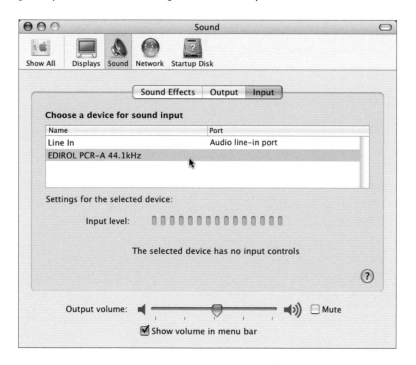

For this exercise, I'm using the EDIROL PCR-A30 audio interface/MIDI keyboard controller as an input device. As you can see in the screen shot, this device does not have an Input Volume slider in the Sound Preferences pane.

Preparing the Project

Before you can record a Real Instrument region, you'll need to open the project **6-1 Recording Test** and save it to your projects folder.

1   Open the project **6-1 Recording Test** from the Lesson_06 folder.

2   Choose File > Save As and save the project to the My GarageBand Projects folder on your Desktop.

Adding a Real Instrument Track

The **6-1 Recording Test** project includes one Real Instrument track containing a Guitar Recording region. In this exercise, you'll create an additional Real Instrument track for your own recording. You'll also need to set up which channel or channels you wish to record to, whether you're recording mono or stereo, and whether you want to monitor (hear) the sound through your speakers or headphones.

For this exercise, you will create a guitar track with no effects recorded on Channel 1, in mono, and with the monitor on.

1   Click the Add Track button (+) located in the bottom-left corner of the GarageBand window to add a new basic track.

2   Select Real Instrument from the New Track dialog, then click Create.

A Real Instrument track appears in the Timeline, and the Track Info pane shows on the right side of the window.

3 In the Track Info pane, select Guitars as the instrument and No Effects as the type of guitar.

Stereo vs. Mono Recording

How do you know when to record mono and when to record stereo? Well, it depends on the instrument and the recording. A single instrument with only one output jack is a mono output. An instrument such as a keyboard with multiple outputs (left and right) gives you a choice of stereo (both left and right outputs) or mono (only the left output).

If you're recording a number of musicians at the same time through a mixing board or console, the signal from each musician may be routed into the mixing board as a mono input. Then the signals are mixed in the board and sent out of the mixer into the computer as a stereo signal.

You can also record a single guitar as a stereo input by changing the track settings to stereo. It just depends on what type of signal you're working with and what you're trying to accomplish.

Each track in GarageBand has two channels for audio recording and playback: Channel 1 and Channel 2. If you record a track in stereo, you use both channels. If you record mono, you record only Channel 1 or Channel 2. At the bottom of the Track Info pane, you can set which channel you record.

In this exercise, you're working with a single electric guitar with a mono output, so the input into the computer will be mono as well.

1   Locate the Input, Volume, and Monitor controls at the bottom of the Track Info pane.

2   Click the Input pop-up menu and choose Channel 1 (Mono) as the format to record only one channel of audio.

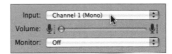

Monitoring Your Input

Monitoring is a musical term for being able to hear yourself play. Musicians monitor their performance in the recording studio and on stage. If you've ever performed live, you know it's nearly impossible to play if you can't hear the sound coming from your own instrument. That would be like painting a picture blindfolded.

Just as you would in a recording studio, you will probably want to monitor your performance when you record a Real Instrument track in GarageBand. If the Monitor setting is off, you won't hear the sound of your instrument going to the computer.

You should always turn off Monitor when you're not recording. Leaving a microphone input on can cause feedback, which is painful to the ears. Avoiding feedback is the reason that Monitor is set to Off by default.

> **TIP** ▶ Don't wear headphones when connecting, disconnecting, or moving an instrument or microphone. There is always the possibility of hearing loud pops when you plug and unplug, as well as feedback that can be a real pain in the ear! Also, if you're using more than one microphone, don't put them too close together, or they are likely to cause feedback.

When do you turn Monitor on? When you're practicing or recording a specific track and can't otherwise hear the instrument as it is played—such as an electronic keyboard. If you are recording vocals with an open microphone, you can turn Monitor on to listen to the recording through headphones. You wouldn't want to listen through speakers while recording in the same room as the microphone because the sound or feedback from the speakers will contaminate the recording.

Once any instrument part is recorded into the Timeline, you will hear it on playback, just as you would any other region in the Timeline.

1   Click the Monitor pop-up menu and change it to the On setting.

2   Adjust the Volume slider as needed to raise or lower the input volume of the track and close the Track Info pane.

Plan Before Recording

There are a few obvious yet essential things to consider before you start recording. First, make sure that the instruments or microphones you plan to use are connected properly and working. Second, be sure you have enough hard-drive space for your recordings. Audio recordings use a fraction of the space of video, but they can accumulate over time, especially if you record many takes. The last thing you want to do is stop your recording session because you're out of drive space.

Stereo audio recorded at CD (44.1 kHz) quality uses around 10 MB of disk space per minute. So 10 recorded stereo tracks, for a song that is 3 minutes long, would fill up around 300 MB.

Recording and Saving a Real Instrument Part

Before you start recording, there are some recording techniques to consider. Should you record the entire song in one take, or break the instrument part into smaller pieces? I think the answer depends on the musician. If there is a song you have played so many times you don't even have to think to play it, feel free to record it in one long and perfect take. Some musicians record multiple takes of a whole song, then edit together the best parts from each take into a master track that becomes the final song. If playing the entire song flawlessly is unlikely, it is very easy to record smaller sections, then put them all together in the Timeline. Most songs in the world of music recording are recorded in smaller pieces, then arranged together to form the final master track. You can also record punch-ins to replace a specific part of a song if necessary.

Let's start with the basics—recording a short musical part, also known as a *riff*.

> **NOTE** ▸ The following recording exercise uses a guitar as an example. However, you are welcome to record whatever instrument you have available.

Setting Up Your Instrument

Take a moment to set up your guitar, keyboard, bass, microphone, or whatever instrument you want to use for the recording exercise. If you don't have an instrument, and your computer has a built-in microphone, you can record finger snaps, or you can whistle. If you don't have an instrument or a microphone, read through the following steps anyway to get a sense of how recording a Real Instrument works.

If you do have an instrument, play a riff on it now. Do you hear a delay between when you play and when you hear the sound? Depending on the audio hardware and computer you are using, there may be a slight delay when playing and recording Real Instruments. The short amount of time the Real Instrument input takes to reach the computer's input port and be processed is referred to as *latency*. You may not be able to eliminate latency completely, but you can reduce the amount of latency in the GarageBand Preferences. Let's take a look at the Preferences setting to reduce latency.

1   Choose GarageBand > Preferences.

2   Click the Audio/MIDI button to open the Audio/MIDI pane.

3 Locate the "Optimize for" section. Select the "Minimum delay when playing instruments live" option if you are experiencing latency delays when you play your instrument.

Selecting "Minimum delay when playing instruments live" will reduce latency by using more of the computer's processing power to process the audio input signal faster. However, this option can affect performance on slower computers. If you don't have latency issues and plan to record multiple tracks simultaneously, change the setting to "Maximum number of simultaneous tracks."

4 Click the General button to return to the General Preferences pane. Locate the metronome controls and select the "During playback and recording" option, if it's not already selected.

5 Press Cmd-W to close Preferences.

Recording a Short Take

Since the track you are about to record has no effects applied to it, the sound of whatever instrument you record will not be altered. You will learn to add effects to the tracks later.

1   On the upper No Effects track, click the Mute button to mute the track.

2   Select the empty No Effects track and make sure the Record Enable button for the track is on.

3   Press the spacebar to start the metronome and playback of the empty track in the Timeline. If you do not hear the metronome, press Cmd-U to turn it on.

NOTE ▸ You can only hear the metronome if the playhead is moving— that is, only while you are playing a song in the Timeline or while you are recording. If you turn on the Count In feature (Control > Count In), GarageBand will count in the first measure (four clicks) before the play-head moves and recording begins.

4   Play a simple musical riff. Practice a few times until you're ready to record. Press Return to move the playhead to the beginning of the Timeline.

TIP▸ The keyboard shortcut to start recording is the R key. This is often easier than using the mouse to click the Record button—especially if you're holding a guitar or another instrument.

5   Choose Control > Count In to turn on the Count In feature.

GarageBand will count in the first four beats before recording begins.

6   Press R, or click the Record button, to record your musical riff.

7   Press the spacebar to stop recording when you're finished.

8   Press Cmd-S to save your project.

That's it! You've recorded an instrument part into GarageBand.

Project Tasks

Now that you've successfully recorded one part, why not try another? Create a new track in the same project and record another part to go along with the first piece you recorded. Don't forget to mute the other tracks before you record if you're not playing along with them. Listen to the finished recording and save your progress when you are finished.

Recording a Long Take

There is nothing wrong with recording the entire song—or even a long part of the song, such as the first half—in one take. If you can play it, by all means record it.

This method is also fantastic for recording song ideas. If you have a melody, lyrics, or instrumental parts floating around in your head, I strongly encourage you to sit down right away and record it. Who cares if it's a rough draft and full of mistakes? The important thing is to document it so you won't forget the subtle creative nuances of the idea while it's fresh. The human brain isn't the most reliable storage medium. Instead of carrying 50 songs around in your head, trying to remember all of them, commit them to your computer instead. You can always delete them or finish them later.

Another thing to remember about recording one long take is that you can always punch in and record over, or rerecord any mistakes you make along the way.

Adding Preset and Custom Effects

In the old days of recording an electric guitar, the particular sound the guitar made was determined by the amplifier, stage, and additional recording equipment used by engineers to alter the sound. Amplifiers were just big black speakers used to project the sound of an electric instrument. Now that digital recording has emerged, the new amplifiers have settings to alter the sound of the guitar itself.

GarageBand builds this extraordinary technology into the software with an effect called amp simulator. Amp simulation lets you change the sound of the guitar as you play and record. All you have to do is play your guitar and then select the type of amplifier simulation sound and feel for your guitar. For those of you raised on a computer, this may not seem like a big deal, but for those of us who used to perform on stage with amplifiers and racks of equipment, it's huge.

Using Amp Simulation

At this time, there should be three tracks titled No Effects in the Timeline; two of them include your recorded Real Instrument regions. In this exercise, you'll apply amp simulation effects to the upper No Effects track containing the Guitar Recording region I provided. Later, you can try the different effects on your recordings.

1   Unmute all of the tracks. In the upper No Effects track, click the Solo button (looks like headphones).

When a track is soloed, the sound is isolated, and other unsoloed tracks will be temporarily muted.

2   Press Cmd-U to turn off the metronome during playback.

3   In the Timeline, play the Guitar Recording region so you can hear the part with no effects.

Now let's listen to it with one of the different guitar amp simulators. To change the sound, all you have to do is change the track info.

4   Double-click the upper No Effects track header to open the Track Info pane, if it is not already showing.

5   In the Track Info pane, click Arena Rock to change the sound of the guitar amplifier.

The icon and name of the track change as well as the sound.

6   Play the track from the beginning and listen to the guitar part using the Arena Rock amplifier sound.

7   Press C to show the Cycle Region Ruler. Create a cycle region above the recorded guitar region in the Timeline.

8   Play the track again. This time, click through some of the different guitar amplifier sounds as the track plays to hear them one at a time.

TIP ▶ Once you've clicked a new amp simulator, you can use your up and down arrow keys to move through the other guitar amplifier sounds. If you press the up and down arrows before you click in the Track Info pane, you'll change which track is selected in the Timeline instead.

Notice that each guitar amp simulator sounds different.

NOTE ▶ Additional amplifier sounds are available in the Jam Pack expansion packages.

9 In the Track Info pane, select No Effects.

The track icon changes back to a speaker.

The next step will be to add some effects to the No Effects track.

Adding Custom Effects to a Track

Even though your current track is called No Effects and has no effects doesn't mean that you can't add effects to it. This exercise will acquaint you with the effects included in GarageBand and how to add one to a track. You will work more with effects later in this book. For now, you will just add a simple effect like Reverb.

1 Select the upper No Effects track, if it isn't already selected.

2 In the Track Info pane, click the Details disclosure triangle to get more details about the effects used in the track.

The Track Info pane expands to reveal additional detailed information about the track. Notice that all of the sliders to the right of the effects are dimmed (gray) because the track currently has no effects applied to it.

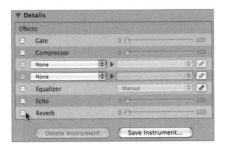

3 Click the Reverb box to add reverb to the track.

You can now adjust the slider to the right of the Reverb effect. By default, the slider is set to 0 (no reverb). The highest setting is 100.

4 Drag the Reverb slider about halfway (to approximately 50).

5 Play the selected track to hear it with the reverb. While the track plays, adjust the Reverb slider to hear the track with different levels of reverb. Repeat this process until you get the reverb just the way you like it. I'm going to stick with around 50 on mine. Don't close the Track Info pane.

You have successfully added the Reverb effect to your track.

Viewing Selected Instruments

Before you save the instrument effect you created, let's take a look at the View Instrument pop-up menu at the top of the Track Info pane (below the Real Instrument and Master Track buttons).

With this pop-up menu, you can choose which instruments to view in the Track Info pane.

1   Click the View Instrument pop-up menu to see the different options.

The View Instrument pop-up includes three default settings: Show All, My Settings, and GarageBand. If you have any of the Jam Pack expansion packages installed on your computer, they will show up on the list, too.

NOTE ▶ Your pop-up menu may vary from mine depending on which custom loops, instruments, or Jam Packs you have installed on your computer.

2   Choose Show All from the View Instrument menu.

This setting will show all of your instruments in the instrument list, including customized settings you create and save.

Saving an Instrument

Now that you've added an effect to your track, you can save the instrument with your custom effect to your list of instruments. Once you have saved an instrument sound, you can use it again on different tracks or projects.

1   In the Track Info pane, click the Save Instrument button.

The Save Instrument dialog appears.

2   Type *Guitar with Reverb* in the "Save as" field and click Save.

Guitar with Reverb appears in the Guitars instrument list.

3 Click the Details disclosure triangle to hide the details portion of the window. Press Cmd-I to close the Track Info pane.

The track in your Timeline is now called Guitar with Reverb.

4 Save the project.

You can use this method to create and save different instruments you want to use later.

NOTE ▶ To delete a saved instrument, select it in the instrument list and then click the Delete Instrument button. You can also revise an instrument anytime by selecting the instrument, changing the settings, and then saving the changes.

Repairing Recording Problems

As discussed earlier, many musicians record an entire song in one take, then go back and record punch-ins to fix mistakes in the performance, or they record multiple long takes and edit the best parts of each take together. Others record songs in multiple short takes, which are then arranged in the Timeline to form the complete song.

When people listen to your finished song, they'll have no idea if you recorded it all in one take or in small sections. So your job is to do whatever is necessary to get the song recorded—period. There are several common recording issues when working with Real Instruments, including tuning, timing, and mistakes. Let's start with tuning.

Working with the Instrument Tuner

If you play a guitar, you probably need to tune it often. Most professional musicians keep an electronic tuner with them so they can tune their guitars with precision. GarageBand includes an instrument tuner you can use before you record. For this exercise, you'll need to hook up an instrument such as a guitar to the computer. You can use the same instrument you used to record in the previous exercise. If you don't have an instrument handy, just read through the steps so you'll know how to use the tuner the next time you want to record an instrument. I'll be using an acoustic guitar and microphone pickup.

1 Open **6-2 Tuning** from the Lesson_06 folder.

2 In the time display, click the Instrument Tuner button, which looks like a tuning fork.

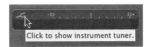

The time display changes from the normal setting into the instrument tuner.

3 Play a C note on your guitar (or other instrument). If you're a vocalist, try singing a C.

When you play a note on your instrument, the name of the note appears at the left end of the instrument tuner, and a colored light appears under the scale that takes up most of the display. If your note is perfectly in tune, a green light appears under the 0 mark. If it's not, a red light appears to the left of 0 if the pitch is flat, to the right of 0 if sharp.

4 Tune your instrument until you get a green light in the center of the time display, indicating that your instrument is perfectly tuned for that note.

5   Try tuning your instrument for several other notes.

6   When you are finished, click the Musical Time button (a note icon) below the Instrument Tuner button to return the time display to its normal setting.

> **NOTE** ▶ The instrument tuner is designed to work with one note at a time. It will not work with chords or combined notes. And sorry folks, but you can't hook up a bunch of instruments at once and try to tune them all at the same time.

Enhancing Tuning and Timing in the Editor

The editor includes two advanced features to enhance the tuning or timing of your recorded Real Instrument regions. Both are turned off by default until they are needed.

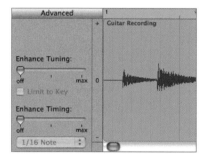

The Enhance Tuning slider affects all regions in the selected track for both your own recordings and loops. Enhance Tuning works accurately only on single notes within a track, so be sure the selected track doesn't include chords.

When you use the Enhance Tuning feature, it enhances the tuning of notes by moving them to the closest note in the project's key. If you want to move them to the closest note that is not in the project's key, deselect the "Limit to Key" option. The default setting is to use the project's key.

You can also enhance the timing of a Real Instrument track. This is useful if the pitch and performance are good, but the notes aren't perfectly in time with the project.

The Enhance Timing slider enhances all Real Instrument regions, your own recordings, or loops. You can enhance the timing of a single note, chord, and even percussion. This feature works best with regions that contain patterns of notes rather than pads of long sustained notes.

This feature is similar to the Fix Timing feature for Software Instrument regions, except the Fix Timing feature fixes the timing of every selected note event in a region, whereas the Enhance Timing feature for Real Instruments adjusts the timing of peaks within the waveform and is less exact.

> **TIP** ▶ The Enhance Tuning and Enhance Timing features may not work equally well with all types of musical recordings. Experiment with the different values and listen carefully to the results to find the best timing enhancement for each individual track. To enhance a track, select the entire track in the editor.

Recording Over a Mistake

This project includes the different stages of repairing a recording mistake by recording over the mistake. The top region contains the original Dry Horn Section recording used in the song "Alaska Sunrise" and includes a major mistake in the middle. Fortunately, this process is easy. You can use a cycle region to narrow down the section you wish to rerecord. This is known in recording circles as *punching in*.

Recall that when you recorded with a cycle region using a Software Instrument, you were able to record multiple passes and keep adding to the part within the cycle region.

Recording Real Instruments with cycle regions is different because GarageBand records only the first pass. After the first pass, you can only monitor the newly recorded section. This is a good thing. If you don't like the recording, you can undo and try again. But if you got lucky and recorded the perfect take, you won't accidentally record over it because you took too long to hit the spacebar to stop the recording.

Let's take a look at a Real Instrument region with mistakes that I had to punch in and record again.

1 Open the project **6-3 Punch-Ins** and save it to the My GarageBand Projects folder.

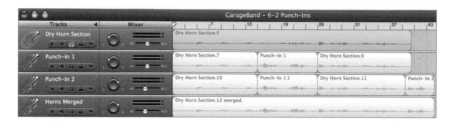

2 Select the Dry Horn Section track and make sure the track is soloed. (Solo button is on.)

3 Play the soloed track and listen for the most obvious mistake near the middle of the region.

Once you have located a mistake, you can set up a cycle region over the mistake to designate which part of the region you want to rerecord. When you begin recording in the new cycle region, a new region is created that matches the length of the cycle region.

4 Press C, or click the Cycle button, to see the cycle region that I used to punch in and rerecord over the original mistake.

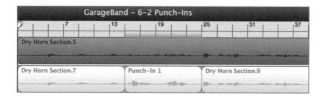

5 Play the cycle region to hear the section isolated by the cycle region.

Normally, you can rerecord directly in your original recorded region. Since I was creating this project as a demonstration of punch-ins, I copied my original recording to two other tracks so you could see the different takes and compare the recordings.

The next step is to select the track you want to record.

6   Unsolo the upper track and click the Solo button on the Punch-In 1 track.

Before you record a part of a region, turn on the metronome, and choose Control > Count In so you can hear the measure prior to the region you are about to record. Both selections will be checkmarked in the Control menu if they are on.

7   Play the cycle region on the Punch-In 1 track to hear the rerecorded section.

8   Press C to turn off the cycle region, then play the track from the beginning to hear the entire repaired track.

When you rerecord part of a region, the new recording will be named after the track instead of the original region.

9   Unsolo the Punch-In 1 track and solo the Punch-In 2 track. Play the last part of the track to hear the recording I added at the end.

> **TIP** If you're adding a recording to the end of a region, you don't have to use the cycle region. Instead you can just start recording from the play-head position. If you think you may need to try several recording attempts, use the cycle region so you can easily cover up one recording with another until it is fixed.

10   Hide the cycle region and unsolo the Punch-In 2 track.

Rerecording part of a region is a great method for masking mistakes in an otherwise terrific performance.

Joining Noncontiguous Real Instrument Regions

Now that you know how to punch in and fix a Real Instrument region, let's look at an advanced technique for joining Real Instrument regions that were recorded in different takes or at different times, also referred to as *noncontiguous regions*.

Why would you want to join noncontiguous Real Instrument regions? Sometimes you edit a recording, or arrange a series of different takes together in a track, and you want to keep the edited track as one region to make it easier to move to another project and archive. Also, if you plan to duplicate a region on another track, it's much easier to do so if you have to move only one longer region instead of many shorter edited regions.

When you join recorded regions to create a new file, the original recordings and the new merged file will be stored together in the project's Media folder.

Let's use this technique to select and join all four regions in the Punch-In 2 track.

1   Click the Punch-In 2 track header to select all the regions in that track.

2   Choose Edit > Join, or press Cmd-J, to join all of the regions into one merged file.

A mixdown progress window appears. If the regions you want to join come from different recording sessions, you may see a dialog warning you that a new file will be created. If you see this dialog, click the Create button.

The new region appears in the Timeline track, replacing the original regions.

All of the separate regions in the track have been merged into one new region.

The new merged file will be added to the project file once you save the project.

3   Press Cmd-S to save the new version of the project.

This technique can be very useful for archiving an edited Real Instrument recording or for doubling a track that consists of numerous shorter edited regions.

Project Tasks

Now that you've seen how I recorded a punch-in to fix the song, it's your turn to try recording and punching in. Use the same instrument you recorded with earlier in this lesson. Record a region with a mistake, then create a cycle region to punch in and fix the mistake. This exercise will truly be an example of learning from your mistakes. Be sure to save your project before moving on to the next exercise.

> **NOTE** ▸ Always select the track you want to record and make sure that the Record Enable button is turned on for that track.

Punch-ins get easier the more you practice with them.

Multitrack Recording

GarageBand allows you to record up to eight Real Instrument tracks and one Software Instrument track at the same time. This lets you record instruments and vocals together, as well as additional backing tracks in any combination you choose. To record multiple tracks simultaneously, you will need to use an audio interface with at least two input channels for recording.

I'm currently using the Edirol FA-101, which connects to the computer through FireWire and has up to 10 inputs and 10 outputs. Although my interface can handle up to 10 different channels at a time, GarageBand is still limited to 9 (8 Real Instrument tracks and 1 Software Instrument track).

In the next lesson, you'll work with a podcast interview of the Seminole, Florida, band Speakeasy, featuring Jimmy Kaufholz (vocals and guitar), Kyle Chason (lead and rhythm guitar), and Amy Harwood (vocals). The multitrack project you'll open for this exercise includes the first two minutes of their song "Take a Bow."

1   Open the project **6-4 Multitrack** from the Lesson_06 folder.

The project opens with six Real Instrument recorded tracks and a Real Instrument mixed version of the song in the top track. The mixed version has been muted so you can focus on the other tracks. As you can see, these are long recorded regions that were done in one take. (Actually, the entire song was laid down in one take—this is just the first two minutes.)

2   Play the first part of the project to get a feel for the song.

This song could have been recorded one track at a time or in a group of tracks at the same time. The method you use really depends on the band and the limitations of the musicians. If a musician plays more than one instrument and sings, you won't be able to record all of his or her parts at once. However, you could record his or her vocals and one instrument at the same time.

Since this is a folk band, and they are used to playing and singing at the same time, it's a good idea to try recording the vocals and their acoustic instruments at the same time to capture the *feel* of their music. You can always punch in to repair problems, or you could rerecord the instrument or vocal parts later if needed. For this example, I would record the two acoustic guitar leads plus the vocals at the same time. Then, I'd go back and record the solo guitar part (which doesn't come in until the middle of the song). Finally, I'd record the Block (percussion) track because it can easily be played last to fit the groove of the other acoustic instruments, instead of the other way around.

3   Mute the Kyle solo and Block tracks, then play the project from the beginning to hear the first four tracks, which were recorded simultaneously.

The Kyle Solo region does not include a waveform because the actual solo part occurs later in the song.

4   Unmute the lower two tracks.

To record multiple tracks simultaneously, you must first create the tracks, assign the input channels, and turn on the Record Enable button for each track. If you enable more than eight Real Instrument tracks or one Software Instrument track, the first track you enabled will be disabled for recording just to prevent you from exceeding the maximum number of recording tracks. If you need to record more than eight Real Instrument tracks, you can always record the first group of tracks, then enable a new set of tracks and record them as a second recording session.

Working with Vocal Effect Presets

The vocals in this song were recorded *dry* (without effects). However, just like other Real Instrument recordings, you can add vocal preset effects. In fact, GarageBand includes a wide variety of vocal preset effects you can use to enhance, distort, or modify the sound of recorded vocals. You'll work more with the vocal effects in the next lesson when you create a podcast. For now, let's just experiment with a few to see how they enhance the vocals.

1   Double-click the Amy vocals track header to select the track and open the Track Info pane. Click the Solo button to isolate the sound of her vocal track.

2   Move the playhead to the 14th measure and start playback.

3   In the Track Info pane, select Female Basic as the preset vocal effect. Listen to the subtle change in Amy's vocals.

4   Select the Helium Breath vocal preset to hear what she might sound like singing after inhaling a dose of helium.

When you stop laughing, use the up and down arrow keys to try different vocal effects. The Male and Female presets are designed to accentuate those respective voices, but they will not make a female vocalist sound like a male, or vice versa.

5   Select Female Basic as the preset vocal effect, and unsolo the track to hear her enhanced vocal with the other tracks.

The name of the track changes to reflect the applied preset, but the region within the track maintains its original name.

TIP You can only use one preset on a track at a time. If you like more than one preset on your vocals, double the track, or split the region and place the parts on separate tracks, and add different effects presets.

Project Tasks

Take a moment and add a vocal preset to the Jimmy vocals track. The Male Basic preset will work fine, but feel free to try others. When you're finished, save your changes to the project.

Tips for Recording Multiple Tracks

▶ Practice, practice, practice. I don't mean to sound like your music teacher here, but if you're recording five musicians plus a vocalist at the same time and somebody hasn't done their homework, it's going to be a very long day.

▶ If you're used to playing a song along with the other musicians, it will be more comfortable for you to record multiple tracks at once. If you are a vocalist who also plays guitar, piano, or some other instrument, this is a terrific way to record your song demos. It's much easier for many artists to get into the groove if they can play their instruments while singing, or vice versa.

▶ Don't rush it, and don't try to record the entire song at once if you're not ready. You can always edit the parts together later.

▶ Record the difficult parts separately. If your song contains a tricky section, record it separately so you can focus on that section, rather than try to perfect it along with the rest of the song. Also, if you have one musician who is having trouble keeping up or is continually making mistakes, have him sit this one out while you record the other parts. Then create a practice CD the musician can use for homework (see Lesson 10). The musician can come back in and record his part solo when he's ready.

▶ Don't forget to tune your instruments *before* you record. It's much easier to record in tune than try to fix it later.

▶ Record your tracks, especially vocals, clean—that is, without too many effects from external devices. You can always add effects, like the guitar amplifier simulators or vocal effects presets that come with GarageBand, *after* you record the track. If you record a vocal instrument with too many external effects, you won't be able to change your mind later—or remove the effects.

▶ Have fun, learn from your mistakes, and remember you can always undo, try again, record a punch-in, or fix mistakes in the editor.

TIP ▶ When you're recording long takes, consider creating edit-friendly moments within the take by inserting a brief pause and releasing the sustain pedal. This will produce a clean break in the waveform, and you will be able to try different takes and build a better song. (Obviously, you wouldn't do this in a live performance, or if the song requires a solid single take.)

Reusing Your Real Instrument Recordings

Have you ever wondered how Real Instrument recordings are stored on your computer? GarageBand stores all of the Real Instrument recordings in a Media folder inside of your project. Understanding how your Real Instrument recordings are stored will enable you to find the recording files and reuse them in other projects.

In this exercise, you'll locate the Real Instrument recordings for the project **Alaska Sunrise**. Let's start by quitting GarageBand.

1   Choose File > Quit, or press Cmd-Q, to quit the program.

2   On the Desktop, double-click the GarageBand 3 Lessons folder.

3   Click the Column View button to change to Column view.

4 Click the Lesson_02 folder to show the Lesson_02 files in the next column.

Notice that there are two GarageBand projects.

OK, so you found the projects. Where are the Media folders for the projects? They're inside the project files themselves. GarageBand project files use a special format called a "package," which acts as a container for a number of files and folders but looks like a single file in the Finder. Let's locate and open the Media folder for the **2-2 Alaska Sunrise Final** project.

5 Ctrl-click the project **2-2 Alaska Sunrise Final** and choose Show Package Contents from the shortcut menu.

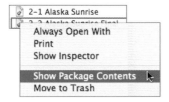

The Finder window shows the contents of the **2-2 Alaska Sunrise Final** project. The contents include a Contents folder, Freeze Files (rendered files), the project data, and a Media folder.

6   Click the Column View button to view the contents in columns.

Now that you have located the Media folder and changed the view to columns, you can preview the recordings directly in the Finder. Your goal is to locate the timpani recording.

7   Click the Media folder to reveal its contents in the next column.

Recordings are always saved with a project. Loops, movie files, and still images stored in other locations on the computer are only saved in a project if it is saved as an archive.

Six different recording files appear in the right column.

These recordings are numbered according to the recorded take that was saved in the finished project. Let's preview the different takes to find the timpani recording.

NOTE ▶ This was not an actual recording of a timpani drum. However, the region in the song was called Timpani because that was the sound I played from the samples on my external keyboard.

To preview the recording, click the recording to open it in the Preview pane.

8 Click Recording#48.aif to open the file.

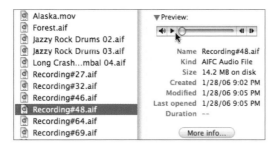

Recording#48.aif opens in the Preview pane.

9 In the Preview pane, click the Play button to preview (listen to) the file.

You may not hear audio right away, depending on when that actual sound starts after the beginning of the recording. Remember, Real Instrument recordings begin at the playhead position when you click Record, not when you play the first note.

So what does locating and previewing recordings have to do with your projects? The biggest thing is that you can duplicate and import (option-drag) these files directly into the Timeline of your GarageBand projects so you can reuse them whenever you want. You can also drag your recordings to the Loop Browser to add them to your loop collection. You can learn how to save files as loops in "Adding Loops to GarageBand" (Bonus Exercises > **Add_Loops.pdf**) on the accompanying DVD.

When you save a project, all of the Real Instrument recorded regions, which are purple (if original) or orange (if imported), are saved to the Media folder of that project.

Now you know how to locate and reuse recordings from one song to another.

Archiving Your Recordings

You can archive your recordings by saving all of your best takes in one project. You'll then have your best recordings available to reuse for new projects.

The specific steps for archiving are simple. When you first record a project, save all of the best takes to that project and add the word "recordings" to the name of the project—for example, Alaska Sunrise Recordings. Save this version of the song, then choose File > Save As, and save the song again with just the song name (Alaska Sunrise). For this version, you'll delete everything except the takes you want to use for the actual song. Resave the song when you finish deleting the unwanted recordings. The result will be two versions of your song—one version with all of the best recordings archived, and the other with just the best takes you actually use in the finished song.

After the song is completed, you can always delete the recordings version of the song if you want to clear some disk space and don't think you'll ever need the other takes again.

Archiving Your Projects

As I mentioned earlier, in GarageBand you can archive an entire song and all of its contents. Normally when you save a song, the project file references the movies, loops, and Software Instruments you have stored on your computer. But what if you want to take that song to a different computer that doesn't have all of the same loops and media? Perhaps you are using loops from one of the Jam Packs, or you recorded and saved your own loops. Whatever the situation, you now have the option to save a song and all of its regions to the project file's package contents. Then, when you open the archived song on a different computer, it contains all the regions needed to play and edit the project.

To save your project as an archive, choose File > Save As, then select the Save As Archive option in the Save As window.

> **NOTE ▶** Saving a song as an archive greatly increases the size of the song file because it contains media for all of the regions in the song, not just Real Instrument recordings and references to loops and Software Instruments on the computer.

That's it—the end of the Real Instrument lesson, and the beginning of your recording careers! You now have a solid working knowledge of recording, saving, editing, and archiving your recordings. Now that you can record and arrange your original music, the next lesson will show you how to mix your tracks to polish the overall sound.

Lesson Review

1. How many tracks can be recorded simultaneously in GarageBand?

2. What does monitoring input mean during Real Instrument recording?

3. How does a cycle region affect a Real Instrument recording?

4. What steps are necessary to hear different effects, such as amp simulators, applied to a track?

5. Can you modify and save effects that are applied to a track?

Answers

1. With the use of an approved audio interface, you can record up to eight Real Instrument tracks and one Software Instrument track.

2. Monitoring input means that you can hear the instrument you're playing before and during recording.

3. Recording a Real Instrument using a cycle region will only record during the first pass. The second pass of the playhead in the cycle region will play back the newly recorded region.

4. You can hear different effects as you apply them to a track by playing the track in the Timeline and changing the instrument or effects in the Track Info pane while the track is playing.

5. Yes. You can save your effects settings as instruments in the Track Info pane and use them again on different tracks or projects.

7

Lesson Files   GarageBand 3 Lessons > Lesson_07 > 7-1 Highway Brothers unmxd; 7-2 HB volume mixed; 7-3 HB rough mix; 7-4 HB with effects; 7-5 HB dynamic; 7-6 Highway Brothers mixed; 7-7 Highway Brothers Major

Time   This lesson takes approximately 1 hour and 30 minutes to complete.

Goals   Understand basic mixing

Work with the Track Mixer

Set volume levels and pan controls for each track

Fix the timing of a Software Instrument note and region

Add effects to a track

Adjust a track's Volume and Pan curves

Adjust the Master track's Volume and Master Pitch curves

Adjust the master output volume levels to avoid clipping

Compare minor and major scale type loops

Work with ducking

Lesson 7
Mixing and Effects

With GarageBand, you can record and create professional-quality music. However, to make your finished songs actually sound professional, you need to understand the fine art of mixing music.

Fortunately, the GarageBand interface includes an easy-to-use Track Mixer with controls for volume level and pan position.

In Lesson 4, you arranged a song in the Timeline using basic and advanced music arrangement techniques. Your goal in this lesson is to take an arranged song to the next level to make it sound like a professional composition. To accomplish this, you'll need to apply professional mixing techniques, including balancing volume, panning, fixing timing, changing velocity, and adding effects. Along the way, you'll also learn some handy shortcuts for features you're already familiar with, such as soloing, muting, and showing cycle regions.

Understanding Basic Mixing

Mixing a song is the art of carefully blending all of the different sounds and musical textures into one cohesive, balanced piece of music. Arranging regions in separate tracks is easy once you get the hang of it—in fact, you've been arranging music since you started this book. Mixing takes a little more practice. It also takes some ear training.

Ear training means being able to listen beyond the basic music to analyze the full panoramic scope of a song. Chefs train their palates so they can taste food beyond the basics. For instance, an Italian chef can taste the full array of spices in a marinara sauce, from oregano to fresh ground pepper. Some chefs can even tell you what type of tomato was used and how ripe it was. It's great to be able to taste the spaghetti sauce and know whether you like it not. It's even better if you know why.

Throughout this lesson, you'll be training your ear so that, by the end of the exercises, you too will be able to hear beyond the music and notice the subtle elements within the mix of a song.

Let's start by listening to the finished song titled **Highway Brothers**.

1   Open **7-6 Highway Brothers mixed** from the Lesson_07 folder.

This finished song includes 11 music tracks plus 2 empty tracks at the bottom for you to record your own Real Instrument or Software Instrument parts after the lesson.

2   Play the finished song.

I wrote this song about a nomadic Southern rock band that lives on the road traveling from gig to gig. They're always the opening act, never the headliner, and they never play in the same town twice. It might make for an interesting documentary, and if so, this would be the opening title music.

Now that you've heard the finished piece, let's compare it to the unmixed song.

3 Choose File > Open and select **7-1 Highway Brothers unmxd** from the Lesson_07 folder.

4 Play the first half of the unmixed song and listen for anything that stands out, in either a good or bad way.

As you play the song, listen for the following:

▶ How is the overall pacing/tempo of the song?

▶ Are some parts difficult to hear? Do some parts seem too loud? Is the overall volume of the song even?

▶ Does the song sound and feel finished?

▶ Does it sound like something you'd buy, or does it sound more like something homemade?

What was your impression of the unmixed song? My first impression is *wake up!* The tempo seems really slow; if this were a live performance, the audience would have a hard time staying focused, let alone awake. Otherwise, all of the musical elements (instruments and parts) are there, but the levels are all over the place. The unmixed song doesn't sound or feel very professional.

Stepping up the tempo of the piece is so easy, let's go ahead and take care of it before moving on and saving the project. The current tempo is 95, which we've already established feels a bit slow. 110 ought to be fast enough to pick up the pace without feeling like they've had way too much coffee.

5 In the time display, click the current tempo (95) and drag the Tempo slider up to 110.

6 Play the song again at the new tempo.

Much better. Too bad you can't actually change the tempo of a live performance that easily.

Now that you've modified the tempo and listened to the unmixed song,
let's save it so you'll be able to compare your work to the unmixed version.

7   Press Shift-Cmd-S to open the Save As window.

8   Change the name to *Highway Brothers* and save it to your My GarageBand
   Projects folder.

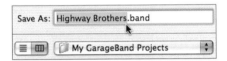

Working with the Track Mixer

The first step to mixing a song in GarageBand is a basic understanding of the
Track Mixer.

The Track Mixer is located between the track header and the Timeline. You can
hide or show the Track Mixer by clicking the disclosure triangle next to the
word "Tracks" at the top of the window.

1   Click the disclosure triangle next to the word "Tracks" at the top of the
   window to show the Track Mixer. (The Track Mixer has been showing in
   all of the previous lessons.)

The Track Mixer appears between the track headers and the Timeline.

The Track Mixer contains three separate tools: the Volume slider, the Pan wheel, and the Level meters.

Let's start with the Volume slider.

Adjusting Levels with the Volume Slider

You can adjust the volume levels for an individual track with the Volume slider. The overall goal is to blend the different levels of all the tracks so that all the instruments can be heard, but the right tracks are emphasized.

By default, the Volume slider is set to 0 dB (decibels) for all tracks. 0 dB doesn't mean the volume of the track is 0 decibels. It actually means that there has been no change applied to the track's volume level. This applies whether the track contains recorded regions or loops. To change the track's volume level, you can drag the slider to the right to raise the volume level and to the left to lower the volume level. You can adjust the volume for an individual track while the playhead is static or while you are playing the song.

There are 11 different tracks—which levels should you adjust first? Great question. Generally, you prioritize your tracks and start with the lead vocals or lead instruments. Since this song doesn't contain vocals, the two acoustic guitar tracks containing the melody are the lead instruments, and therefore they take priority. Once the levels of the lead tracks are good, you then move on to the rhythm tracks.

Let's start by adjusting the volume level on the Acoustic Guitar 1 track (near the middle of the track list). Before you adjust the volume, you'll need to solo the track so you can hear the level change without the other tracks.

1   Click the Acoustic Guitar 1 track header to select the track in the Timeline.

The track turns brighter blue to indicate it has been selected.

2   Press S, or click the Solo button, to solo the track.

The soloed track becomes the only audible track in the Timeline.

3   Drag the Volume slider all the way to the left.

The slider turns blue when you click it to indicate it has been selected. The lowest volume level is –144.0 dB (silence). That means the level has been lowered by 144.0 dB from the original volume level.

Next, you'll raise the volume while the track is playing.

4   Press Return, and then play the soloed track from the beginning of the song.

5   Drag the Volume slider to the right to raise the volume level while the track is playing.

6   Release the slider when you think you've reached a good volume level.

How do you know if your volume level is good? You can look at the Level meters.

Reading the Level Meters

The Level meters use colored bars to visually represent the volume level for the track.

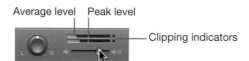

The lower the volume, the shorter the solid colored bars. If the color is green, the level is within a safe range and isn't too loud. If the color turns from green to yellow, that means caution—your sound is bordering on being too loud. If it turns red, you need to stop and turn the volume down immediately. The two circles at the end of the Level meters are the clipping indicators. Clipping means your music is not only too loud, but it could be distorted.

The Level meters in GarageBand are "sticky," which means a single line of the colored bar will stick to the highest position on the meter while the average levels continue to change. The average volume level is marked by the solid colored bar, and the peaks are marked with the vertical line.

Let's create a cycle region and take a look at the Level meters in action.

1   Move your playhead back to the beginning of the Timeline.

2   Press C to open the cycle region.

3   Drag the ends of the yellow cycle region bar to resize the cycle region until it is approximately the length of the first region in the selected track.

4   Press the spacebar to play the Acoustic Picking region in the soloed track.

5   As the region plays, watch the average levels and the peak levels in the meter.

If any of the levels in the meter turn yellow or red, lower the volume for the track. You'll know your level is acceptable when the average stays within the green "safe" region of the meter, and the peaks remain within the green and yellow regions.

Keep in mind that you can use the Level meters to see the levels, but the only way to make sure the levels are right for the song is to hear the track with the rest of the song.

6   Press C to hide the cycle region.

Project Tasks

Now that you've set the volume level of the Acoustic Guitar 1 track, let's take a moment to find a good level for the Acoustic Guitar 2 track. You'll start by unsoloing the Acoustic Guitar 1 track, soloing the Acoustic Guitar 2 track, and finding a good level. Then solo the Acoustic Guitar 1 track again so you can hear both guitar tracks and make sure the combined levels are good. Instead of using the cycle region, play the entire song with the guitar tracks soloed, and watch their Level meters. I used a volume level of 3.1 dB on both acoustic guitar tracks.

Using the Pan Wheel

The Pan wheel controls the left-to-right placement of a track within the stereo field. The "Pan" in Pan wheel stands for "panoramic." A panoramic photograph is an image that includes your full visual spectrum from the far left to the far right. In other words, it's everything you can see without turning your head. A stereo field is everything you can hear from the far left to the far right, without turning your head.

Imagine a panoramic photograph of the Rocky Mountains with a train cutting through the far-left side of the image. Visually, you place the train on the left side of your field of view. You would also place the sound of the train on the far-left side of the stereo field.

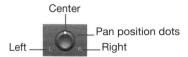

By default, all of the tracks in GarageBand start with the pan position set to the center. With center pan position, the sound is heard equally out of both speakers—it sounds like it is directly in front of you in the center of the audio space.

To adjust the pan position of a track, click the small white dots around the Pan wheel. Let's adjust the pan position of the selected track.

This exercise works best if you are listening through headphones, so take a minute and put on your headset before you start. Make sure your headphones have the right speaker (R) on the right ear and the left speaker (L) on the left ear.

1   Unsolo the Acoustic Guitar 2 track.

2   On the Acoustic Guitar 1 track, click the dot next to the L on the lower-left side of the Pan wheel to change the pan position to the far left of the stereo field.

3   Press C to show the cycle region. Press the spacebar to listen to the cycle region.

Notice that the guitar part sounds like it is coming from the far left.

NOTE ▶ If you hear the guitar coming from the far right, you probably have your headphones on backwards.

4   Click the dot next to the R on the lower-right side of the Pan wheel to change the pan position to the far right of the stereo field.

Notice that the sound of the guitar jumps to the far-right side.

5   Click the dot on the middle-right side between the center position and the far-right position.

If the Pan wheel were a clock, the dot would be at 2:00.

Notice that the guitar still sounds like it is on the right, but closer to the middle of the stereo field. Now let's add the other guitar and make it sound like it is playing on the opposite position from the center of the stage (10:00 on the Pan wheel).

6   Solo the Acoustic Guitar 2 track so that both acoustic guitar tracks are soloed.

7   Press C to hide the cycle region.

8   On the Acoustic Guitar 2 track, click the dot on the middle-left position between the center position and the far-left position (10:00).

9   Listen to the panned guitar tracks.

Notice how it sounds like two different guitar players sitting on the right-center and left-center of the stage.

10 Press the spacebar to stop playback.

NOTE ▶ To quickly reset the Volume and Pan controls to the default settings, Option-click the controls. The default volume level is 0 dB, and the default pan position is Center.

Now that you have a better understanding of the Track Mixer and how to use it, let's start mixing the song.

Creating a Rough Mix

When mixing, you start with a rough mix, then fine-tune the mix, and finally polish the mix in the final master. There are five basic steps for creating the final mix:

1. Adjust the volume levels of the individual tracks to balance the sound of the different instruments.

2. Adjust the pan positions of the individual tracks to place them in the correct location in the stereo field.

3. Find and fix any musical imperfections in timing, velocity, or performance. (This may require editing in the editor, or rerecording a section of the song.)

4. Add and adjust effects to enhance the sound of individual tracks or the whole song.

5. Create dynamic volume and pan changes over time using the Volume and Pan curves on individual tracks and the Master track.

Let's start with step 1, adjusting the volume levels of the different tracks.

As you can imagine, there are hundreds of combinations of volume levels you could try on this song. Instead of experimenting, let's use logic and come up with a plan.

Planning Your Volume Mix

To mix the volume levels, you need to know what type of sound you are going for in your song. What style of music is this song? A vocal ballad might favor the vocal tracks and the lead instruments and keep the drums low in the mix. A club song might favor the drums and synth bass tracks and bury the supporting tracks. Rock songs often favor the lead guitar and vocals and keep the drums about midlevel. Every song is different, every style is different, and every mix is different.

As I mentioned before, this song is about a nomadic Southern rock band, and I want the style to feel like a live performance. The guitars are the lead instruments and should be played higher (louder) in the mix. The shaker, tambourine, and strings are supporting background parts that should be lower (quieter) in the overall mix.

Mixing Volume Levels for Individual Tracks

The first step is to adjust the volume levels to balance the song. Mixing tracks of music is very much like mixing cooking ingredients. You start with the main ingredients, like water and tomatoes if it is a marinara sauce. Then you slowly add more ingredients, tasting along the way to make sure there isn't too much or too little of anything before moving on to the next. Following this analogy, the main ingredients (lead tracks) of the song have already been adjusted. Time to work on the next track, which in this case will be the Electric Bass. To save time in selecting tracks, you can simply use the up and down arrow keys.

1   Press the down arrow key to select the Electric Bass track. You may need to press it more than once if you started with the Acoustic Guitar 1 track selected.

2   Press S to solo the selected Electric Bass track, then play the song from the beginning and listen to the bass along with the soloed guitar tracks.

The default volume level (0 dB) is a good starting point for the Electric Bass track. However, you may find it a little too heavy in the mix, which takes away from the lead guitars.

3   Lower the Electric Bass track to –4.6 dB. Feel free to raise or lower it to your own liking.

Next, you'll add all four Drum Kit tracks, one at a time.

4   Begin playback from the beginning of the song. Press the up arrow key until the upper Drum Kit track is selected. Then press S to solo the track. Press the down arrow, then press S to select and solo each of the drum tracks while the song is playing.

How do the drums sound and *feel* with the other tracks? They seem a little dominant and distracting to me. In other words, they're too loud! Remember your goal isn't to raise the volume of each track to match, it is to find balance between the tracks. If your marinara sauce had equal parts tomato, onion, and garlic it would taste completely different and would probably not be very popular except among vampire slayers.

5   Start playback again from the beginning of the song and lower the volume level of each Drum Kit track to –8.5.

NOTE ▶ Adjusting track volume is like adjusting water temperature in a sink with separate cold and hot controls. If you are running both hot and cold water, and you want to make the overall temperature hotter, you can just turn down the cold instead of turning up the hot. The same goes for volume—instead of making a track louder to hear it better, you might need to turn down the other tracks a bit.

Before you mix the rest of the tracks, it's a good idea to mute the remaining tracks, then unsolo all the soloed tracks. That way you simply unmute the final tracks as you go. There's no sense in soloing all of a song's tracks; that kind of defeats the purpose of solo. You can click the Mute button on the remaining Tambourine, Shaker, Acoustic Guitar, and Hollywood strings tracks, or select the tracks and press M to mute.

6   Mute the four remaining tracks, then unsolo all of the soloed tracks.

7   Press Cmd-S to save your progress.

Project Tasks

Now that you understand the principle behind mixing the volume levels of music tracks, it's your turn to finish the job. Start with the Hollywood Strings track. It sounds pretty good in the mix at the default level. To add the muted tracks, start playback, select the track, and press M to unmute. Next, add the shaker and tambourine tracks. They both seem about twice as loud as they need to be, so let's lower them to half of their current volume. Finally, add the Acoustic Guitar track below the Shaker track. This track includes only one region at the end of the track, so you'll need to play the ending to hear that part with the other tracks. If you're not sure which volume levels to set for the tracks, try the following:

▶   0 dB (default) for the Hollywood Strings track

▶   −16.7 dB for the Shaker and Tambourine tracks

▶   −4.6 dB for the lowest Acoustic Guitar track

NOTE ▶ If you didn't complete any of the previous exercises, feel free to open the project **7-2 HB volume mixed** to catch up. Then save the project as *Highway Brothers* to your My GarageBand Projects folder.

Panning the Individual Tracks

Now it's time to place the individual tracks in their proper position within the stereo field. There are many different styles for panning the tracks. The important thing is to spread the tracks out within the stereo field. Remember the panoramic photo of the Rocky Mountains? Imagine a beautiful panoramic picture with mountains spread from the left to right side of the frame, birds in the air, a stream in the foreground, a grove of trees on the right side, and a train cutting through the lower left of the frame. The photographer utilized the full stereo field when composing the picture.

Right now, your song has all of the tracks panned to the center. To re-create that onstage in the real world, all of the musicians would have to line up one behind the other in the center of the stage, or on top of one another like a musical totem pole. That wouldn't look very natural, and it doesn't sound natural either. Your ears, trained or untrained, are accustomed to hearing *where* a sound is coming from, as well as hearing the sound itself.

Let's use the pan controls to place the different musicians where they would be if they were performing this song onstage.

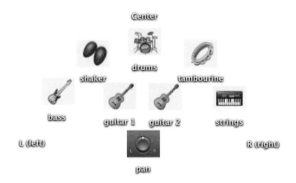

The illustration shows the relative position of the musicians performing "Highway Brothers" onstage. The drums are in the middle of the stage (center pan position). The tambourine and shaker are performed by the backup singers on the left and right of the drums. The two guitars are next to each other, just to the left and right of center stage. The bass is on the left side of the stage, and the keyboard (which plays the strings) is on the right.

To set the panning control for each instrument, simply adjust the Pan wheel so it is pointing in the direction of the instrument in the panoramic field of the stage.

Let's start with the lead Acoustic Guitar tracks. They are currently panned in the 2:00 and 10:00 positions and are panned a little too far left and right for this scenario. Imagine two guitar players standing next to each other in the center of the stage. They can't both be in the center at the same time, so instead they are slightly right and left.

1 On the Acoustic Guitar 1 track, click the first dot to the left of center on the Pan wheel to place the sound of that track just to the left of center.

2 On the Acoustic Guitar 2 track, click the first dot to the right of center on the Pan wheel to place the sound of that track just to the right of center.

If you compare the pan positions of the two guitar tracks to the picture of the band, you'll see that the controls for each track point to the actual instrument.

Using the picture as a guide, let's set the panning controls for the rest of the tracks.

3 Pan the Tambourine track to the second dot to the right of center.

4 Pan the Shaker track to the second dot to the left of center.

5 Pan the Hollywood Strings track to the third dot to the right.

6   Pan the Electric Bass track to the third dot to the left.

The lower Acoustic Guitar track that plays only at the end of the song can stay panned to the center.

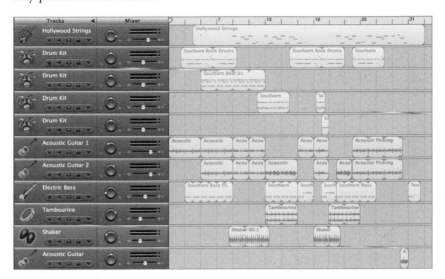

7   Play the first half of the song from the beginning to hear the rough mix.

So, what did you hear this time? Did it sound like the same old song, or did you hear the different instruments (tracks) performing from different places in the stereo field?

Did you notice that the bass seems out of place so far to the left? Some ears are more sensitive to bass than others. However, anytime you pan the bass too far from center, it has a tendency to sound a little strange. Low, bassy sounds feel better if they are closer to the center of the mix, regardless of where they might be on the stage.

8   Change the pan position for the Electric Bass track to one click to the left of center.

Take a closer look at the guitar tracks for a moment. You're probably wondering why I doubled some of the regions but not all of them. I was going for a live performance feel, where one guitar starts, the other joins in, and they mirror each other (not easy to do live). Then the first guitar drops out to let the second lead, and then they play together again, alternating from time to time. The idea is to give the feeling that this was performed by two real guitar players playing on separate tracks from different locations onstage, instead of sounding like a bunch of Software Instrument loops on tracks in the Timeline.

9   Play the entire song from the beginning and listen with your trained ear to the different guitar tracks as well as the other tracks.

10 Press Shift-Cmd-S and save this version of the song as *HB rough mix*.

Excellent! You just completed your rough mix of the song. You're ready to proceed to the next steps.

> **NOTE ▶** If you missed any of the previous steps, please feel free to open the project **7-3 HB rough mix** to catch up. Save the project as *HB rough mix* to your My GarageBand Projects folder.

Locking Tracks to Improve Processor Speed

Now that you've adjusted the volume and panning levels of all the music tracks, it's a good idea to lock the tracks that are finished. Track locking serves two primary purposes:

▶   It prevents unwanted changes.

▶   It renders the track to the computer's hard drive, which frees up processor speed for the rest of the tracks.

You certainly don't need to lock tracks unnecessarily. However, when you're working with a lot of Software Instrument tracks that require more processor speed, locking tracks and rendering them to the hard drive can improve GarageBand's performance.

Let's lock all of the Drum Kit tracks in order to free up some of the processing required to play those Software Instrument tracks.

1 On each of the Drum Kit track headers, click the Lock button.

The Lock button turns green to indicate that the track is locked.

2 Play the song from the beginning to render the locked tracks.

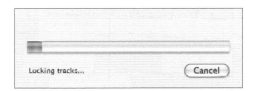

A progress window appears, showing you that the tracks are locking and rendering. When rendering is complete, the window closes automatically, and the song plays from the beginning.

NOTE ▶ You can unlock a track anytime by clicking its Lock button. If you do unlock a track, any other locked tracks will remain locked and rendered until you unlock them.

That's it. You've rendered those four tracks to the hard drive, which frees up processor speed for effects and other advanced features.

It's time to move on to some more advanced mixing features, which include fixing timing and velocity, creating dynamic volume and pan changes over time using track curves, and working with the Master track to apply changes to the overall song.

Fixing the Timing and Velocity of a Software Region

The next step toward creating the final mix is to fix any problems in the recordings or tracks. Now that you've mixed the volume and pan levels for the song, it'll be easier to hear any mistakes and take care of them.

There are no glaring mistakes, but when I listen to the song, I notice that the timing of some of the notes in the Strings track seems a little off.

These notes are off because that's how I recorded them. Fortunately, you can fix the timing of the notes in any Software Instrument region.

Evaluating Timing in the Editor

To appreciate timing that is not right, it's a good idea to look at an example of timing that is perfect.

Let's examine one of the drum regions in the editor. This is a prerecorded Apple Loop, and it has perfect timing. Then we'll take a look at a Hollywood Strings region where the timing is a little off.

1   Double-click the first region in the first Electric Bass track to open it in the editor.

    Now, let's resize the editor for a larger view of the Southern Rock Drums region. You can resize the editor the same way you resize the Loop Browser.

2   Drag the dark gray area to the left of the Record button upward to make the editor larger.

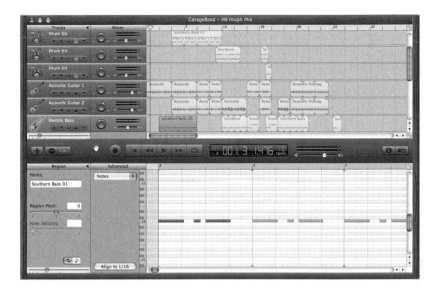

3   If needed, drag the vertical scroller to move the note events into view. Then, drag the editor's Zoom slider to the right to zoom in on the region.

The note events in the editor move farther apart as you zoom in on the region. The beginning of each MIDI note event in the editor is perfectly aligned to the grid, which means that each note is perfectly in time with the grid and the song.

Let's take a closer look at the grid.

4   Locate the Fix Timing button in the Advanced section of the editor.

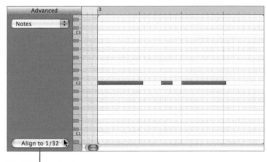

Fix Timing button

The ruler and grid are currently set at ¹⁄₃₂ notes. Notice how detailed the grid is at that level, and how many lines there are in the Beat Ruler for one measure.

5   Drag the editor's Zoom slider to the left until the Fix Timing button changes to ¼ notes.

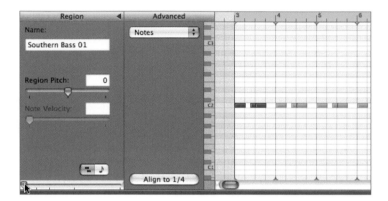

When you have zoomed out of the editor, the Fix Timing button will indicate that the ruler grid is now showing ¼ notes.

NOTE ▶ Zooming in and out of the editor doesn't change the timing of the existing notes. However, it modifies the detail of the grid and how far the notes will move if you automatically fix the timing.

Now let's evaluate the timing of the first Hollywood Strings region.

6   In the Hollywood Strings track, click the Hollywood Strings region to open it in the editor.

7   Drag the horizontal scroller to view the note at the beginning of the 9th measure.

The timing looks OK when you are zoomed out of the editor. Now let's zoom in to see how well aligned it really is.

8   Drag the editor's Zoom slider to the right until the grid is set to ¹⁄₃₂ notes. Then move the scroller to view the note at the beginning of the 9th measure.

> **NOTE** ▶ You can zoom in as far as 1/64 notes for the finest detail, but ¹⁄₃₂ is plenty for this exercise.

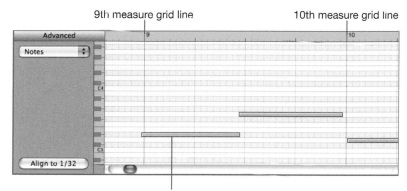

Note event (not aligned to a grid line)

Notice that the note doesn't start exactly on the grid line.

> **NOTE** ▶ If you use the scroller to view some of the other notes in the region, you notice the same thing. Many of them are close to the grid lines, but most of them are slightly off.

Fixing the Timing of a Note

Now that you know how to use the editor to tell if the timing is off, it's time to fix it. To fix the timing of a note, all you need to do is drag the note to the nearest grid line. Let's fix the note at the beginning of the 9th measure.

1   Move your playhead to the beginning of the 9th measure to use as a guide for aligning the note.

2 Drag the note event to the right so it lines up with the playhead and the grid line at the start of the 9th measure.

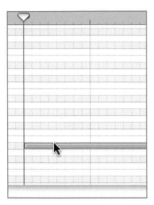

As you can see, to adjust the timing of a single note in a Software Instrument region, all you have to do is move the note.

Fixing the Timing of an Entire Region

Instead of manually adjusting every note in the Hollywood Strings region, wouldn't it be nice if you could do it all automatically? Well, you can.

Keep in mind that very few people (if any) can play an instrument in perfect time. So you probably wouldn't want to do this on a lead guitar region or on an instrument that was played with feeling. The music will sound like it was performed by a computer.

If you want to fix the timing of all the notes in a track, click the track header to select it. If you want to fix the timing of all the notes in a region, click the region in the Timeline (not in the editor) to select it. Shift-select or drag-select to add more regions in the track to the selection.

1   Open the editor, if it's not already open. Click the Hollywood Strings region to load it into the editor.

2   Check the Fix Timing button to make sure the grid is set to $\frac{1}{32}$ notes.

> **NOTE** ▶ Remember to select the region in the Timeline to load it into the editor. If you select the region in the editor, the Fix Timing button will be dimmed.

3   Drag the scroller in the editor to the right to view the 14th measure.

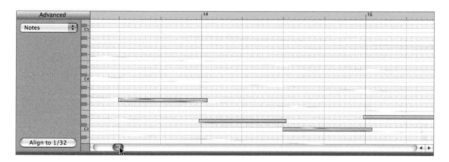

Notice that the note at the beginning of the 14th measure is not aligned with the grid. The note at the beginning of the 15th measure is off as well.

4   Click the Fix Timing button to fix all of the notes in the entire region.

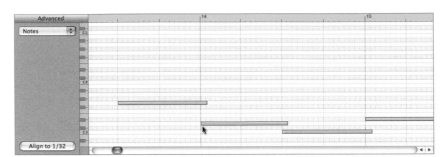

Notice that the notes at the beginning of the 14th and 15th measures are now both aligned to the grid.

The Fix Timing button will align the beginning of every note in the region to the nearest grid line. When you set up the grid to 64th notes, the grid is at the finest level of detail, with the most lines per measure, and the notes will move the shortest distance to the nearest grid line. If you moved to the nearest 8th note, the notes that are off would have to move farther to a grid line. This, in turn, would move them farther from the original place in the song at which you wanted them to play.

The moral here is that you need to be careful when you use the Fix Timing button. If you move the notes too far when you are adjusting the timing, they will play at the wrong time in the song, and it will sound terrible even if they are aligned to the grid.

Changing Velocity for an Entire Region

Now that the timing is right for the Hollywood Strings region, I noticed that the notes are a very light shade of gray. You can gauge the velocity (loudness) of a note by the shade of gray. The darker the shade, the louder the note was originally played. The notes in the Hollywood Strings region were recorded at a very low velocity. Just as you adjust the timing of note events, you can change the velocity for one note or all of them at once.

To change all of the notes at once, you first need to select them all.

1   Move the scroller in the editor until you can see the 15th measure.

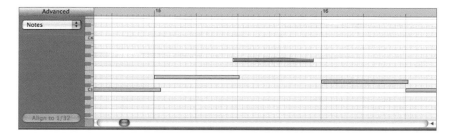

Notice that the different note events are different shades of gray.

2   Click the first note event in the 15th measure to hear it, and check the velocity in the Note Velocity field in the editor.

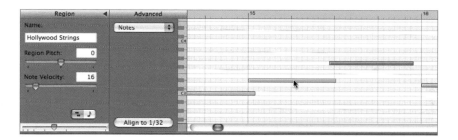

The velocity of the note is 16. That's pretty low considering that 0 is the lowest and 127 is the highest.

3   Click the 2nd note in the 15th measure to check the velocity.

The velocity is 41. This note is definitely played with more intensity than the first note, but it's still relatively low.

Let's raise the velocity for all of the notes in this region simultaneously.

4   Press Cmd-A to select all the notes in the region.

All the notes turn green to indicate that they have been selected.

The Note Velocity field shows the level of the last note you selected. That level is 41. With all of the note events selected, you will raise the velocity of each note by the same amount. Let's raise the velocity from 41 to 61. This will also raise the velocity of every note in the region by the same amount (in this case, 20).

5   Type *61* in the Note Velocity field and press Return.

The velocity of each note in the region has been raised by 20.

6   Click the empty track space above a note in the editor to deselect all of the notes.

7   Click the 2nd note in the 15th measure.

The velocity of this note had been 41 and was raised by 20. The velocity is now 61.

8   Click the 1st note in the 15th measure.

The velocity was originally 16 and now reads 36, which means it was also raised by 20.

9   Press Cmd-E to close the editor, then press Cmd-S to save the project.

10 Listen to the first half of the song to hear the new and improved Hollywood Strings in the mix.

You've fixed various problems in the timing and note velocity for the song, and in doing so, you have just completed the third step in the mixing process. Now you can move on to the next step—adding effects.

Adding Effects to a Track

Effects enhance the sound of the overall song. Each Real Instrument and Software Instrument comes with a set of professional-quality effects.

Each different effect has a slider or pop-up menu you can use to adjust the parameters of the effect. In Lesson 6, you learned how to add effects to a Real Instrument track. You use the same method to add effects to a Software Instrument track in the Timeline.

Let's add some echo, reverb, and EQ to the Hollywood Strings track. You'll start by soloing the track and creating a cycle region so you can hear how the track sounds before and after we adjust the effects.

1   Select the Hollywood Strings track and press S to solo the track. Then, press C to open the cycle region.

2   Create a cycle region over the first part of the Hollywood Strings track (approximately the 9th to the 18th measures).

3   Play the cycle region of the Hollywood Strings track and listen to how the track sounds before we adjust the effects.

4   Double-click the Hollywood Strings track header to open the Track Info pane.

5   Click the Details disclosure triangle in the lower-left corner of the Track Info pane to reveal the instrument details.

Notice the blue checkboxes for Equalizer, Echo, and Reverb. Those boxes show which effects are being applied to the track. Let's adjust all three of those effects.

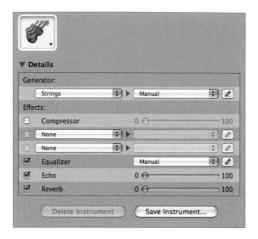

6 Drag the Echo slider to around 25.

The slider starts with 0 and ends at 100. So 25 will be about one-quarter of the distance from the left edge of the slider.

7 Drag the Reverb slider to around 33, one-third of the distance from the left edge of the slider.

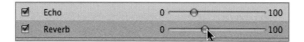

Both the Reverb and Echo effects use sliders. Now let's try the Equalizer, which has a pop-up menu of preset sounds.

TIP ▶ Make sure that you like the way an effect sounds on a soloed track before you add it to the mix. Also, keep in mind that a little echo and reverb go a long way, so use them sparingly.

8 Click the pop-up menu to the right of the Equalizer and choose Add Brightness to listen to this setting.

Add Brightness is one of the preset EQ settings.

NOTE ▶ You may see a dialog asking if you want to save the instrument settings. Don't save the settings for this exercise. When you are working on your own, feel free to save all the effects settings you want.

9 Select a different EQ setting.

10 Try all of the different settings to hear how they sound.

Notice that some settings make a difference you can hear, and some do not. These presets are made for a variety of different instruments, so not all the settings will be noticeable with the strings sound.

11 Choose Brighten Strings from the Equalizer pop-up menu.

12 Close the Track Info pane and stop playback. Then, press C to close the cycle region, and press S to unsolo the selected track.

13 Press Cmd-S to save your work.

Manually Adjusting the EQ for a Track

Now that you've added effects to the Hollywood Strings track, let's add effects to the Acoustic Guitar 2 track. Our goal is to make it sound slightly different from the Acoustic Guitar 1 track.

To accomplish this, you'll add Reverb and manually adjust the EQ. Just to keep things interesting, let's use keyboard shortcuts to select the track and open the Track Info pane. Also, feel free to adjust the settings with the playhead moving, or not, whichever method you prefer.

1   Press the down arrow six times until the Acoustic Guitar 2 track is selected.

2   Press Cmd-I to open the Track Info pane for the selected track. The details should still be showing in the Track Info pane. If they are not already showing, click the Details disclosure triangle.

3   Drag the Reverb effect to around 25 on the Reverb slider, then select the Equalizer option to enable the Equalizer effect.

4   Click the Edit button (which looks like a pencil, to the right of the Equalizer pop-up menu).

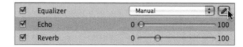

The Equalizer settings window opens with all parameters set to Neutral.

5   Press S to solo the Acoustic Guitar 2 track. Press C to turn on the cycle region. Listen to the soloed track.

6   Experiment with the different EQ sliders to manually adjust the EQ.

You can save your changes and create your own presets. You can also adjust the settings of the default EQ presets as well.

1 At the top of the Equalizer window, click the EQ pop-up menu to choose a different EQ preset.

You may see a dialog asking if you want to save the file (effect setting) before changing effects.

2 If you see the dialog, click Discard.

As you can see, you can save any of your effects settings as presets. For now, let's stick with a built-in preset.

3 Choose Bass Boost from the pop-up menu.

This EQ setting boosts the bass end of the selected track.

4 Click the Details disclosure triangle to hide the details portion of the Track Info pane, then press Cmd-I to close the Track Info pane.

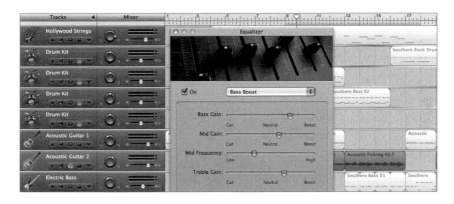

The Equalizer window stays open in case you want to adjust the EQ with the Track Info pane closed.

5 Close the Equalizer window.

TIP ▶ Adding effects to a track can often raise the volume of the regions within that track as well. Before moving on, it's always a good idea to check the new volume level of a track once the effects have been applied.

6   Press the spacebar to play the cycle region and watch the Level meters for the Acoustic Guitar 2 track.

The track is now too loud at times due to the added effect.

7   Lower the Volume level slider on the Acoustic Guitar 2 track to –2.9.

8   Press the up arrow to select the track above (the Acoustic Guitar 1 track), then press S to solo the selected track.

Now you hear both guitar tracks together.

9   Press the spacebar to stop playback.

10   Press C to turn off the cycle region, then unsolo both the guitar tracks.

11   Press Shift-Cmd-S and save this version of the project as *HB with effects*.

Mission accomplished. You've added effects to the Acoustic Guitar 2 track to make it sound slightly different from the Acoustic Guitar 1 track.

That's the end of the fourth step in creating a final mix—adding and adjusting effects.

NOTE ▶ If you didn't complete all of the previous exercises, feel free to open the project **7-4 HB with effects** to catch up. Save the project as *HB with effects* to the My GarageBand Projects folder on your Desktop.

Working with Volume and Pan Curves

So far, you have adjusted the different track volume and pan levels for each individual track by using the controls in the Track Mixer. This method is great for setting one volume or pan level for an entire track. But what if you need the level to change during the song?

This next series of exercises will show you how to change the volume and panning within a track by setting control points along the Volume or Pan curve. To make changes to a track's Volume or Pan curve, you first need to show the curve in the Timeline.

Showing Volume Curves

There are two ways to show the Volume curve for a track:

▶   Press A (for Audio) to show the Volume curve for the selected track.

▶   In the track header, click the disclosure triangle to the right of the Lock button.

Our goal in the next two exercises is to show the Volume curve and then set control points on the Volume curve to fade the volume of the Hollywood Strings track up and down during the song.

First, you need to show the Volume curve.

1   Select the Hollywood Strings track.

2   Click the disclosure triangle next to the Lock button to show the track's Volume curve.

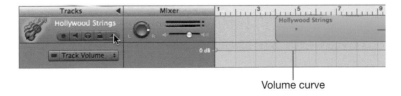

Volume curve

The Volume curve appears below the Hollywood Strings track.

In this case, the Volume curve isn't actually a curve. It's a straight line that represents the steady volume of the track.

3 Drag the Hollywood Strings track Volume slider all the way to the left and watch the movement of the Volume curve.

As you can see, the Volume slider moves the Volume curve.

4 Option-click the Hollywood Strings track Volume slider to reset the slider back to the default position.

If the Volume curve does not move to the default position, click the Hollywood Strings track Volume slider once to apply the new position to the Volume curve.

Adding and Adjusting Control Points

Now that you can see the Volume curve, you can make adjustments to it using control points. Control points set a fixed volume level on the Volume curve at a specific point along the Timeline. Changing the position of a control point allows you to bend the Volume curve, which raises or lowers the volume between the control points.

Control points are often used to fade music in or fade music out. With music, when you slowly fade the volume of a song up from silence or slowly fade the music down to silence, this is *fading in* or *fading out* the music.

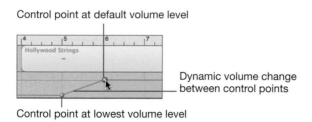

Control point at default volume level

Dynamic volume change between control points

Control point at lowest volume level

You need two control points to change the volume dynamically. The first control point is for the starting volume level. The second control point is for the new volume level. You can add a new control point by clicking the Volume curve. You can move a control point by dragging the point.

Let's add some control points to fade in the Hollywood Strings track.

1   Drag the control point at the beginning of the Volume curve down to the bottom of the track to lower the volume of the track to the lowest possible volume (silence).

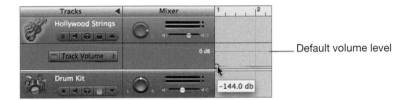

Default volume level

This control point sets the volume for the overall track. Notice the gray horizontal line above the current Volume curve position. This line indicates the default volume level.

2   Move the playhead to the beginning of the 5th measure.

NOTE ▶ You may wish to zoom in to the track one or two levels (Ctrl-right arrow) to see the numbered measures you are looking for in the Beat Ruler.

3   Click the Volume curve at the playhead position (bar 5) to set a control point where the first note is played in the Hollywood Strings region.

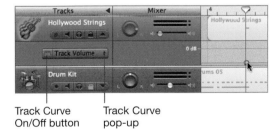

Track Curve
On/Off button

Track Curve
pop-up

A new control point appears in the Volume curve at the playhead position. This control point has a value that is the same as the lowest volume level.

Notice that the Track Curve pop-up is set to Track Volume and that the Volume curve is on (blue). The track curve turns on automatically whenever you select or create a control point in the Volume or Pan curve. You can turn the track curve on or off by clicking the Track Curve On/Off button located to the left of the pop-up menu. If you turn on either the Track Volume or Pan curves, they both become activated and both the Volume slider and the Pan wheel are disabled.

4   Click the Volume curve at the beginning of the 6th measure to set a new point at that position.

Let's change the value of the new control point so that it is the same as the default volume level for the track (0.0).

5   Drag the new control point (at the 6th measure) up to the horizontal gray default volume line. The default volume level is 0.0 dB.

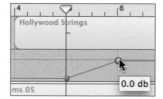

The volume of the track gradually changes between the 5th and 6th measures to fade the volume of the track up from silence.

6   Press the left arrow key to move the playhead to the beginning of the Hollywood Strings region. Press S to solo the track, then play the first part of the song and listen to the first note in the Hollywood Strings track fade in.

7   Unsolo the track and play the beginning of the song again to hear the fade-in mixed with the rest of the tracks.

Now that you've added control points to the Volume curve for the Hollywood Strings track, let's hide the Volume curve.

8   Press A to hide the Volume curve on the Hollywood Strings track, then press Return to move the playhead back to the beginning of the Timeline.

Notice that the Volume slider for the Hollywood Strings track is at the lowest volume position. That's because the Volume curve is now at its lowest position, which is at the beginning of the Timeline.

9 Try to click-drag the Volume slider on the Hollywood Strings track.

The Volume slider is disabled because the Volume curve has been changed. Once you add the first control point, the Volume slider becomes disabled.

10 Play the beginning of the song. Watch the Volume slider in the Hollywood Strings track as the song plays.

The Volume slider moves to reflect the value of the Volume curve. By setting the control points, you have automated the Volume slider.

11 Press Cmd-S to save your work.

Now that you know how to add control points to dynamically change the volume of an individual track, let's try setting control points on the Pan curve.

Dynamically Panning a Track

Just as you added control points to the Volume curve, you can also add control points to the Pan curve so that the sound moves from one speaker to the other. Then let's say that the backup vocalist holding the shaker is pacing back and forth—maybe she had a little too much coffee, or maybe she's just trying to liven things up. Whatever the reason, panning a sound from one speaker to the other is an advanced mixing technique that can add a little excitement to an instrumental part.

Let's add some control points to the Pan curve on the Shaker track to give it some dynamic movement within the stereo field.

1 On the Shaker track, click the disclosure triangle to reveal the active track curve (either Volume or Pan).

2 Click the Track Curve pop-up menu and choose Track Pan, if it is not already showing.

3 Drag the control point at the beginning of the Pan curve and drag it up to the highest position (–64), which is panned all the way to the left.

4 Drag the control point to the lowest position (+63), which is panned all the way to the right.

Zero (0) is the center panning position.

5 At the beginning of the first region in the Shaker track, click the Pan curve to add a control point.

6 Set the control point to +47, which favors the right speaker but is not panned all the way.

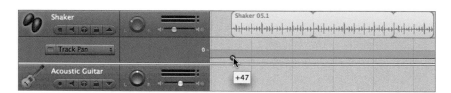

7   Add another control point at about halfway through the first shaker region (the beginning of the 11th measure). Set the control point value to −48.

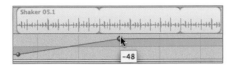

This position in the stereo field is opposite that of the first control point and will favor the left speaker.

8   Set one more control point at the end of the first shaker region. Make the value of the control point the same as that of the first point (+47).

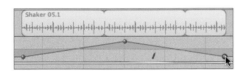

9   Solo the Shaker track and listen to the panned region.

Sounds like someone moving from one side of the stage to the other with the shaker. You have just successfully created a dynamic panning effect.

TIP ▶ You can select multiple control points at once by dragging the pointer along the track curve to select the points. You can also select all of the points on a curve by clicking the empty space at the left of the curve, below the mixer. Once the points are selected, you can raise or lower them all at the same time by dragging one of the selected points up or down. To delete selected points, press the Delete key. You can deselect points by clicking the empty space in the track curve.

Project Tasks

Now we'll dynamically pan the second region in the Shaker track.

1   Add three control points (beginning, middle, and end) to the Shaker track's Pan curve.

2   Set the three control points so that the sound will pan from one speaker to the other and then back.

> **TIP** ▶ You need to move only the middle control point, since the other two are already in position.

3   Press A, or click the disclosure triangle on the Shaker track, to hide the track curves. Then unsolo the Shaker track and listen to the song with the dynamically panned shaker.

4   Save your changes as *HB dynamic* to your My GarageBand Projects folder.

Excellent. Now it's time to move on to the Master track.

> **NOTE** ▶ If you didn't complete all of the previous exercises, feel free to open the project **7-5 HB dynamic** to catch up. Save the project as *HB dynamic* to the My GarageBand Projects folder.

Working with the Master Track

Throughout this lesson, you have been mixing the song by adjusting the individual tracks. The song has come a long way since the arrangement you started with, and the mix is almost finished.

There's one thing left to work with, and that is the Master track. Unlike individual tracks, the Master track controls the entire song. In the next series of exercises, you'll work with the Master track to change the volume and effects for the overall song.

There are two ways to show the Master track:

▶   Choose Track > Show Master Track.

▶   Press Cmd-B.

Let's try it now.

1   Choose Track > Show Master Track.

The Master track appears at the bottom of the Timeline. The Master track's Volume curve shows by default.

2   Click the Master Track header to select it, if it is not already selected.

The Master Track header appears purple.

The Master Track Curve pop-up menu lets you show either the Master Volume curve or the Master Pitch curve. You can set control points on the Master Pitch curve to dynamically change the pitch of (transpose) the overall song.

Understanding the Different Volume Controls

There are four different volume controls to consider as you finish your song. Each volume control adjusts a particular level.

Track Volume

Track volume is the volume level of an individual track. You adjust it using either the track's Volume slider or the track's Volume curve. The purpose of adjusting the track volume is to make it higher or lower in the overall mix in order to balance the levels of the different tracks.

Master Track Volume

To dynamically adjust the volume levels of the overall song, you adjust the volume of the Master track, which is a combination of all the mixed individual tracks. To change Master track volume, you adjust the control points in the Master track's Volume curve. The time to adjust Master track volume is after you have balanced the levels of all the individual tracks.

Master Output Volume

It is important to understand the difference between the overall song volume, which you control through the Master track, and the master output volume. The *master output volume* is the volume level that goes out of GarageBand to the computer. This output level determines the level your song will have when it is exported—for example, when it is output from GarageBand to iTunes.

You can control the master output volume of the song by using the Master Output Volume slider, located in the lower-right corner of the window.

This slider should only be adjusted after you have mixed the levels of the individual tracks and then adjusted the Master track volume. Once the overall song is mixed, you use the Master Output Volume slider to raise or lower the output level. This step ensures that you avoid clipping and that the export volume of the finished song is not too high or too low. You'll adjust the Master Output Volume slider in Lesson 10 when you learn to export and share projects.

Computer Output Volume

The computer output volume is how loud you hear your GarageBand project through your headphones or computer speakers. You should always use volume controls for your computer to adjust the loudness in your headphones and speakers. You should not use the Master Output Volume slider in GarageBand for this purpose. Adjusting your computer's output volume level lets you listen to your GarageBand music as loudly or quietly as you like without changing the output level of the actual project so that it exports too loudly or too quietly.

NOTE ▶ You can access the volume controls for your computer through the speaker icon in the menu at the top of the screen, using the volume control keys on the computer keyboard, or in the Sound pane of your System Preferences window.

Now that you understand the different volume controls, let's focus on the Master track volume and the master output volume.

Adding Control Points to the Master Track

One of the most important features of the Master track is that it can be used to dynamically change the Volume curve of the overall song. Let's add control points to the Master track Volume curve to fade out the end of the song.

1   Move the playhead to the beginning of the 29th measure and play the end of the song to hear how it sounds.

    Did you notice that the strings keep going long after the last bass note? Let's fade out the Master track after the last note in the Electric Bass track.

2   Click the Master track Volume curve at the beginning of the 31st measure to add a control point.

3   Add another control point on the Master track Volume curve at the beginning of the 32nd measure.

4   Drag the control point at the beginning of the 32nd measure down to the lowest volume level.

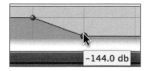

5   Play the end of the song and listen to the Master track volume fade out at the end.

    Now the song has a nice clean fade after the last note.

Adding Effects to the Overall Song

To add an effect to an individual track, you used the Track Info pane for the track. The Master track also appears in the Track Info pane so that you can make changes to the overall song.

Let's open the Master track Info pane and add an effect to the entire song.

1   Press Cmd-I, or click the Track Info button, to open the Track Info pane.

The Track Info pane opens with the Master track info showing.

2   Select Rock from the effects presets list.

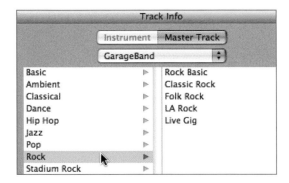

3   Select Rock Basic from the list of specific presets on the right.

You may see a dialog that asks if you want to save the file before opening a new one. Click Discard.

You just added a Rock Basic preset to the overall song. Let's listen to the song to hear how it sounds.

4   Play the song from the beginning. While the song is playing, press the down arrow to hear the other Rock preset effects applied to the song. Stop playback when you have selected an effect.

Did you find a favorite preset? I like the way the Classic Rock and LA Rock presets sound. You can select whichever you like best. The Master Track Info pane includes the Tempo, Time signature, and Key controls for the entire song.

5   Click the Details disclosure triangle to view the other effects options for the Master track.

The Details area includes other controls that work the same way they do for the individual track effects. You can even save master effects settings to create your own presets.

6   Click the Details disclosure triangle again to hide the details portion of the pane, and then press Cmd-I to hide the Master Track Info pane.

7   Press Cmd-B to hide the Master track.

Now that you've added control points and effects to the Master track, it's time to check the output level for clipping. This is the last thing you do to your final mix to prepare the song for export or sharing with other iLife applications.

Checking for Clipping

You've finished your final mix, adjusted all of the track levels individually, and made adjustments to the overall song. The last thing you need to do is play the song from the beginning and watch the Master Output Volume meters to make sure the song output levels are good, and not clipping.

The yellow and red indicate that the output level is clipping.   Good output level

When the output level is good, the average volume levels (solid green bars) move as high as the middle or upper third of the meters, and the peaks (green lines) never turn yellow or red.

To change the output volume for the song, you drag the Master Output Volume slider.

Let's raise the master output volume to illustrate clipping.

1   Drag the Master Output Volume slider to the right so that it is near the highest level.

It doesn't need to be at the highest level to cause clipping.

NOTE ▶ You may want to lower the volume of your computer because the playback will now be louder than normal.

2   Play the song from the beginning. Watch the Master Output Volume meters for any signs of clipping. If the clipping indicators turn red, press the spacebar to stop playback.

3   Click the red clipping indicators to reset them so you will know if the problem has been corrected the next time you play the project.

4   Drag the Master Output Volume slider to the left to lower the output volume of the song.

5   Repeat steps 2 through 4 until you find a good level for the Master track volume.

Make sure your output level isn't too low. Try to set the output level as loud as you can safely, without the meters reaching the yellow or the red clipping range.

NOTE ▶ If the peak indicators reach one or two lines of yellow, that is still acceptable, just make sure that they never peak into the red.

6   Press Shift-Cmd-S and save the finished mix as *HB mixed* to your My GarageBand Projects folder.

Testing Your Trained Ear

Now that you understand how to mix a song in GarageBand, let's put your ear to the test. In this exercise, you'll listen to the original, unmixed song, then the mixed song. See if you hear the difference in the two versions.

1   Choose File > Open Recent > **7-1 Highway Brothers unmxd** to open the original unmixed version.

2   Play the first half of the song.

3   Choose File > Open Recent > **Highway Brothers mixed** to open your finished mix. If you didn't complete all of the mixing steps, you can open **7-6 Highway Brothers mixed** from the Lesson_07 folder.

4 Play the finished mix.

As the song plays, ask yourself the following questions:

▶ Does the mixed version of the song sound better than the unmixed version?

▶ Do you notice the left-to-right placement of the different tracks in the stereo field?

▶ Do you notice the overall balance of the volume between the tracks?

▶ Can you hear that the lead instruments (guitars) are louder in the mix than the supporting instruments?

If you heard any or all of these things, you've trained your ear to hear beyond the basic song.

Congratulations! Now you know how to mix your songs to make them sound professional. Before moving on to the next lesson, there are two other elements of mixing and arranging that are good to know.

Comparing Loops from the Major and Minor Scale Types

Musical instruments such as the piano or guitar play a variety of scale types including major, minor, and both. You don't have to be a music major to understand and recognize the difference. In fact, the important thing for GarageBand is just working with parts that sound good together.

Music played in the minor scale has a serious feel that is often used to evoke tension or drama. The song you've been working with—"Highway Brothers"— used a lead instrument in a minor scale type.

Music played in the major scale has a happier, more positive feel and is often used for more upbeat, feel-good songs.

Let's open a different version of the Highway Brothers song. It has the same rhythm tracks (drums), but all of the guitar and bass parts were replaced with loops from the major scale type.

> **NOTE ▶** Major guitar parts usually sound good together, and minor guitar parts also sound good together. On the other hand, you generally don't want to mix major and minor guitar parts, at least not at the same time.

1 Open the project **7-7 Highway Brothers Major** from the Lesson_07 folder, and save it as *Highway Brothers Major* to your My GarageBand Projects folder.

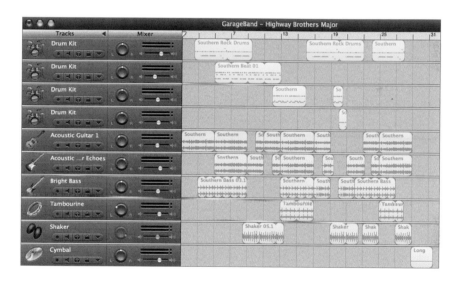

2 Play the first part of the song to hear the difference of using major scale type loops.

It's a totally different feeling and a much happier song. This version feels like the Highway Brothers are really excited about their lives on the road traveling around and playing different venues every night. The original minor version was a bit more depressing and seemed much more serious.

I also noticed that the new major version of the song feels a little rushed, and it could benefit from a slightly slower tempo. Did you notice that, too? If so, your ear training is also leading you toward song producing as well.

3   Lower the project's tempo to 100. Then play the first part of the song again to hear it with the revised tempo.

That's better. This would be good opening music for a documentary about the brothers heading out on their lifetime highway tour. The minor version would be better for the end of the documentary after they've been on the road for 20 years together.

So, how do you sort loops by scale type? Simple. Just choose the scale type in the Loop Browser using the Scale pop-up menu.

4   Press Cmd-L to open the Loop Browser, and select the Guitars keyword button.

The Scale pop-up menu at the bottom of the browser shows the current scale type. There are five different choices in the Scale pop-up: Any, Minor, Major, Neither, and Good For Both. These different categories are self-explanatory.

The default setting is Any scale, which you have been using on all of the songs you've created in this book.

There are more than 70 guitar loops included with GarageBand.

5   Change the Scale pop-up to Minor and notice how many guitar loops match the minor scale.

There are 22 minor guitar loops included with GarageBand.

NOTE ▶ The specific number of minor guitar loops may vary on your computer if you have added more loops to the original installation.

6   Preview some of the minor scale guitar loops in the results list to hear the serious, dramatic sound of minor scale loops.

7   Change the Scale pop-up to Major.

There are almost twice as many major guitar loops as minor ones because major loops are more common.

8   Preview some of the major scale guitar loops in the results list to hear the happier, more feel-good sound of major scale loops.

9   Change the Scale pop-up back to Any. Then hide the Loop Browser.

The next time you want to build a song using Apple Loops, you can adjust the scale type to fit the song.

Ducking Background Tracks

The last mixing feature you'll explore in this lesson is the new ducking feature. Ducking was designed for easy mixing of your podcasts and movie soundtracks, so you'll work more extensively with it in Lessons 8 and 9. However, this is a good time to introduce you to ducking since it can also be used to automatically lower (duck) the levels of backing tracks to favor the levels of other tracks.

You apply ducking by setting which tracks are lead tracks and which are backing (background) tracks. Whenever there is sound on the lead tracks, the volume of the backing track is lowered. Tracks that aren't designated as lead or backing stay the same.

The term *duck* comes from the shape a Volume curve would take if you had to lower the volume of a track every time a part played, or voice spoke, in another track. It would look like the Volume curve is ducking (bending down) out of the way of the waveform in the other track.

The best part of the new ducking feature is you don't have to use control points to create the same ducking effect.

You can turn on the ducking feature by pressing Shift-Cmd-F, or by choosing Control > Ducking.

1   Choose Control > Ducking to turn on the ducking controls in the current project.

A ducking control with arrows pointing up and down appears in each track's header. The arrows let you set whether the track is background (ducked with a blue down arrow), is not ducked (gray), or causes other tracks to be ducked (lead track with an orange up arrow).

The ducking controls in the middle tracks are set so that the lead instrument tracks (Acoustic Guitar 1 and Acoustic Guitar 2) are causing background tracks to duck. The Tambourine and Shaker tracks show blue down arrows in the ducking controls so both tracks will automatically lower the volume levels whenever sound is playing in the lead instrument tracks. The ducking feature works only while the controls are active.

2   Play the project with the ducking controls active.

Notice that the volume levels of the Shaker and Tambourine tracks stay below the lead instrument tracks, and they rise only in the parts of the song where the lead guitars aren't playing.

The ducking controls are most common for podcasts or working with voice-over or narration to automatically lower the music levels whenever someone is talking. You'll work more with this feature in the next lesson as you build a podcast.

Project Tasks

This is a good time to practice some of the skills you've learned throughout this lesson. Try changing the effect on the Acoustic Guitar Echoes track to change the sound. Apply effects to other tracks. Modify the volume and pan levels, and add dynamic changes within the track curves. Since the Master track is showing, you can open the Track Info pane and try different effects on the overall song. You can even record your own parts in the lowest tracks, or add more major scale type loops to enhance the song. Finally, feel free to experiment with the ducking controls. When you're finished, don't forget to save the project.

Lesson Review

1. What features are included in the Track Mixer for each track?

2. What happens to a track's Level meters if a track's volume level is too loud?

3. How do you change where a sound is placed in the stereo field?

4. Where can you add or change effects applied to a track?

5. How do you add or change the effects for the overall song?

6. How do you change the volume or panning of a track over time?

7. How do you add control points to a track's Volume or Pan curve?

8. What track curves are available for the Master track?

9. What feature allows you to automatically lower the level of a track or tracks based on the sound in another track or tracks?

10. Which volume controls should you use to adjust the volume level in your headphones or speakers while working with GarageBand?

Answers

1. The Track Mixer includes a Volume slider, Pan wheel, and Level meters with clipping indicators for each track.

2. The Level meters peak in the red, and the clipping indicators turn red.

3. Change the pan position of a track to change the placement of that track to a different location in the left-to-right stereo field.

4. In the Track Info pane.

5. Change the Master track settings in the Track Info pane.

6. You can dynamically change the volume or panning of a track over time by adding control points to the Volume or Pan curves.

7. You can add control points to the Volume or Pan curve by showing the curve, and clicking it where you want to add a point.

8. The Master track includes a Volume curve for dynamically adjusting the volume of the overall song in the Timeline. You can also dynamically transpose a song by adding control points to the Master Pitch curve.

9. The Ducking feature automatically lowers the level of background tracks to favor lead tracks based on the settings in the ducking controls.

10. To change the volume of your playback in your headphones or speakers, use the volume controls for the computer, not the Master Output Volume slider.

8

Lesson Files GarageBand 3 Lessons > Lesson_08 > 8-1 Podcast start;
8-2 Podcast 6min

Time This lesson takes approximately 1 hour and 30 minutes to complete.

Goals Create a new podcast episode

Add and adjust the Speech Enhancer effects to voice tracks

Import and edit a project within a project

Add artwork to the Media Browser and Podcast Track

Edit marker regions

Build a title sequence in the Podcast Track

Crop and resize artwork in the Artwork Editor

Add a URL and URL title to a marker region

Record sound effects in the Timeline

Edit the project's episode information

Creating Podcasts

Podcasts are like radio or TV shows that can be downloaded over the Internet, and they are one of the fastest growing forms of multimedia. With GarageBand 3, you can create your podcast episodes and then upload them to the Internet using iWeb or another application.

There are four primary types of podcasts: audio podcasts; enhanced podcasts with markers, artwork, and URLs; video podcasts containing a movie; and enhanced video podcasts containing a movie, markers, artwork, and URLs.

In this lesson, you'll first learn how to create a new podcast episode and set up the voice tracks for recording. Then you'll work on a real-world enhanced podcast with multiple voice tracks, markers, artwork, and a URL. Along the way, you'll also build an opening title sequence, learn how to add a project to another project, edit marker regions and artwork, and record sound effects directly to the Timeline.

Creating a New Podcast Project

Many of the previous projects you've worked on were already in progress when
you started. Since you'll be creating your own podcasts from scratch once you
finish this book, let's take a look at the New Podcast Episode template available
in the GarageBand welcome screen.

1 Launch GarageBand. If GarageBand is already open, choose File > New.

2 In the GarageBand welcome screen, click the New Podcast Episode button.

3 Save the project as *Podcast Template* to your My GarageBand Projects
folder.

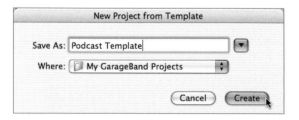

4 Click Create.

The Podcast Template project opens, with the empty Podcast Track, editor with marker information, and Media Browser already showing. The Media Browser contains buttons for different types of media files (Audio, Photos, Movies), a browser where you can navigate to the media files you want to use, and a media list showing the media files in the current location.

Notice that the Photos button and the iPhoto icon in the Media Browser are selected. If the iPhoto library on your computer includes movie files, they will appear in the lower pane of the Media Browser whenever you select the iPhoto icon. Any files in the Photos pane of the Media Browser can be used as episode artwork for your podcast.

You can also add other folders of still images and photos to the Photos pane so you can access artwork files anywhere on your computer.

Showing and Hiding the Podcast Track, Browser, and Editor

Because you created a new podcast episode using the template from the Garage-Band welcome screen, all of the basic tracks and panes are already showing. However, as you work on your own podcast projects, chances are you'll need to show and hide the different tracks and panes as needed to maximize your Timeline workspace. Many of these elements use the same shortcuts you'd use if you were working on a music project.

1   Choose Control > Hide Editor, or press Cmd-E, to hide the editor.

2   Choose Control > Hide Media Browser, or press Cmd-R, to hide the Media Browser.

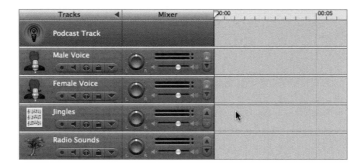

The podcast template includes a Podcast Track and four prebuilt audio tracks, including Male Voice, Female Voice, Jingles, and Radio Sounds. You can always add more tracks or delete unneeded tracks from the Timeline. Also, the ducking controls are on and have the voice tracks set as priority tracks; the Jingles and Radio Sounds tracks are set as backing tracks that will be ducked as needed to favor the voice tracks.

3   Choose Track > Hide Podcast Track, or press Shift-Cmd-B.

You generally won't hide the Podcast Track while you're working. In fact, you're more likely to want to show the Podcast Track in a project you may not have originally designated as a podcast.

4 Choose Track > Show Podcast Track, or press Shift-Cmd-B.

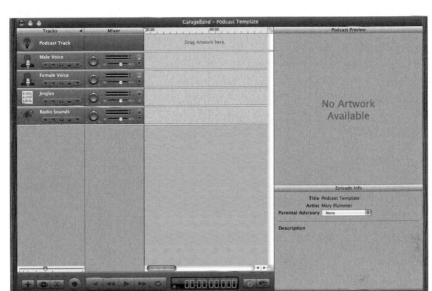

The Podcast Track reappears along with the Track Info pane for the selected track (in the above screen shot, the Podcast Track has been selected). You'll also see a Podcast Preview pane in the upper-right corner of the window. The Podcast Preview pane—which is similar to the Video Preview pane—allows you to see the podcast's artwork as you play the project.

5 Press Cmd-R to show the Media Browser and automatically hide the Track Info pane.

6 Press Cmd-R again to hide the Media Browser.

Hiding the Media Browser will not make the Track Info pane reappear. When a pane is hidden to make room to show another pane in its place, the previous pane remains hidden until you choose to show it again.

Now that you are comfortable with showing and hiding the various panes you'll be using during this lesson, let's move on to setting up your podcast recording equipment.

> **NOTE** ▶ A project can include either a Podcast Track or a Video Track, but not both. If you try to show the Video Track for a project that contains a Podcast Track, a dialog appears asking if you want to replace the Podcast Track with a Video Track and vice versa.

Choosing Podcast Recording Equipment

Recording audio for a podcast in GarageBand 3 can be as easy or complicated as needed for your particular project. For example, if your podcast needs only one voice track, you can record the narration to an enabled Real Instrument track by connecting a microphone to your computer or by using the built-in microphone (if it has one). An iSight camera will also work because it includes a fully functioning microphone that is perfect for recording podcast audio as well as visuals. In fact, you can even record remote interviews with iChat users.

Remember that the voice tracks you record for a podcast are Real Instrument tracks, so they follow the same recording rules you learned in Lesson 6. You can record a maximum of eight Real Instrument tracks and one Software Instrument track simultaneously. To record more than one track at a time, you'll need to use an external audio interface.

Due to the popularity of GarageBand, a variety of third-party recording equipment is available. When I'm creating projects for these books, I try to find equipment that is both GarageBand-friendly and modestly priced.

The podcast you'll be working on later in this lesson includes four Real Instrument voice tracks, plus a Software Instrument track used for sound effects. To record all four voice tracks at the same time, I used the Edirol FA-101, which is the same audio interface I used for recording Real Instruments in Lesson 6.

To record my narration, I used the new Blue Snowball USB microphone, which plugs into any USB port. It doesn't require any additional software or drivers, and it works well for these types of projects.

To trigger sampled MIDI sound effects during the podcast recording, I use the small Edirol PCR-A30 MIDI keyboard/audio interface. This is the same keyboard I used to record Software Instrument parts in Lesson 3.

Finally, I use the M-Audio iControl for GarageBand, which I have to confess I've been using throughout the process of writing this book.

The iControl is a GarageBand-specific USB device that allows you to select, mute, solo, record enable, pan, and adjust volume on tracks, as well as operate the transport controls, add effects, and adjust the master volume.

For me, using the external iControl device to control the tracks and transport controls, and an external MIDI keyboard to trigger sounds, enables me to focus on the live podcast interviews without using the mouse or computer keyboard.

In addition to my various MIDI keyboards, I also keep an iGuitar handy for recording riffs, guitar parts, and song ideas. The iGuitar.USB by Brian Moore Guitars is an exciting development in the world of digital music recording. It is the first guitar to offer on-board, class-compliant USB audio to streamline the guitar-to-computer connection, eliminating the need for an external audio interface. In other words, you can use a standard USB cable to hook the iGuitar to the computer and record real guitar parts into GarageBand without any other equipment.

MORE INFO ▶You can find more information on GarageBand accessories at www.apple.com/ilife/garageband/accessories.html. You can find out more about the iGuitar at www.brianmooreguitars.com.

Again, let me stress that none of this equipment is necessary to create a podcast, and you can often get along with minimal equipment. I just wanted you to see some of the other options, especially if you plan to create a lot of enhanced podcast episodes or music projects.

Before recording, make sure that your equipment is turned on and properly connected to the computer. For more specifics on the operation of your equipment, refer to the equipment manuals.

Exploring the Vocal Track Presets

GarageBand includes microphone settings and vocal enhancement effects that can be applied to a vocal track before or after recording. These effects—available in the Details area of the Track Info pane—are designed to improve the quality of your vocal recordings.

1   In the Timeline, double-click the Male Voice track header.

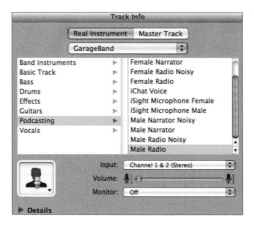

The Track Info pane appears for the selected track. Notice that the Podcasting instrument category has been selected, and Male Radio is the specific preset.

There are five Male Voice presets: iSight Microphone Male, Male Narrator Noisy, Male Narrator, Male Radio Noisy, and Male Radio.

The presets that have *Noisy* in the title include automatic noise reduction to help eliminate unwanted background noise in the recording.

The iChat and iSight presets are designed specifically for tracks using those methods of recording.

2   In the Track Info pane, select the Male Narrator preset.

The preset effect changes, and the Track Header's name changes to reflect the new preset.

3   In the Track Info pane, click the Details disclosure triangle to reveal the effects details.

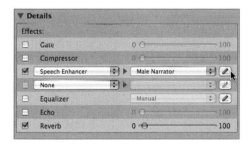

You can see that the preset includes a little bit of Reverb effect and a Speech Enhancer effect set to Male Narrator.

The Manual settings for the Speech Enhancer also let you choose which type of microphone you are using. This is very useful to enhance the quality of recordings if you are using a built-in microphone.

4 To open the Speech Enhancer controls, click the Edit button (looks like a pencil) for the Male Narrator preset.

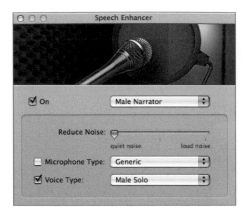

The Speech Enhancer controls include a preset pop-up menu, which will automatically change to Manual if you modify any of the current settings. There is also a Reduce Noise slider, which is currently at the lowest setting. In the Microphone Type menu, you can choose the type of microphone, and in the Voice Type menu, you can select the type of voice.

5 Select the Microphone Type box, then click the Microphone Type menu to see the different choices, ranging from PowerBook G4 Titanium to iMac G5 with iSight. Choose the microphone type that best fits your recording situation. Use Generic if you are using an external microphone.

6 Choose a preset from the Preset menu at the top of the Speech Enhancer dialog. Try a preset that best suits the type of recording you might use in a podcast. If you're unsure, try Male Narrator or Female Narrator.

An alert appears, showing that you've made changes to the current instrument settings.

7 Name the preset My Podcast Voice, and click Save.

8 In the Speech Enhancer dialog, choose your new preset from the menu. Then close the Speech Enhancer dialog to add your custom settings to the selected track.

NOTE ▶ Once you've made changes to a track's preset vocal effect, you may want to change the name of the track to reflect the current effects.

Project Tasks

If you have a microphone attached to your computer, take a moment and try recording to the track you just set up. Remember the shortcuts R to start recording and spacebar to pause. Also make sure that the track you want to record is selected and the Record Enable button is turned on. Record a little narration about yourself, or your family, or read a few paragraphs from this book. The important thing is the practice, not the content of the recording. When you have finished, save and close the project.

Adding Speech Enhancer Effects to Recorded Vocals Tracks

Now that you know how to create a new podcast project and set up your vocal tracks, let's fast-forward to a podcast project that is a little further along. In this exercise, you'll apply the Reduce Noise control to some of the tracks. Along the way, you'll also use many of the skills you've learned throughout this book.

1   Open the project **8-1 Podcast start** and save it as *Podcast start* to your My GarageBand Projects folder.

   The project contains a lot of media files and is fairly large, so it may take a few minutes to save.

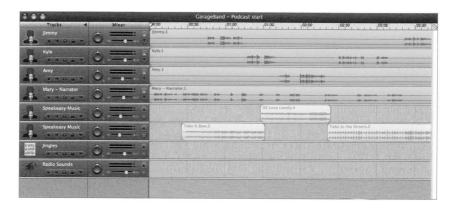

This podcast project-in-progress is an interview with the band Speakeasy, featured in Lesson 6. It includes four recorded Real Instrument voice tracks, two Speakeasy music tracks containing orange (imported) Real Instrument regions, and two empty tracks: Jingles (Real Instrument) and Radio Sounds (Software Instrument). The Podcast Track has been hidden so you can focus on the recorded tracks first.

Notice that the ducking controls are showing, and the recorded voice tracks are the priority tracks; the music and effects tracks are ducking (lowering volume) to favor the priority tracks.

2   Move the playhead to 00:45 (45 seconds) in the time display. This is right before Jimmy speaks for the first time.

3   Press C to show the Cycle Region Ruler, and create a yellow cycle region over the first section of waveform in the Jimmy region (from 00:45 to around 01:14).

4   Double-click the Jimmy track header to open the Track Info pane for the selected track. Then click the Details disclosure triangle to see the track's details.

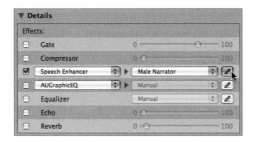

The track has the Speech Enhancer effect applied, with the Male Narrator preset.

5 Click the Edit button to open the Speech Enhancer controls.

6 Press the spacebar to begin playback of the cycle region.

7 Press S to solo the selected track.

You can hear a bit of room noise when Jimmy speaks. You may not be able to get rid of all the noise, but you can certainly remove some of it.

8 Continue playback and drag the Reduce Noise slider from the lowest setting (quiet noise) to the highest setting (loud noise). Feel free to choose a setting in-between that you like better.

Can you hear the difference in the noise while he's talking? Let's also change the Voice Type effects preset on his track.

9 Continue playback and change the Voice Type pop-up menu from Male Solo to Male Voice Over.

10 Close the Speech Enhancer dialog and pause playback.

11 Press S to unsolo the Jimmy track, then press C to hide the Cycle Region Ruler.

NOTE ▶ Normally, when you choose a new preset in the Track Info pane, the name of the track also changes. Podcast Tracks are commonly named after the subjects or contents. If you have manually named a Podcast Track, the name will stay with the track, even if you change to a different preset.

As you can see, it is easy to apply the Speech Enhancer effects to a track before or after it has been recorded.

Project Tasks

Now it's your turn to apply the same changes to the Kyle track. You can choose whether or not you want to solo the track and use a cycle region. Your main goal is to open the Kyle track's info and manually adjust the Speech Enhancer effect to add the Reduce Noise feature, as well as change the preset to Male Voice Over. When you are finished, save your progress. Also, be sure to close the cycle region and unsolo all of the tracks.

Importing a GarageBand Project

If you have listened to the beginning of the podcast, you'll notice that it is pretty darn boring without any music. Not to mention it's just a voice without any visuals, which you will also fix shortly. First, let's add a good podcast jingle to the beginning and end of the project. You could choose from one of the many professional jingles included with GarageBand 3. However, since you'll be using them extensively in the next lesson, let's instead use one of the projects you built from scratch.

Remember the project SpaceBass from Lesson 4? That musical piece was designed for a podcast, so let's use it. You could mix and export the finished song, then import it into the podcast project, or simply import the GarageBand project. That's right, import a project into another project. If you save a project with iLife preview, you can preview and use it in any of the other iLife applications, including GarageBand.

Saving a Project with iLife Preview

In this exercise, you'll open the project **SpaceBass final** from your My Garage-Band Projects folder and save it with iLife preview. If you didn't complete and save the project in Lesson 4, you can open the project Lesson_04 > **4-4 SpaceBass final**. You may also remember at the beginning of the book I had you turn off the alert that asked if you want to save a project with iLife preview. It takes longer to save projects with iLife preview, and the feature is only for the projects you want to share with other iLife applications—or GarageBand itself. So this is the first time you've needed that feature.

1   Save the current project. Then choose File > Open and select either **SpaceBass final** from your My GarageBand Projects folder or **4-4 Space Bass final** from the Lesson_04 folder.

2   Play the project once for nostalgia's sake.

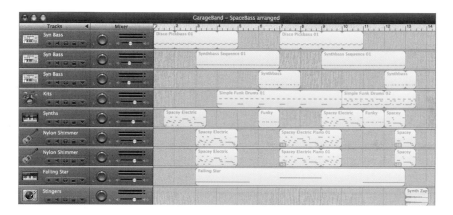

You've come a long way since you built this project. Luckily, it still sounds cool and will work well for your podcast project. Feel free to mix the track levels and add effects if you'd like before continuing, or you can always tweak it later.

3   Choose GarageBand > Preferences. In the Preferences window, click the General button.

4   At the bottom of the General Preferences dialog, select the iLife Preview option, if it is not already selected.

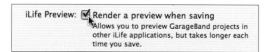

Now, each time you save this project, a rendered preview of the project will be created so you can preview it in other iLife applications.

NOTE ▶ If you turn on this feature, an alert about saving with iLife preview will appear when you save other GarageBand projects until you turn it off again. When the feature is on, saving each project will take longer. You can always go back to Preferences and turn off iLife preview as needed.

5 Close the Preferences dialog.

6 Press Cmd-S to save the project with iLife preview. If you see an alert asking if you'd like to save with iLife preview, click Yes.

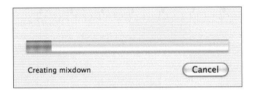

A progress alert appears, showing you that the iLife preview is rendering as you save.

That's it. The project has been saved with an iLife preview.

Adding GarageBand Projects to the Media Browser

Saving the project with iLife preview means that you can add it to your Garage-Band Timeline. First, you'll need to place it in the Audio pane of the Media Browser. By default, the Media Browser gives you access to your iTunes library in the Audio pane of the Media Browser. You can also add other folders containing audio files, including GarageBand projects. Let's reopen the Podcast start project and show the Media Browser.

1 Choose File > Open Recent and choose the Podcast start project you were working on earlier in this lesson.

2   Press Cmd-R to show the Media Browser. Click the Audio button to show the Audio pane within the browser.

Your iTunes folder and default GarageBand folder are automatically show-ing in the Audio pane. You've been saving your projects to a folder on your computer's Desktop, so they won't show in the browser until you add your folder.

3   In the Dock, click the Finder icon to switch to the Finder.

4   In the sidebar of a Finder window, select the Desktop.

5   In the Finder, scroll through the Desktop contents and locate your My GarageBand Projects folder.

> **NOTE ▶** If you used the **4-4 SpaceBass final** project from the Lesson_04 folder, navigate on the Desktop to the GarageBand 3 Lessons folder and locate the Lesson_04 folder.

6   Drag the folder containing the SpaceBass project saved with iLife preview from the Finder to the Audio pane of the Media Browser.

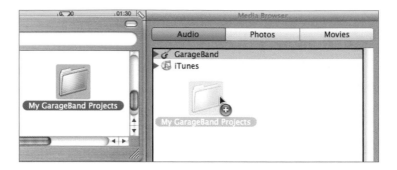

7   Switch back to GarageBand.

The folder appears in the Audio pane of the Media Browser.

8   In the Media Browser, click the folder you just added (either My GarageBand Projects or Lesson_04).

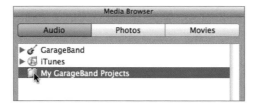

9   Scroll through the folder contents in the lower pane of the Media Browser.

Normal GarageBand project file icons look like a document (paper) with a guitar printed on it. GarageBand project files saved with an iLife preview show only a guitar icon.

10 Drag the **SpaceBass final** (or **4-4 SpaceBass final**) project from the Media Browser to the beginning of the Jingles track in the Timeline.

The project file appears in the Timeline as an orange Real Instrument region. The small guitar icon in the upper-left corner of the region shows that it is a GarageBand project instead of a normal audio file.

11 Play the first part of the project to hear the SpaceBass project as the intro music for the podcast.

Notice that the ducking controls are working as they should and automatically ducking (lowering) the volume level of the Jingles track to give volume priority to the narration track.

12 Press Cmd-S to save your progress.

You will see an alert asking if you'd like to save the project with iLife preview.

13 Click No.

There is no reason to save this project with iLife preview at this time.

You've successfully added a GarageBand project to the Timeline of another project. Of course, you might wonder what the big deal is about that. You can also export a finished mix of a song and just add the mixed audio file to a project the same way. Well, what if you change your mind? More importantly, what if your clients change their minds? It happens —more often than not, depending on the client. What if someone wants you to make changes to the song in the Timeline? Then what? If it is an audio file, you have to find the original project, or re-create it, then make the changes and export it again, then add the exported mix to the project. On the other hand, if you have a project in the Timeline, you simply open the project in the editor, click the Open Original song button, and voila! You're working on the original song again. Best of all, when you save the changes, the project automatically updates in the Timeline. It sounds more complicated than it is. Let's just try it.

Editing a GarageBand Project Within Another Project

To demonstrate editing a project within a project, you're going to open the SpaceBass project from the Podcast start project, change the panning on several tracks, then save it so it automatically updates in the Podcast start project.

1 In the Timeline, select the SpaceBass project. Then press Cmd-E to open the editor.

2 In the editor, click the Open Original button to open the original song project.

A dialog appears, asking if you want to close the current project and open the other.

3   Click Open Original Project.

NOTE ▸ If another dialog appears, prompting you to save the changes to the Podcast start project, click Save to continue.

The original **SpaceBass final**, or **4-4 SpaceBass final** project opens.

4   Pan the Elec Piano track two dots to the left (10 o'clock position).

5   Pan both Nylon Shimmer tracks two dots to the right (2 o'clock position).

6   Press Cmd-S to save the changes to the project. If prompted with an alert, click Yes to save with iLife preview.

7   Press Cmd-W to close the current project.

The Podcast start project automatically reopens. An alert appears, asking if you want to update the changes to the SpaceBass final region.

8 Click Update Region to update the project within the current project.

The project updates, and the Podcast start project automatically saves. You've just witnessed a very advanced maneuver, new to GarageBand 3.

NOTE ▶ If you choose not to apply the changes when you return to the project you started from, the link between it and the imported project is permanently broken. Also, extending the length of the imported project can result in regions being deleted when you apply the changes to the project it is imported into.

There's just one more thing to do: add the SpaceBass project to the end of the project. No problem. You'll just copy the file and paste it at the end of the song.

9 Hide the editor if it is showing. Select the SpaceBass project at the beginning of the Timeline and choose Edit > Copy, or press Cmd-C. Then move the playhead to 00:05:30 in the Timeline.

10 Make sure the Jingles track is selected, then choose Edit > Paste, or press Cmd-V to paste the project at the playhead position.

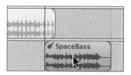

11 Play the end of the project from the playhead position to hear the **SpaceBass final** song with the rest of the tracks.

Excellent! The song works well at both the beginning and end of the project.

Now that the audio tracks are in place, including a jingle at the beginning and end of the project, it's time to add some artwork.

Working with Artwork and Markers

The next step in building the podcast is to enhance it with artwork and markers. When you add episode artwork to a podcast, the artwork appears when you play the podcast episode in iTunes and when you work with it in iWeb. Artwork added to the Podcast Track creates a marker region the same length as the artwork in the Podcast Track. Marker regions are used in podcasts to literally *mark* a specific region in the Timeline to include artwork, a chapter title, or a URL. When you publish your podcast, iWeb or other software will use these marker regions to include the designated information for that region in the project.

You can edit, move, and resize marker regions anytime while creating your podcast project. You can also add and edit chapter title markers and URL markers to the Podcast Track. In addition to the artwork used as marker regions in the Podcast Track, you can also designate the episode artwork in the editor. The episode artwork appears in the Podcast Preview pane whenever there is no artwork for the current marker region.

Adding Artwork to the Media Browser

The artwork you'll be using for this project is in the Photos for GarageBand folder inside the GarageBand 3 Lessons folder on your Desktop. You can add artwork folders to the Media Browser in the same way you added your projects folder earlier in this lesson. The difference is that you need to place podcast artwork in the Photos pane of the Media Browser.

1   In the Media Browser, click the Photos button to show the Photos pane.

     If you recall, this is the default Media Browser pane when you create a new podcast episode in GarageBand.

2   In the Dock, click the Finder icon to open the Finder window. Locate the GarageBand 3 Lessons folder on your computer's Desktop.

3 In the Finder, open the GarageBand 3 Lessons folder and select the Photos for GarageBand folder. Drag it to the Photos pane of the Media Browser. Return to GarageBand.

The Photos for GarageBand folder appears in the browser.

4 Click the disclosure triangle at the left of the Photos for GarageBand folder to view the folder's contents, if they are not already showing

You'll see that it contains two folders: Images and podcast titles.

5 Press Return to move the playhead to the beginning of the project.

6 Choose Track > Show Podcast Track to show the Podcast Track in the Timeline.

The Podcast Track appears at the top of the Timeline, above the other tracks.

7 Select the Podcast Track to see it in the Track Info pane.

The Podcast Track is where you can view and edit marker regions for a podcast episode.

Adding Episode Artwork to the Project

Episode artwork represents the entire project—like a movie poster or CD cover. People will see it when they choose your podcast to download or preview. The project can only have one piece of episode artwork. Let's take a moment and assign a file as the episode artwork for this podcast.

1 Press Cmd-E to show the editor.

The editor appears for the Podcast Track. The Episode Artwork well on the side of the editor is currently empty. The marker area of the editor shows the marker regions and artwork already added to the Podcast Track.

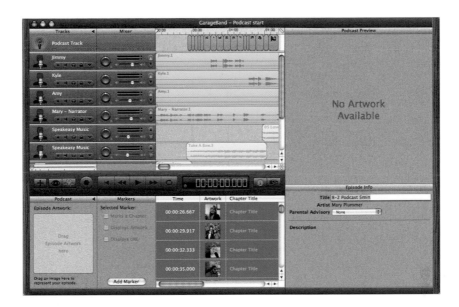

The Podcast Preview pane shows that no artwork is available, because the playhead is at the beginning of the project where there is no artwork in the Podcast Track.

2   Press Cmd-R to show the Media Browser.

3   In the upper pane of the Media Browser, select the podcast titles folder located inside the Photos for GarageBand folder.

These titles were created in Motion. You can create title stills in virtually any graphics program, such as the iWorks applications. As long as the files are QuickTime-compatible, you'll be able to include them as podcast artwork.

4   Select the file Podcast Title 1.jpg and drag it to the Episode Artwork well in the editor.

The episode artwork appears in the editor.

5   Press Cmd-I to show the Track Info pane.

The episode artwork appears in the Podcast Preview pane because there is no other artwork in the playhead position of the Podcast Track.

What if you change your mind after you've added episode artwork? You can drag the artwork from the well, and it will vanish in a puff of smoke—really. Or just add another piece of artwork to the well to replace the original.

6 Drag the episode artwork out of the well and release the mouse.

Poof—the well is empty again. You'll add another piece of artwork later in the lesson.

Adding Artwork to the Podcast Track

Since you already have the titles showing in the Media Browser, let's go ahead and build the opening title sequence and create marker regions as we go. The opening title sequence will include images that go with the SpaceBass theme song for the podcast. Let's zoom in to the Timeline for a larger view of the Podcast Track as you add the artwork.

1 Press Cmd-E to hide the editor.

Notice the empty space in the first 26 seconds of the Podcast Track. You'll fill that space momentarily with a marker region.

2 Press Ctrl-right arrow several times until the ruler shows 10-second increments instead of 30-second increments.

3 Click the empty space at the beginning of the Podcast Track to deselect all of the marker regions within that track.

If marker regions are selected when you add new artwork to the Podcast Track, the new artwork may replace the first selected marker region, instead of creating a new marker region.

4 Press Cmd-R, or click the Media Browser button, to show the Media Browser.

If you add artwork to the beginning of an empty space in the Podcast Track, it will automatically fill the space.

5 Drag one of the Podcast Title blank files from the Media Browser to the beginning of the Podcast Track in the Timeline and release the mouse.

A marker region appears and fills the empty space at the beginning of the Podcast Track. The new marker region shows Podcast Title blank as the artwork for the region.

NOTE ▶ If you released the artwork too far to the left or right, it will not start at the very beginning of the track. Simply drag the beginning of the marker region toward the left until it extends to the beginning of the track.

6 Press Cmd-I to see the artwork for the current playhead position in the Podcast Preview pane.

7 Play the project from the beginning to see the artwork in the Podcast Preview pane.

What do you think of the title sequence so far? It's a start but still a little boring. Some art is better than no art, but it could use more titles and a little something to lead into the first title. Keep in mind, there is nothing wrong with having one long piece of artwork at the beginning of a podcast. However, in this case, since there is more artwork available, we'll use it. Let's add Podcast Title 1 to the Podcast Track. When you add a new piece of artwork, it won't replace the entire existing artwork. Instead, it will split the original and replace the marker region from the position you release the artwork to the next marker region.

8   Select the first marker region in the Podcast Track, if it is not already selected. Press Return to move the playhead to the beginning of the Timeline.

9   Press Ctrl-left arrow to zoom out of the Timeline one level until you can see the entire first marker region in the Podcast Track.

10   Press Cmd-R to show the Media Browser. Then select the Podcast Title 1 file and drag it to the middle of the first marker in the Podcast Track.

The marker region splits in two, with the Podcast Title blank region first and the Podcast Title 1 region second.

11   Press Cmd-I to show the Track Info pane and Podcast Preview pane.

12   Watch the beginning of the project and listen to the audio.

Any thoughts? I think it would be much better if the "New Artists in Action" title actually appeared when the narrator says, "Welcome to New Artists in Action." No problem.

Editing Marker Regions

Your goal in this exercise is to change the timing of the second marker region to match the narration. The first thing you need to do is find the narrator's waveform and visually identify where the first line of narration begins.

1   Locate the Mary – Narrator region in the Mary – Narrator track. (Yes, it's me. I couldn't find anyone else to narrate this project in time.)

2   Press Ctrl-right arrow to zoom in one level for a closer view of the wave-
    form and Timeline.

3   Move the playhead to the beginning of the waveform in the Mary –
    Narrator region (00:00:04).

4   In the Podcast Track, drag the beginning of the second marker region left
    to the playhead position.

When you release the mouse, the second marker region begins at four seconds, and the first marker region with the blank title artwork fills the first
four seconds of the project, before the narrator speaks.

Finishing the Title Sequence

Now that you understand how to add artwork and edit the marker regions,
let's finish the title sequence. You'll use the narrator's voice and the SpaceBass
music as a guide for placing the remaining artwork. Once you have the artwork in place, you can always trim or adjust the marker regions to improve
the timing.

1   Move the playhead to 00:00:10 in the Timeline, around the beginning of
    the first pause in narration.

2   Drag one of the Podcast Title blank images from the Media Browser to the
    playhead position in the Podcast Track.

3 Press Cmd-I to see the Podcast Preview pane. Play the first part of the project to see and hear the timing of the artwork to the audio.

The music plays a little synth riff during the pause in the narration that works well with the blank title background.

4 Press Cmd-R to show the Media Browser. Then move the playhead to 00:00:12 in the Timeline and drag Podcast Title 2 from the Media Browser to the playhead position in the Podcast Track.

5 Move the playhead to 00:00:15 and add Podcast Title 3 to the playhead position.

6 Move the playhead to 00:00:20 and add Podcast Title 4 to the playhead position.

7 Move the playhead to 00:00:24 and add one of the Podcast Title blank images to the playhead position.

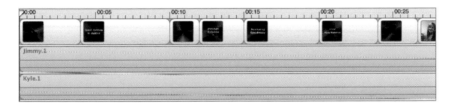

8 Press Cmd-I to see the Podcast Preview pane, then play the title sequence.

9 Save your progress.

TIP Including blank backgrounds with title images gives you more editing flexibility as you build your podcasts. The blank backgrounds make an interesting transition at the beginning and end of the sequence, as well as between titles and the main project artwork.

Good job. You've completed the title sequence.

Viewing Marker Information

You can see more information about a project's markers, artwork, and marker regions in the editor. You can also select markers and change or update their information.

1 Press Cmd-E to open the editor.

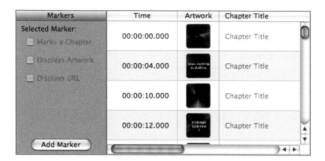

The marker regions are listed in chronological order from the beginning of the project. The editor includes columns that show Time, Artwork, Chapter Title, URL Title, and URL for each marker.

2 Drag the vertical scroller to scroll down through all of the project's markers.

As you can see, there is a title sequence at the end of the project similar to the one at the beginning.

The checkboxes in the Markers area of the editor show how the marker will be designated. Adding artwork to a marker region automatically selects the Displays Artwork checkbox for that marker. You'll work with chapter title markers in the next lesson.

Adding a URL to a Marker

You can add a URL (Web site address) to a marker region in a podcast or a marker in a movie and view the URL when you play the movie or podcast in iTunes. Not only will viewers see the URL when they play the finished project, but they can also click the URL onscreen to open the Web page in their browsers.

If you add a URL title, the title appears in the Album Artwork window of iTunes (in a published podcast) and clicking it opens the Web page for the URL. An example of a URL title might be "For More Information," or "Check out our Web site."

Let's add a URL title and link to the end of the project. You'll add the URL to an existing marker region. To get there, you could navigate in the Timeline or simply double-click the marker in the editor.

1 In the editor, locate the marker that begins at 00:05:23.583. Then double-click any blank area on the marker's row in the marker list to jump to the marker's location in the Timeline.

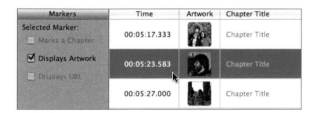

The playhead jumps to the marker's location in the Timeline.

2 Press the spacebar to play the project from the playhead position.

The dialog content includes Jimmy saying the band's URL address.

3 Press Cmd-I to hide the Track Info pane so you can see all of the marker info columns in the editor.

4 For the selected marker, click the URL Title field. Type *speakeasyhome.com* and press Return.

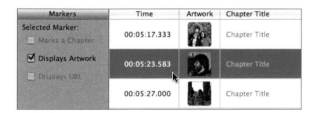

5 For the selected marker, click the URL field. Type *www.speakeasyhome.com* and press Return.

GarageBand will automatically add the *http://* to the address.

Notice the checkmark for the Displays URL option after you add a URL to the marker.

URL also appears on the marker region in the Podcast Track to show that the marker includes a URL.

6 Press Cmd-I to show the Track Info pane. Play the marker to see the URL title appear in the Podcast Preview pane.

Feel free to click the URL title in the Podcast Preview pane to open the Web page. If your computer is not currently connected to the Internet, your browser will try to open the page and then tell you that you're not connected.

Project Tasks

The URL title and link you added works great. But it's not onscreen very long. To give viewers enough time to see and click the URL, let's add the same information to the next marker as well. Select the marker region that starts at 00:05:27.000 and add the same URL title and URL as you did in the previous marker. You can retype the information in each field, or copy and paste the information from a field in one marker to the same field in another. When you are finished, save your progress.

Using Marker Artwork for Episode Artwork

While you are in the editor, this is a good time to pick a new image for the episode artwork. Earlier you used the title of the show, but it didn't really say much about the content. Instead, let's choose one of the pictures of the band to use as the episode artwork. You could look through all of the images in the Media Browser or simply drag one of the images from the Artwork column in the editor to the Episode Artwork well.

1   In the editor, locate the marker that starts at 00:05:17.333.

2   Select the artwork image for the marker and drag it to the Episode Artwork well.

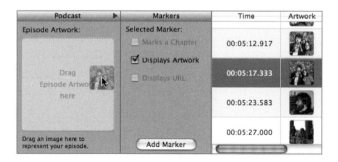

It's that easy. In fact, you can replace the image in the Episode Artwork well anytime by simply dragging another image to the well.

Resizing and Cropping Artwork

GarageBand includes a handy Artwork Editor you can use to resize and crop your artwork to show all or part of the original image. To access the Artwork Editor, double-click the artwork in the project.

1 Double-click the artwork in the Episode Artwork well.

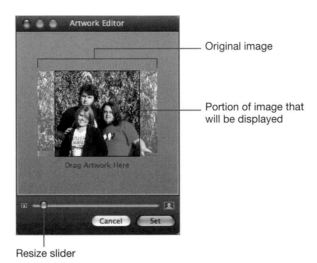

Original image

Portion of image that will be displayed

Resize slider

The Artwork Editor opens with the artwork. The square frame represents what will be displayed in your podcast.

2 Drag the Resize slider toward the right to zoom in on the image until all three heads and shoulders just fit within the black square frame.

3   Drag the image left or right within the editor until you're happy with the framing of the image.

4   Click the Set button to set the changes to the image. Close the Artwork Editor.

The episode artwork updates according to the changes you made in the Artwork Editor.

Project Tasks

Now it's your turn to use the Artwork Editor to fix an artwork image in the podcast. Play the first minute or so of the podcast. The image at 00:00:40:0000 shows Amy's back, but it doesn't include the other two band members. In the Timeline, click the marker region to open it in the editor (double-click if the editor is not already open). In the editor, double-click the artwork for the selected marker to open the Artwork Editor and resize the image until you can see all three members of the band in the image. When you're finished, save your progress.

Adding Loops and Sound Effects

Now that the main podcast sound and artwork is in place, you can add a few extra audio touches to enhance the overall project. In the next series of exercises, you'll add several loops from the Loop Browser to emphasize the content of the interview. Then you'll add some applause to the beginning and end of the project to give it more of a radio-show feel.

1   Close the editor, if it is still open.

2   Play the project from around 00:01:06 to 00:02:00 (about a minute) and listen to the content of the interview as you watch the artwork in the Podcast Preview pane.

What do you think? The project works fine as is, but I thought it would be even better to add a few instrument loops to go with their comments. When Kyle says he played tuba, it would be fun to hear a little tuba. When he says he went from tuba to bass guitar, you could add a little bass riff. Also, when Amy says she was a hip-hop girl, I'd really like to hear a cool hip-hop beat under that section. Sure, these parts won't go with the Speakeasy song that is playing in the background, but it will enhance the content of the interview.

We could break out our favorite tuba from the closet and record a riff, or we could simply use one of the loops that come with GarageBand. I vote for the latter. There isn't a specific tuba loop, but there's an orchestral brass loop that will work perfectly.

3   Press Cmd-L to open the Loop Browser.

4   Change the browser to Button view, if it's not already.

5   In the Loop Browser, type *horn* in the search text field and press Return. Then scroll down through the results list and locate the Orchestra Brass 03 loop.

6   Select the Orchestra Brass 03 loop to preview it.

Sounds good enough. Plus you can always transpose it an octave lower once you've added it to the Timeline.

7 Move the playhead to 00:01:26.000 in the Timeline. This is where Kyle is talking about the tuba as the first instrument he played.

8 Drag the Orchestra Brass 03 loop from the browser to the empty space below the Radio Sounds track and release it at the playhead position.

A Trombone track appears at the bottom of the Timeline with the Orchestra Brass region in the track starting at 01:26.

9 Change the name of the Trombone track to *Music Loops.*

10 Play the loop in the project to hear it with the other tracks.

Good stuff. The only problem is that the ducking is lowering the sound of the music loop too much when Kyle talks. You can either turn off ducking on the track or raise the track's volume level.

MORE INFO ▶ For more information about ducking, read the "Ducking Background Tracks" section at the end of Lesson 7.

11 On the Music Loops Track Mixer, drag the Volume slider a bit to the right to 4.6 to raise the track's volume by 4.6 dB.

12 In the Timeline, double-click the Orchestra Brass region to open it in the editor.

13 In the editor, change the Region Pitch value to −12 to lower it by one full octave.

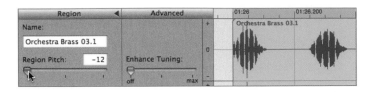

14 Hide the editor and play the transposed loop in the Timeline.

It sounds great and will pass for a tuba, no problem.

Project Tasks

It's your turn to add two more loops to the Music Loops track. Find a cool electric bass loop in the Loop Browser and add it to the Timeline when Kyle says "My brother goes, hey, why don't you play bass guitar…."

Feel free to extend the Orchestral Brass loop so it continues to play until the bass loop starts.

Then find a hip-hop beat drum part in the Loop Browser and add it to the track when Amy says "I was definitely a hip-hop girl…." Resize the loop to last as long or short as you'd like. Save your progress when you're finished.

Recording Sound Effects

The last audio element to add to the project is the applause at the beginning and end of the show. It doesn't have to be roaring stadium applause, but a little applause can go a long way in making a show feel authentic. In some of the previous lessons, you've added sound effects to the Timeline by finding them in the Podcast Sounds view of the Loop Browser and dragging them to the Timeline. In this case, you'll play them in the Musical Typing window and record them to the Timeline.

1 Double-click the Radio Sounds track header to open it in the Track Info pane.

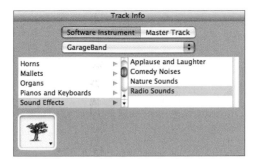

GarageBand 3 includes four different Software Instrument sound effects instruments with preassigned effects for different MIDI keys. Using this feature, you can play the MIDI sounds live during your podcast recording, or you can record them later into the Timeline.

2 Choose Window > Musical Typing, or press Shift-Cmd-K, to open the Musical Typing keyboard.

NOTE ▸ If you have an external MIDI keyboard connected to your computer, you can use it for this exercise if you prefer.

3 Click the different keys on the Musical Typing keyboard (or the corresponding keys on your computer keyboard) to trigger the preassigned Radio Sounds effects.

4 In the Track Info pane, select the Applause and Laughter instrument for the Sound Effects to change the instrument and preassigned sounds.

The Radio Sounds track name changes to Applause and Laughter.

5 Play the different keys to hear the variety of applause and laughter sounds.

There are several different light applause sounds that would work for this podcast. If you hover the pointer over a key on the Musical Typing window, a tooltip will appear, showing you the name of the sound effect assigned to that key.

6 Press D on your computer's keyboard to trigger the light Clapping Crowd Studio 03 sound effect. Hold the D key to play the entire effect until it fades out.

This is the effect you'll record at the beginning of the podcast.

7 Move the playhead to 00:00:32.000 in the Timeline. This is where the narrator says "Speakeasy…" and welcomes the band members to the show.

8 Choose Control > Count In, or press Shift-Cmd-U, to turn on the Count In feature, if it isn't already on.

When the Count In feature is turned on, the playhead will back up one full measure before reaching the record position so you'll have time to prepare before recording. When you click Record, a red line appears at the recording position so that you can see the playhead approach the recording start point during the count-in process.

9 Make sure that the Applause and Laughter track is selected, the Record Enable button is turned on for that track, and the playhead is in the starting position (00:00:32.000). Also move the Musical Typing window upward onscreen so that you can clearly see the Applause and Laughter track in the Timeline.

10 Click the Record button to start the count-in and recording. Watch the playhead approach the red line. Press and hold the D key on your computer's keyboard until the sound ends. Release the key and press the spacebar to stop recording.

Nice applause.

NOTE ▶ If you don't like your recording, press Cmd-Z to undo the recording and repeat steps 9 and 10.

11 Close the Musical Typing window and save your progress.

Project Tasks

There's one last applause sound to record. Move toward the end of the project (around 00:05:32.000) and record another applause region to the Applause and Laughter track. Choose any of the applause sounds you like. Try mixing several effects by pressing more than one key at a time, or simply record the same applause sound effect you recorded at the beginning. When you are finished, close the Musical Typing window and save your project.

Adding Episode Info to a Podcast

The last step needed to complete your podcast episode is to add the episode information, which includes the title, artist information, a description of the episode, and a parental advisory. The episode information is available when you work on the podcast in iWeb and when you view the podcast in iTunes.

1 Select the Podcast Track in the Timeline.

2 Show the Track Info pane, if it is not already showing.

3   Click the Description area and type *An interview with the band Speakeasy.*

4   From the Parental Advisory menu, choose Clean.

5   Change the Artist name field to *Speakeasy.*

6   Change the Title field to *New Artists in Action – Episode 1.*

The description could be more in-depth if you'd like. You might include the names of the band members, list the songs included in the podcast, and provide other information.

7   Press Cmd-S to save the finished podcast.

8   Play the podcast from start to finish to see the completed project.

All of the artwork images are included in the Images folder in the Media Browser if you want to change or edit some of the images.

NOTE ▶ If you didn't complete all of the steps in this lesson and would like to see the finished six-minute version of the podcast, open the project **8-2 Podcast 6min** from the Lesson_08 folder.

Applause! You added many of the advanced podcast features to this project and have a good working knowledge of how to build your own podcasts. Once you have created a podcast episode, you can send it to iWeb to publish it to the Internet. You'll learn more specifics on exporting and sharing your finished podcast in Lesson 10.

Lesson Review

1. How do you create a new podcast using the Podcast Episode template?

2. Where can you add and adjust the Speech Enhancer effects for a voice track?

3. What must you do to a project so that it can be previewed or added to another project?

4. In what two locations can you add artwork to a podcast?

5. How do you crop or resize artwork in a podcast project?

6. Where do you add URL titles or URL information to a marker region?

7. Where do you edit the podcast episode information?

Answers

1. You can open a New Podcast Episode template from the GarageBand Welcome screen.

2. In the Track Info details area, click the Edit button to open the Speech Enhancer dialog and modify the effects settings on the selected track.

3. You must save a project with iLife preview in order to preview it in the Media Browser and use it in another project.

4. You can add artwork to a podcast as a marker region in the Podcast Track and marker information in the editor.

5. You can crop or resize podcast artwork by double-clicking the artwork in the editor and modifying it in the Artwork Editor.

6. You add URL titles or URL information to a marker region in the editor.

7. You can edit a podcast episode's information in the Track Info pane for the Podcast Track.

9

Lesson Files	GarageBand 3 Lessons > Lesson_09 > 9-1 Movie Score start; 9-2 Movie with Music; 9-3 Movie with M&E; 9-4 Movie Score final
Time	This lesson takes approximately 45 minutes to complete.
Goals	Find and preview video files in the Media Browser
	Import a video file into a project
	View a video as you work
	Edit a video's audio track
	Add and edit markers
	Assign chapter titles to markers
	Add music and sound effects
	Customize the Musical Typing window
	Save an instrument

Lesson 9

Scoring an iMovie or Video

How you score a movie depends greatly on the scope of the project. Feature film scores often require composers, large recording stages, and a full orchestra of musicians. Smaller projects, such as training videos, corporate projects, or home movies, can easily be scored using GarageBand 3.

Not only can you create your own music for your iMovies and QuickTime-compatible video files, but you can also choose from hundreds of finished musical pieces and sound effects to complete the soundtrack.

In Lessons 1 and 2, you worked with an original musical score that was recorded and arranged in GarageBand, then added the Alaska video clip to go with the song. In this lesson, you'll try the opposite approach and import a finished video, then create a soundtrack from scratch using some of the musical pieces and sound effects that come with GarageBand 3. Along the way, you'll also add and label chapter markers that will be used in iDVD when you export the finished piece. You'll also learn how to place sound effects at your fingertips as you design your own Musical Typing instrument track and save the customized settings.

Creating a New Movie Score Project

In Lesson 8, you used a GarageBand template from the welcome screen to create a new podcast project. GarageBand also includes a template for movie score projects. Instead of opening a project that has already been started for you in the GarageBand 3 Lessons folder, let's create a new movie score project using the GarageBand 3 templates, just as you might if you were working on your own.

1   Launch GarageBand. If GarageBand is already open, choose File > New.

2   In the GarageBand welcome screen, click the New Movie Score button.

3   Save the project as *Lesson 9 Movie Score* to your My GarageBand Projects folder.

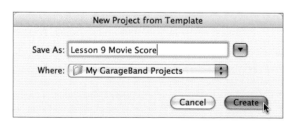

4   Click Create.

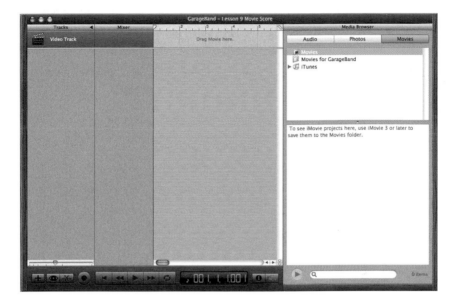

The Lesson 9 Movie Score project opens, with the empty Video Track and Media Browser already showing. The Media Browser contains buttons for different types of media files (Audio, Photos, Movies), a browser where you can navigate to the media files you want to use, and a media list showing the media files in the current location.

Notice that the Movies button and the Movies folder in the Media Browser are selected. If the Movies folder on your computer includes movie files, they will be displayed in the lower pane of the Media Browser whenever you select the Movies folder.

The Movies pane of the Media Browser may include iTunes if you have created your own mp4 files compressed for your video iPod. Protected iTunes media will not appear in the Media Browser. You can also add other folders to the Media Browser so you can access media files anywhere on your computer.

5 In the Media Browser, select the Movies for GarageBand folder, which you added in Lesson 1.

The thumbnail for **Lesson 9 movie.mov** is black because this video fades in from black at the beginning and fades out to black at the end. It will also appear black in the Video Preview pane when the playhead is at the beginning and end of the project.

NOTE ▶ If you didn't add the Movies for GarageBand folder to the Media Browser back in Lesson 1, turn to the "Adding Movies to the Media Browser and Timeline" section at the end of Lesson 1. Follow the steps to add the folder to the Media Browser before continuing to the next step.

Working with Video Files in the Media Browser

The Movies for GarageBand folder in the Media Browser includes two video clips. For this lesson, you'll use the **Lesson 9 movie** file. Once you have located a media file, you can preview it and import it into the project.

Before you import the video file to your project, it's a good idea to preview it. Finding the right video file in this case is easy because the name is very obvious, and there are only two video clips from which to choose. However, in your real-life workflow you may have dozens, or even hundreds, of video clips in your Media Browser, and the selection process may not be as easy.

Previewing a Video File

There are two simple ways to preview a video clip in the Media Browser: select the file and click the Play button, or double-click the clip.

1   Double-click the **Lesson 9 movie** file to preview it in the Media Browser.

Lesson 9 movie.mov

The movie icon becomes a small preview of the movie.

2   Click the Play button, or select another file to stop the preview.

If the file you previewed included puppy footage, you have the correct file. Don't worry, I'm not trying to bore you with home movies of the life and times of my dog, Niki. I just used this footage as an example of the type of movie you could score. It could just as easily contain footage of kids, family, vacation, company picnics, business meetings, or a video about how to snowboard a half-pipe. Truth is, I chose this footage because I've been looking for an excuse to use some of the fun cartoon sound effects and stingers that come with GarageBand 3—this video is perfect.

Importing a Video File from the Media Browser

You can import any one iMovie project or QuickTime-compatible video file from the Media Browser. The movie you'll use in this lesson was originally edited in Final Cut Pro. Then it was exported to a highly compressed H.264 format.

Let's add the **Lesson 9 movie** to the project.

1   Drag the **Lesson 9 movie** file from the Media Browser to the Timeline.

GarageBand creates a new AIFF file that contains the soundtrack of the movie. The original movie file remains unchanged.

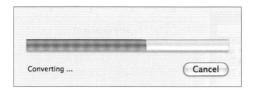

Once the video file is imported into the project, the video appears in the Video Track at the top of the Timeline, showing still frames from the video file. The Track Info pane also appears in place of the Media Browser, with the Video Preview pane at the top where you can see the video as you play the project.

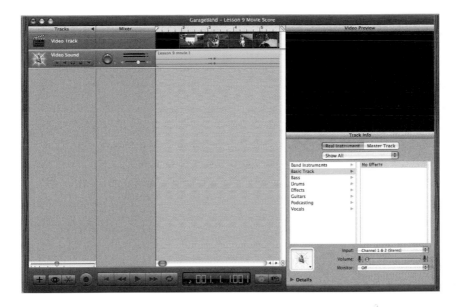

The video file always starts at the beginning of the project. Once added to a project, video files cannot be edited or repositioned in the Timeline. Below the Video Track is a new Video Sound track containing the video file's audio. The Video Sound track is a Real Instrument track, and it includes an orange (imported) Real Instrument region.

2   Select the Video Track to see the its info in the Track Info pane. Then select the Video Sound track to see its information.

The Video Preview pane will be visible as long as the Track Info pane is showing, no matter which track is selected in the Timeline.

NOTE ▶ A project can only contain one video file. If you import a video file into a project that already contains one, you'll see a dialog asking if you want to replace the existing video with the new one.

Preparing the Project for Scoring

Once the video file has been added to the project, it's ready to start scoring. However, there are a few things you should do first:

▶ Watch the video to get ideas about what type of sound you want to add.

▶ Clean up any problems in the video's audio track.

▶ Add markers that might be useful for planning the soundtrack or separating the project into chapters.

Viewing the Video

The Video Preview pane is available to view your project's video as long as the Video Track and Track Info pane are both showing. Since this project is based on video instead of music, you can change the time display to absolute time rather than musical time.

1 In the time display, click the Absolute Time button to view the project in absolute time (Hours:Minutes:Seconds.Fractions).

2 Press the End key to move the playhead to the end of the project.

The time display indicates the project is a little over three minutes in length.

3 Press Return or the Home key to move the playhead to the beginning of the project.

4 Play the project once from the beginning to see the movie file in the Video Preview pane. Feel free to use the Fast Forward button to watch it quickly.

The black-and-white puppy is my dog Niki, and the white dog is Ayla (who belongs to my dad in Montana).

5 Press Return to move the playhead back to the beginning of the project.

This movie was edited in sections that can be divided into chapters for a DVD or played consecutively as a movie. You'll add chapter markers later in the lesson. First, let's clean up the audio track.

Working with the Video's Audio Track

You can edit and mix the Video Sound track exactly like any Real Instrument track. You can also mute it, solo it, adjust the volume level and pan position, and even add effects. Although you can edit the Video Sound track anytime, it's always a good idea to clean up any obvious problems early, before you build the rest of the soundtrack.

The biggest problem I noticed in the existing audio is during the section when Niki is chasing her tail and loses her balance. You can hear me behind the camera ask her if she is dizzy before I laugh. The laugh is okay, but it's hard to understand what I'm saying. The solution is to simply delete the unwanted audio.

You won't need the Video Preview pane for this audio procedure, so let's close it temporarily to make more room in the Timeline for the task at hand.

1   Press Cmd-I to close the Track Info and Video Preview panes.

2   Double-click the orange **Lesson 9 movie.1** audio region in the Video Sound track to open it in the editor.

3   Move the playhead to around 1 minute 36 seconds in the Timeline (00:01:36:000).

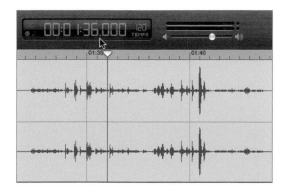

TIP ▶ You can use the time display to navigate to a specific time by double-clicking the numbers in the display and typing the desired time. Press the right or left arrow keys to select a different field within the display. Press Return to send the playhead to the location in the display. You can also move the playhead in the Timeline two seconds at a time earlier or later by pressing the left and right arrow keys.

4 Press Ctrl-right arrow several times to zoom in to the waveform in the editor.

5 Listen to the track between 01:38 and 01:41.

The laugh doesn't start until 01:40, so let's select and delete the two seconds of audio leading up to the laugh.

6 Move the pointer over the waveform in the editor until the pointer changes to crosshairs. Click and drag the crosshair pointer from 01:38 to 01:40.

7 Once the selection is complete (blue), release the mouse and click once on the selected area to make it a separate selected region.

8 Press Delete to remove the unwanted section.

9 Move the playhead back to around 01:36 and play through the edited section.

My talking is gone, but the laugh remains. Mission accomplished. You'll add music and sound effects that will mask the silence in the Video Sound track.

As you can see, the audio in the Video Sound track can be edited just like any other Real Instrument region. The only difference is that it is orange to indicate it was imported.

Adding and Editing Markers

In Lesson 8, you added URL markers to the podcast so that the viewers could see and click a link to the band's Web site. For this project, you'll add chapter markers between each section that you can use in iDVD to create chapters. The chapter markers can also be handy for navigation to different parts of the finished movie as you build the soundtrack.

In this exercise, you'll add four chapter markers that separate the different parts of the movie. You can add markers to the video track in the editor. Since the editor is already showing, all you'll need to do is select the Video Track.

1   Select the Video Track to show marker information in the editor.

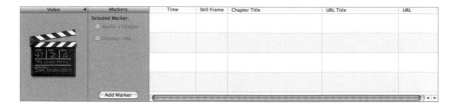

The editor changes to Marker view and contains the marker list with columns showing the start time, still video frame, and chapter title for each marker. The first chapter marker you'll add will be for the montage at the beginning of the video that shows Niki growing up from 9 weeks to 9 years old. (She'll be 11 this year.)

2   Press Cmd-I to open the Track Info and Video Preview panes.

3   Press Return to move the playhead to the beginning.

4   In the editor, click the Add Marker button to add a marker at the playhead position.

The first marker appears in the marker list. Also, the time position where you added the marker appears in the Time column, and the frame of the video at that position appears in the Still Frame column. The beginning of the video fades in from black, so the still frame for the first marker will also be black.

5 Click the Chapter Title text field and type *Montage*, then press Return.

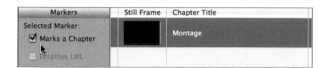

Naming the chapter marker in the Chapter Title field automatically designates the marker as a chapter. If you want to name a marker without making it a chapter marker, you can deselect the "Marks a Chapter" option.

NOTE ▶ To delete a marker, select it in the marker list and press the Delete key.

Chapter markers you create in GarageBand will be recognized when you play the movie in iTunes, iDVD, or QuickTime Player. You'll learn how to share this project with the other iLife '06 applications in the next lesson.

Project Tasks

Now it's your turn to add the remaining three markers. First, you'll navigate to the right position in the Timeline, then click the Add Marker button. Once you've created the marker, you can name it accordingly. There is a fade-in/fade-out between each section of the finished video, so the still frame for each marker will be black. The last step is to press Cmd-S to save your progress.

▶ 00:00:31 – Ayla's Water Dance

▶ 00:01:10 – Tail Spin

▶ 00:01:44 – 1st Grape

> **TIP** ▶ Since you're working with whole timecode numbers and not fractions of a second, start with the playhead at the beginning of the Timeline so you'll have all zeros in the time display. Then you can simply type in the absolute time where you'd like to move the playhead.

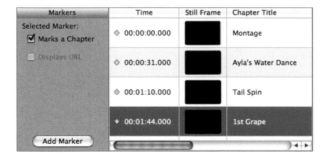

Building a Soundtrack in the Timeline

Now that you've viewed the project and added markers, it's time to add some music. In the previous lessons, you've created and mixed music in the Timeline. For this exercise, you'll use some of the professional quality prerecorded music selections that come with GarageBand 3. Once the music is in place, you'll learn several techniques for adding sound effects to complete the project.

Navigating Between Markers

Before you add the music, let's take a minute to identify and navigate to the markers in the Timeline. Each marker appears as a yellow diamond in the Ruler. To quickly navigate from one marker to another, simply double-click the marker (yellow diamond) icon in the marker list.

1   Press Cmd-I to close the Track Info pane.

2   Press Ctrl-right arrow until you are fully zoomed in to the Timeline.

The more you zoom in, the more thumbnails of video frames you will see in the Video Track, and the more detailed the increments of time will be displayed in the Ruler.

3   Move the playhead to the beginning of the project.

4   In the editor, double-click the yellow diamond (marker icon) for the Ayla's Water Dance marker.

The playhead jumps to that location in the Timeline. That doesn't necessarily mean you'll see the playhead without scrolling to it.

Locking the Playhead

This is a good time to mention the two different ways you can watch the playhead in action. When you play a long take or a full song, or simply navigate to a marker, your playhead may actually leave the screen. If you like to watch your playhead scrub across the tracks, click the Playhead Lock button. It's called that because it also lets you lock the playhead in the Timeline and the playhead in the editor so they remain onscreen.

The Playhead Lock button is located on the far-right side of the window, and it looks like two playheads, one on top of the other.

Playheads   Playheads
unlocked   locked

If the two playheads are lined up in the middle of the button, the playheads in the Timeline and the editor are moving in sync with one another (ganged). It also means that the playheads will stay locked in view in the Timeline, and the tracks will move behind the playhead. By default, the playheads in the Timeline and the editor stay centered in the middle of the GarageBand window once they reach the center.

If the button shows two playheads that are not aligned, the playheads in the Timeline and editor are not locked to the center of the screen. The playhead will continue moving left to right and can continue to move offscreen as it plays the tracks in the Timeline. Sometimes you may want to see a different part of the song in the editor than the one shown in the Timeline. To do this, you can "unlock" the two playheads, so that the Timeline and editor can show different parts of the song.

Let's lock the playheads so that when you navigate to a marker, the playhead will be visible in the center of the screen even if you are zoomed in to the Timeline.

1 Click the Playhead Lock button once to set the playheads in the locked position, if they are not already locked.

The Ruler and playhead scroll until the playhead position is in the center of the Timeline.

2   Press Ctrl-left arrow several times to zoom out of the Timeline until you can see every other second displayed in the Ruler.

3   Press the spacebar to begin playback from the second marker.

Notice that the playhead remains in the center of the Timeline, and the tracks move behind it.

4   While the track is playing, click the Playhead Lock button to unlock the playheads.

Notice the change in the playhead. This time the playhead continues offscreen.

5   Pause playback, then click the Playhead Lock button again until it is in the locked position (two playheads aligned in the center of the button).

6   In the editor, double-click the 1st Grape marker to navigate to it in the Timeline.

The playhead appears at 01:44 in the center of the Timeline.

Browsing and Adding Music to the Project

There are several strategies you can take when adding a soundtrack to your iMovie or video clip. One option is to import the video into GarageBand and add music and sound effects to the edited video. Or, you could create a song in GarageBand, then export it to iTunes, where you can then bring it into your video editing software such as iMovie and edit the picture to the music.

The original song "Alaska Sunrise," which you worked with in Lessons 1 and 2, was actually composed first in GarageBand, then exported as a finished song to iTunes. Once the song was completed, I used it as a guide for editing the video.

For this project, you'll use prerecorded jingles instead of starting from scratch on an original song. GarageBand 3 includes hundreds of prerecorded musical pieces (jingles) to add to your projects. You can find and preview the different jingles in the Podcast Sounds view of the Loop Browser. Your goal in this exercise is to find a piece of music that works well with the montage section at the beginning of the video.

1   Press Cmd-E to hide the editor. Then move the playhead to the beginning of the project.

2   Play the project from the first marker to the second marker (around 30 seconds) and watch the montage.

What type of music do you think would work well with this piece? If I were going to compose an original score for this montage, it would be something upbeat and happy with a touch of sentimentality, without being too heavy or dramatic. What does that sound like? You'll know it when you hear it. Let's use the same criteria to find a finished jingle.

3   Press Cmd-L to open the Loop Browser.

When the Loop Browser opens, the Track Info pane automatically closes.

4   Change the Loop Browser to Podcast Sounds view.

5   Select Jingles from the Loops column.

The Jingles column shows that there are 200 jingles in the All category. It might take a while to wade through all of them. Instead, let's narrow the search to the Cinematic jingles.

6   Select the Cinematic category.

7   Scroll down through the different Cinematic jingles.

8   Select the first jingle in the list, Borealis, to preview it in the Loop Browser.

What did you think? I think it was nice, but a little surreal and mysterious for this montage. Time to try another.

Did you notice that many of the jingles include three versions: long, medium, and short? Many jingles come in three lengths so that they can be used with video scenes that also vary in length. This can also be useful if you are using jingles for a podcast or radio show and want to start with a long version during the introduction and use shorter versions of the same theme music as bumpers between sections of the show or at the end.

9   Preview the Broadcast News Long jingle.

It definitely has an exciting news quality that would be great if the montage included footage of Niki rescuing people from danger. Otherwise, it's too much for this montage.

10   Listen to the Broadcast News Short jingle to hear the difference between the short and long versions.

The short version is perfect for a show that has already used the long version. When the show comes back from commercial, the audience recognizes a familiar theme and knows the show is back.

11   Listen to the Elysium Long jingle.

Thoughts? It sounds perfect to me. Upbeat, happy, a touch of sentimentality, and not too dramatic. Let's check the length.

12 Find the Length column in the results list of the Loop Browser and check the length of the Elysium Long jingle.

The Elysium Long jingle is 31 seconds, exactly the same length as the montage. What luck.

NOTE ▶ If you select a jingle that isn't the exact length, you can always resize it to make it shorter or loop it to make it longer, as you would any Real Instrument region.

13 Drag the Elysium Long jingle from the Loop Browser and drop it at the beginning of the Timeline, below the Video Sound track.

A Jingles track containing the Elysium Long region appears below the Video Sound track in the Timeline.

14 Press Cmd-I to show the Track Info and Video Preview panes.

15 Play the montage from the beginning and listen to the music as you watch the video.

Doesn't get much better than that. It almost feels like the video was edited for that specific music.

16 Press Shift-Cmd-S and save the project as *Movie with Music* to your My GarageBand Projects folder.

Project Tasks

Now it's your turn to add jingles to the remaining three markers. I'll give you specific jingles to use for this exercise, but feel free to try other combinations after you finish the lesson. Use the All category in the Jingles column so you'll be able to browse all of the different jingles. To go back and forth between the marker info in the editor and the Podcast Sounds in the Loop Browser, select the Video Track in the Timeline, then use the shortcuts Cmd-E for editor and Cmd-L for loop.

Remember, each marker will be a new chapter on the DVD, so the song needs to start right after the marker. If you start the song before the marker, it won't start cleanly when the chapter fades in. Most of the jingles have a few frames of blank space at the end, so if you need to overlap the end of one loop to add another, that's fine. You can also place them on separate tracks if you'd like to separate the jingles.

- ▶ Ayla's Water Dance marker – Campfire jingle
- ▶ Tail Spin marker – Carousel jingle
- ▶ 1st Grape marker – Acoustic Sunrise jingle

When you're finished, play the project to see how the video is enhanced by the music.

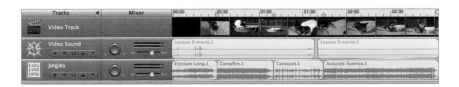

> **NOTE ▸** If you did not complete any of the previous steps, feel free to open the project **9-2 Movie with Music** and save it to your My GarageBand Projects folder.

Working with Sound Effects

Now that the music is in place, it's time to have some fun adding sound effects to the project. You've probably seen an animal bloopers TV show that includes funny music and sound effects when animals slip, fall, bump into things, or act wacky. These shows are funny because of the footage, but the sound effects add a little extra humor to the mix that might push a chuckle into a full-blown laugh. This is your opportunity to add a few cartoon sound effects to animal footage. Keep in mind, GarageBand includes lots of serious sounds, too. Once you finish the lesson, you'll be ready to score your own videos however you'd like.

There are two primary ways to add sound effects to a project in GarageBand:

▸   Add them from the Loop Browser and edit as needed.

▸   Trigger them with a MIDI device and record them into a track.

In the next series of exercises, you'll try both methods.

Adding a Sound Effect from the Browser

Your goal is to add sound effects to the 1st Grape section of the project. If you've watched the video, you've seen that Niki as a puppy (and adult for that matter) has a tough time eating a grape. The darn grape keeps popping out of her mouth. The footage is cute, but when you add a cartoon *boing* to the grape whenever it hits the floor, you'll find it even funnier—at least I did.

1   Press Cmd-L to show the Loop Browser, if it is not already showing.

2   Click the Podcast Sounds View button. In the Loops column, select the Sound Effects category.

3 Type *boing* in the search text field and press Return.

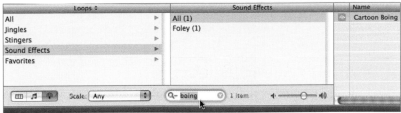

The Sound Effects category includes one boing sound.

4 Preview Cartoon Boing in the results list.

Cute. But it might sound too repetitive if you use the same boing over and over. Let's try the Stingers category to see what's in there.

5 In the Loops column, select the Stingers category.

Without even scrolling, you can see that the Stingers category includes a Cartoon Boing Boing effect, as well as a Cartoon Space Boing, and other cartoon effects that will be perfect for the other parts of this video.

6 Preview the Cartoon Boing Boing effect to see what it sounds like.

The effect actually includes four separate boings—perfect to add variety to the falling grape. Let's add the effect to the Timeline and then cut it into four pieces that can be used for different grape moments.

7 Click once on the last marker (yellow diamond) in the Ruler to move the playhead to the marker.

Double-clicking a marker in the Ruler will start playing the project from that marker position.

8 Press Ctrl-right arrow several times to zoom in to the Timeline until the Ruler displays each second starting with 1:44 (the marker position).

9 Press Cmd-I to show the Track Info and Video Preview panes.

10 Play the video until you see the grape roll out of Niki's mouth around 1:52.

Don't worry about getting the exact playhead position, you can maneuver the sound effect after you've put it in the Timeline.

11 Press Cmd-L to show the Loop Browser.

12 Drag the Cartoon Boing Boing clip from the Loop Browser to the playhead position in the Timeline and release it below the Jingles track.

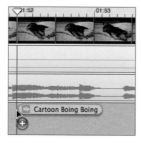

The Cartoon Boing Boing region appears in a Stingers track in the Timeline.

Splitting the Sound Effect in the Timeline

Now that the sound effect is in the Timeline, let's take a moment to split it into four separate boing effects.

1 Select the region in the Stingers track, if it is not already selected.

2 Move the playhead to the empty space in the waveform (flat horizontal line) between the end of the first boing and the start of the second boing.

> **NOTE ▶** If you can't see the waveform clearly enough in the Timeline, you can always press Cmd-E to view the waveform in the editor.

3 Press Cmd-T, or choose Edit > Split, to split the selected region at the playhead position.

4 Repeat steps 2 and 3 to split the region after the 2nd and 3rd boing sounds.

When you are finished, you should have a total of four separate regions in the Stingers track.

5 Click the empty space in the Stingers track to deselect all of the regions in that track.

Aligning Sound Effects to the Video

It's time to place each boing sound effect with the corresponding grape moment in the video.

1 Press Cmd-I to show the Track Info and Video Preview panes, if they're not already showing.

2 Press the left arrow to move the playhead two seconds earlier, and play the video until you see the grape pop out again. Then pause playback.

The first boing effect is late and needs to start earlier in the Timeline.

3 Drag the first region in the Stingers track to the left until it starts at 01:51.

4 Move the playhead a few seconds before the region and play the section.

It's close, but still not quite right.

5 Drag the region a few ticks to the right and play it again. Continue adjusting the placement until you get it just right.

You'll know when it's perfect because the sound effect really looks like it is caused by the grape. Funny stuff.

6 Zoom out of the Timeline several levels until you can see all four regions in the Stingers track, and up through 2:10 or so in the Beat Ruler.

Zooming out will give you easy access to the effects while you continue playing the project.

7 Save the project as *Movie with M&E* (for music and effects) to your My GarageBand Projects folder.

Project Tasks

It's your turn to align the remaining three boing segments to the video. Feel free to try them anywhere you'd like in the 1st Grape section of the video. You don't have to use them in any particular order, so pick the one that works best for the moment you're matching it to. If you want some ideas, use the following guide to place them in specific locations. When you're finished, double-click the 1st Grape marker in the Beat Ruler to play from the marker. It's amazing how much the effects and music enhance the video. Be sure to save your work.

- ▶ Segment 4 starts around 02:04. (Segment 4 works well here because the grape rolls a long distance, and the sound effect accents the move.)
- ▶ Segment 3 starts around 02:15.
- ▶ Segment 2 starts around 02:10.

The video contains more grape moments, and we'll add sound effects to them in the next section.

Playing and Recording Sound Effects

The sound effects that come with GarageBand 3 are also MIDI samples, which means that you can trigger them with a MIDI instrument, onscreen keyboard, or Musical Typing, and record them as needed into a track. This technique is very useful if you're doing a radio show or podcast and want to trigger a sound effect such as applause, laughter, or a rim shot at the touch of a key.

To record sound effects in the Timeline, let's first create the track and assign the track instrument as Comedy Sounds.

1 Choose Track > New Track. In the New Track dialog, select Software Instrument as the track type, then click Create.

   A new Grand Piano Software Instrument track appears below the Stingers track in the Timeline.

2 In the Track Info pane, select Sound Effects as the track instrument category and Comedy Noises as the specific track instrument.

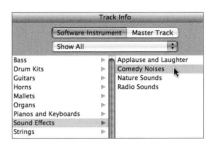

The new track changes to Comedy Noises in the Timeline.

3   Choose Window > Musical Typing.

The Musical Typing window appears. If you have an external MIDI key-board, feel free to use it for this exercise.

4   Click the keys on the Musical Typing window or press the corresponding keys on your computer keyboard to hear the preassigned comedy noises.

The F key triggers the same Cartoon Boing Boing effect you worked with earlier. The longer you hold the key the more boings you'll hear until all four boings have played.

Let's try recording one.

NOTE ▶ You'll probably want to turn off the metronome (Cmd-U) before you start recording, if it is on.

5   Move the playhead back to around 2:16. This is about four seconds before you'll need to trigger the F key (boing).

6   Make sure that the Comedy Noises track is selected. Then, click the Record button to start recording. When Niki loses her grape around 2:20, press the F key on your computer keyboard long enough to trigger the first boing. Then release the F key and press the spacebar to stop recording.

Don't worry if the boing you recorded doesn't line up perfectly with the video. You can always move it in the Timeline. If you really hate your recording, you can press Cmd-Z to undo the recording and try again.

7   Move the recorded Comedy Noises region in the Timeline as needed until the boing sound matches the action in the video preview.

Project Tasks

Now that you know how to record the effects as you play them, let's try a few more. This time, instead of stopping playback after the recording, wait until you've recorded all of the boings for the rest of the video. Don't worry if you trigger them late—that's expected. In fact, there's a good chance you'll trigger all of them late because there is a reaction time from when you see the grape and can actually press the key. Here's the good news. When you're finished, simply move the recording earlier until the first recorded boing aligns with the video. Chances are, the others will all work as well. If not, you can always edit the MIDI events in the editor or split the region and move the segments. When you're finished, save your progress.

> **TIP**   The more familiar you are with the footage, the easier it will be for you to record the sound effects to the Timeline. Also, you can set unnamed markers each time the grape falls to give you a visual cue when the playhead is approaching a marker. If you don't name the markers, they won't become chapter markers later when you export them.

Customizing a Sound Effect Track Instrument

If you liked recording the sound effects by pressing keys, GarageBand 3 also lets you manually design your own track instrument so you can assign any effect or loop to any key. Once you've customized the instrument, you can save it for use in other projects. Let's create a comedy sounds instrument you can use to add sound effects to the other sections of the video. This exercise will use many of the skills you've already worked with in previous lessons.

> **NOTE ▶** If you didn't complete any of the previous exercises, feel free to open the project **9-3 Movie with M&E** to catch up.

1   Create a new Software Instrument track.

2   In the Track Header, change the name from Grand Piano to your first name or initials followed by *Comedy*, then press Return.

3   In the Track Info pane, click the Details disclosure triangle to show the track's details.

4   In the Details area, select Sound Effects from the Generator pop-up menu. Then set the preset pop-up menu to Manual, if it is not already set that way.

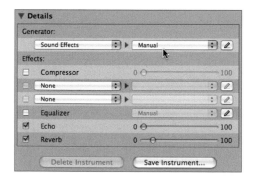

5 Open the Musical Typing window, if it is not already open, and move it to the top of the screen.

You can now manually assign any loop, stinger, jingle, or sound effect to the keys in the Musical Typing window for your comedy track.

6 Press Cmd-L to show the Loop Browser.

7 In the Podcast Sounds view, select the Stingers category.

8 Drag the Cartoon Boing Boing effect from the Loop Browser to the A key (first white key) on the Musical Typing keyboard.

9 Press the A key on your computer keyboard.

The Cartoon Boing Boing sound plays.

10 Move the pointer over the A key on the Musical Typing window.

A yellow tooltip appears, showing you the sound assigned to that key.

11 In the Loop Browser, scroll down to the Cartoon Timpani stinger and preview it.

This sound would be funny in the Tail Spin section when Niki falls the first time. Or it could be used in the Ayla's Water Dance section.

12 Drag the Cartoon Timpani stinger from the Loop Browser to the S key on the Musical Typing window.

13 Browse and add five or six more sound effects to specific keys on the Musical Typing window.

You can always change what is assigned to a key or add more sounds later.

Saving a Customized Track Instrument

Once you've manually customized your sound effects track instrument, you can save it the same way you save other customized track effects in the Track Info pane.

1 Press Cmd-I to open the Track Info pane, if it is not already showing.

The customized track details should be showing. If not, select your custom comedy track.

2 In the Track Info pane, click the Save Instrument button.

The Save Instrument dialog appears.

3 Type the same name in the "Save as" field as you named the comedy track, then click Save.

Your custom comedy track instrument appears in the instrument list in the Track Info pane.

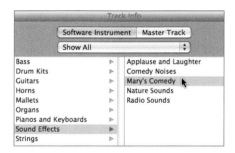

Once you've saved an instrument, you can access it for any of your GarageBand projects. You can also modify it by selecting the instrument, dragging different sounds to the keys of the Musical Typing window, then saving the modified version of the instrument.

4 Click the Details disclosure triangle to hide the details area in the Track Info pane.

Congratulations! You've created a soundtrack in GarageBand that includes both music and sound effects. You'll learn to export the project as a QuickTime file and share it with iDVD in the next lesson. Before you move on to the next lesson, take a few minutes and experiment with adding other effects to the project.

Project Tasks

Now you have all the skills you need to continue adding sound effects to the other sections of the video. Remember, if you're dragging sounds from the Loop Browser to the Timeline, they will be Real Instrument regions and all of the rules of editing Real Instrument regions apply. If you prefer to record regions as Software Instrument samples into the Timeline, all of the rules for recording Software Instrument regions apply.

One great trick with recording sound effects using Musical Typing or a MIDI keyboard is that you can combine different sound effects at the same time, in the same recording. All you need to do is create a cycle region over the portion of the video you want to record, and you can create multipass recordings adding new effects with each pass. I highly recommend that you try this method in the Tail Spin section of the video when Niki gets dizzy and falls over.

Take a few minutes to try adding or recording more effects. You can also feel free to experiment with other musical parts and jingles to vary the piece. Have fun! Don't forget to save your finished project.

Lesson Review

1. What tracks and panes are showing when you open a new movie project template from the GarageBand welcome screen?

2. What types of video files can be imported into a GarageBand project?

3. What is the maximum number of video files you can add to a Garage-Band project?

4. If you import a movie file that includes audio, how does the imported audio appear in the Timeline?

5. Can you edit the audio region in the Video Sound track?

6. How do you add markers to the Video Track?

7. Why do many jingles come in Long, Medium, and Short versions?

8. How can you use the Musical Typing window to add sound effects to the Timeline?

Answers

1. The new movie template includes an empty Video Track and displays the Movies pane of the Media Browser.

2. You can import any iMovie project or QuickTime-compatible video format.

3. A GarageBand project can only include one video file. It will always start at the beginning of the project.

4. A video's audio appears as an orange Real Instrument region in the Video Sound track located directly below the Video Track.

5. You can edit the audio in the Video Sound track in the same way you edit any Real Instrument region.

6. Select the Video Track, move the playhead to the desired marker position, then click the Add Marker button in the editor.

7. Many jingles come in different lengths so that they can be used as a recurring theme in a show.

8. Create a Software Instrument track and choose one of the Sound Effects instruments, or manually create a customized sound effect instrument. Once you've selected the instrument, you can trigger the sound effects and record them to the track.

10

Lesson Files GarageBand 3 Lessons > Lesson 10 > 10-1 Loops

Time This lesson takes approximately 30 minutes to complete.

Goals Set preferences for exporting to iTunes

Evaluate a project's output levels

Send a song to iTunes

Export a project as a QuickTime movie

Send a movie to iDVD

Send a podcast to iWeb

Sharing Your Finished Projects

Now that you know how to record, arrange, and mix your projects in GarageBand, it's time to learn how to share them with other iLife applications, export them to iTunes, download them onto your iPod, and even burn them to a CD or DVD.

All of the iLife '06 applications, including GarageBand, are designed to work together seamlessly. You can write music in GarageBand and export your songs to iTunes; score your iMovie video and export it as a Quick-Time movie or send it back to iMovie; send your finished podcast to iWeb to publish on the Internet; or create a whole playlist of original songs to be shared with any of your applications.

The focus of this lesson is learning how to export or share your projects with the other iLife applications.

Exporting Projects to iTunes

Exporting to iTunes is as simple as choosing Share > Send Song to iTunes. Before you begin exporting, however, there are a few things you'll need to do to prepare your songs.

In the next series of exercises, you'll set your GarageBand preferences to create a playlist in iTunes. Then you'll evaluate a song to make sure that you are exporting the whole song, and you'll check the output levels for clipping. Finally, you'll export your songs to a new playlist in iTunes.

Since you'll be working with a finished, mixed song, this is a great time to practice your "ear for music" so that you can hear beyond the basics.

Setting GarageBand Preferences for iTunes

To prepare a song to export to iTunes, the first step is to set your song and playlist information in the Export pane of the GarageBand preferences.

Let's open the mixed "Highway Brothers" song from Lesson 7 and set up the song and playlist information.

1   Choose File > Open and select **7-6 Highway Brothers mixed** from the Lesson_07 folder.

2   Choose GarageBand > Preferences to open the Preferences window.

3   Click the General button to open the General Preferences pane, if it is not already showing.

Next, you'll need to name your iTunes playlist, composer, and album. By default, GarageBand names the playlist and album after the registered user of the computer.

4   Type *GarageBand 3 Lessons* in the iTunes Playlist field.

5   Type your name in the Composer Name field.

Technically, I composed the music in this book, but you'll want to use your own name for all of your original projects.

6   Type *GarageBand 3 book Album* in the Album Name field.

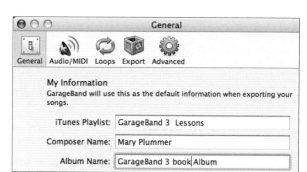

7   Close the Preferences window.

Now that you've set up the export information, iTunes will automatically create a playlist titled GarageBand 3 Lessons and include the composer's name as
well as the album name information in the playlist.

Evaluating the Song's Output Level

Once you've set your information for iTunes, it's time to check the output
levels for the song to make sure they aren't clipping. Remember, the Master
Output Volume meters are located in the lower-right corner of the GarageBand
window. You can use the Master Output Volume slider to raise or lower the
output level as needed.

Also, since training your ears takes practice, remember to listen beyond the
basic song: check the left-to-right placement of the different instruments in
the stereo field, as well as the balance between the volume levels of the different tracks.

Let's play the song and check the output levels. If the levels are too high,
you'll need to lower the output. If the levels are too low, you'll need to raise
the output.

1   Press Return, then the spacebar to begin playback. As the song plays,
watch the Master Output Volume meters for signs of clipping.

If you see any clipping (red) in the meters, stop playback.

You should discover clipping around the 6th and 12th measures.

2   Drag the Master Output Volume slider to –2.4 to lower the output volume and avoid clipping.

3   Play the song again from the beginning and check the new output level in the meters.

Be careful not to set your levels too low. Ideally, your levels should peak between the highest green and yellow portions of the meter.

4   Press Shift-Cmd-S and save the project as *Highway Brothers mix* to your My GarageBand Projects folder.

TIP ▸ Always save your project with the corrected levels before outputting to iTunes. That way, if you decide to output the song again or go back to work on the song later, the levels will be correct.

Sending a Song to iTunes

GarageBand projects are sent to iTunes in AIFF (Audio Interchange File Format) at 44.1 kHz (kilohertz). Your songs can then be burned to an audio CD, downloaded to an iPod, or converted to another format, such as MP3, from within iTunes.

When you export a song to iTunes, the entire song or cycle region, if active—from the beginning of the first measure to the end of the last region—is exported. (If you mute or solo tracks, only those tracks set to play will be exported.) Let's export the song to iTunes.

NOTE ▶ If you have more than one version of iTunes on your computer (for example, OS 9 and OS X versions), GarageBand may export to the older version of iTunes. Launch the most recent version of iTunes before you export.

1   Choose Share > Send Song to iTunes to export the song.

GarageBand begins to mix down your song.

The mixdown process means that all of the different tracks are mixed (at the current levels) into one stereo pair (left and right) for iTunes.

A progress alert shows the progress of the mixdown. You can cancel the export process during mixdown by clicking Cancel.

When mixdown is complete, iTunes launches with your song in the new playlist, and the song automatically plays in iTunes. If your iTunes window does not open, click the iTunes icon in the Dock.

2   Click the playlist you created, GarageBand 3 Lessons, to open the new playlist, if it is not already open.

NOTE ▶ If the playlist appears with your name (user name) instead of GarageBand 3 Lessons, change the playlist name in the GarageBand preferences and export again.

3 In the playlist, double-click Highway Brothers mix to play the song, if it is not already playing.

You don't have to listen to the whole song.

4 Press the spacebar to stop playing the song, then press Cmd-Q to quit iTunes.

Once your song has been sent to iTunes, you can access it from any of the iLife applications through the Media Browser.

5 Select the GarageBand window to make it active, if it is not already active.

6 Press Cmd-R to show the Media Browser. Select the Audio pane, if it is not already showing.

The GarageBand 3 Lessons playlist appears in the iTunes library of the Media Browser.

Your song can now be used in any of the iLife applications, including Garage-Band. If you would like to export individual tracks from a song, perhaps for a musician to practice with, see "Exporting Selected Tracks" (Bonus Exercises > **Export_Selected_Tracks.pdf**) on the accompanying DVD.

Exporting a Project as a QuickTime Movie

GarageBand projects that contain a movie file can be exported as a QuickTime movie. Exporting a project as a QuickTime movie includes both the video and the soundtrack you created. The Video Sound track that came with the original movie file is also included in the soundtrack unless the track is muted when you export the movie. Let's export the finished *Alaska Sunrise* project as a QuickTime movie. First, you can determine what type of compression settings you'd like to use in the Export pane of the GarageBand preferences. By default, the project is exported using the current movie compression settings. Compression settings are stored as part of the GarageBand project until you change them while the project is open.

1   Open the project **2-2 Alaska Sunrise Final** from the Lesson_02 folder.

2   Choose GarageBand > Preferences, then click Export.

The Movie Settings are located in the middle of the Export Preferences pane.

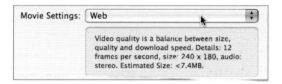

The information below the Movie Settings pop-up menu shows the image size, audio information, and the estimated size of the specific file you plan to export.

3   From the Movie Settings pop-up menu, choose the Full Quality setting.

At the Full Quality setting, the finished project will be around 59.6 MB. Later if you'd like to export a smaller version for an email or the Web, you can go back in and change the export settings.

4   Close the Preferences window.

5   Choose Share > Export as QuickTime Movie.

    The Export QuickTime Movie window appears.

6   Save the project as *Alaska Sunrise* to your Desktop. Click Export.

    You'll see a series of three progress alerts for creating mixdown (mixing all the audio tracks down to a stereo pair), converting, and compressing the movie.

7   When the export is finished, press Cmd-H to hide GarageBand. Locate the exported file on your Desktop.

8   On your Desktop, double-click the Alaska Sunrise movie file to play it in QuickTime Player.

9   Quit QuickTime Player when you are finished looking at the movie.

As you can see, it's incredibly easy to export a scoring project from GarageBand as a QuickTime movie.

Sending a Movie to iDVD

If you have a project containing both video and audio you'd like to burn to a DVD disc, you can send it to iDVD. When you send a project to iDVD, no compression is applied to the project, because in most cases, you'll want to make those compression changes in iDVD. GarageBand projects you send to iDVD can use the chapter markers in the project to move to different parts of the movie. URLs and URL titles will not appear in the finished DVD project. Let's send the **9-4 Movie Score final** project to iDVD.

1   Open the project **9-4 Movie Score final** from the Lesson_09 folder.

This project includes a Video Track, Video Sound track, chapter title markers, music, and sound effects.

2   Choose Share > Send Movie to iDVD.

You'll see progress windows for creating the mixdown and exporting the video.

When the export is complete, iDVD will automatically launch, and your project will be included in the selected iDVD theme.

3   Click the Play button to play the template.

A menu opens named after your project.

4   On the menu, click the Play Movie button to play your movie project.

5   Click the Next Chapter button on the iDVD onscreen remote to jump to the next chapter marker.

6   Quit iDVD. Click Don't Save if you are finished with this example. Click Save if you want to come back and explore this project in iDVD later.

Once the project is in iDVD, you can change the template, modify the buttons, add images to drop zones, and finish any changes you'd like to make to the project before burning the finished DVD disk.

> **MORE INFO** ▶ You can find more information about working with iDVD in the iDVD Help menu.

Sharing a Podcast

When you finish your podcast project in GarageBand, you can either send it to iWeb for publishing on the Internet, or you can export it to disk so it can be finished using another application. Compression settings for podcast episodes are located in the GarageBand Export Preferences pane. Let's open the finished podcast from Lesson 8, change the compression settings, and send it to iWeb.

> **NOTE** ▶ Turning on the cycle region has no effect on the length of the exported project. When you export a project containing a podcast track, the entire project from the beginning to the end of the last region is exported.

1   Open the project **8-2 Podcast 6min** from the Lesson_08 folder.

2   Choose GarageBand > Preferences, then click Export, if the Export pane is
not already showing.

The Audio Podcast Settings are located at the top of the Export Preferences
pane. They affect only the quality of the podcast's audio.

The information below the Audio Podcast Settings pop-up menu shows
the type of compression, kilobytes per second, whether the file is stereo or
mono, and the estimated file size.

3   From the Audio Podcast Settings pop-up menu, choose the Spoken
Podcast setting.

At the Spoken Podcast setting, the finished audio will be around 2.8 MB.

If your podcast project includes artwork or video, you can set the compression in the Movie Settings pop-up menu.

4   From the Movie Settings pop-up menu, choose the Web setting.

At the bottom of the Export pane, you'll see the Publish Podcast settings.

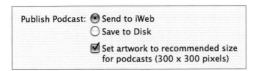

These settings include three publishing choices: Send to iWeb, Save to Disk,
and "Set artwork to recommended size for podcasts (300 x 300 pixels)."

Saving a podcast to disk lets you export your project to a drive to then
publish through iWeb or another application.

If you select Send to iWeb, the project will be sent to iWeb for publishing.
Selecting the "Set artwork to recommended size for podcasts" setting will

keep all of the podcast artwork sized accordingly. Deselecting this setting will publish the artwork at the current size, which may not be optimal for podcast publishing.

5   Select Send to iWeb, if it is not already selected. Also, make sure that the "Set Artwork to recommended size for podcasts" setting is selected.

6   Close the Preferences window.

7   Choose Share > Send Podcast to iWeb.

    Several progress alerts appear sequentially for creating chapter markers, creating mixdown, and converting.

    Once the project is prepared for export, you may see a .Mac Information dialog, which allows you to sign in to your .Mac account or set up an account if you don't already have one. You can set up an account or sign in now, or you can close the dialog.

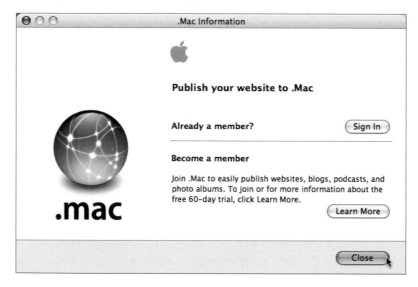

8   Click Close. You can sign in or sign up for your .Mac account after this lesson.

    iWeb launches and prompts you to choose a template for your Web page.

9   In iWeb, scroll through the templates, select the Black template, then select the Podcast webpage type for the Black template.

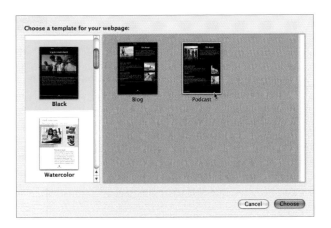

10   Click Choose to choose the selected podcast template.

When iWeb finishes preparing your podcast project, it will appear in the selected template.

11   In the lower-left corner of the podcast player, click the Play button to see the compressed podcast.

12 While the project plays, drag the vertical scroller on the iWeb window downward to see the rest of the page with your other podcast episode information.

Feel free to stop previewing the podcast at any time.

13 When you are finished, save your project and quit iWeb.

There you have it. You've successfully completed the steps to send your podcast to iWeb for publishing. After your podcast is in iWeb, you can make changes to the podcast episode information and publish it to the Web.

> **MORE INFO** ▶ You can find more information about publishing the podcast in iWeb and submitting your podcast to iTunes in the iWeb Help documentation.

What's next? Well that's entirely up to you. This is officially the end of the lesson and also the end of this book, but hopefully just the beginning for you and your GarageBand experience. Make sure to try the four bonus exercises included on the accompanying DVD to learn how to add and index loops, export selected tracks, edit a Real Instrument bass part, and more. If you're interested in taking your songs and recording capabilities up to a professional level, you can easily step from GarageBand to Logic or Logic Express. So have fun, keep the music flowing, and don't forget to let your songs breathe.

Lesson Review

1. What should you do to a music project before exporting it to iTunes?

2. What type of file does GarageBand export to iTunes?

3. Where do you set the information for exporting songs to iTunes?

4. What determines the length of the exported song file to iTunes?

5. How do you export a project that includes a movie file?

6. How do you export a project to iDVD?

7. What are the two ways that you can export or send a podcast project so that it can be published in iWeb or another application?

8. How do you add loops to your library?

Answers

1. Check the master output volume levels to make sure the song is at a good level and not too low or too loud (clipping).

2. GarageBand exports songs to iTunes as 44.1 kHz AIFF files and places them in an iTunes playlist.

3. Set song and playlist information for iTunes in the GarageBand General Preferences window.

4. The length of a song exported from GarageBand is from the beginning of the first measure in the Timeline to the end of the last region in the Timeline. If you use a cycle region, only the portion of the Timeline included in the region is exported.

5. Choose the compression settings in the Export Preferences pane, then choose Share > Export as QuickTime movie.

6. Choose Share > Send Movie to iDVD.

7. You can either send the project to iWeb, or save the project to disk, which exports it to a designated place on your computer.

8. Drag the loops to the Loop Browser.

Logic for GarageBand Users

You've discovered how easy it can be to create your own musical masterpieces in GarageBand. Now you're ready to move up to one of the professional-level music applications from Apple: Logic Pro or Logic Express. After completing the tutorial in Appendix A, you'll understand the similarities and differences between GarageBand and Logic, know how to perform basic tasks in Logic, and be ready to start creating and editing songs. See GarageBand 3 Lessons > **x_App_A_Logic for GarageBand Users** on the DVD accompanying this book.

Exploring Jam Packs

If you really enjoy creating music with GarageBand, you can expand your musical horizons with the GarageBand Jam Pack Series. Each is loaded with over 2,000 new Apple Loops in a wide variety of instruments and genres, plus additional GarageBand Software Instruments, audio effects presets, and new guitar amp settings.

Appendix B, on the DVD accompanying this book, describes the Jam Packs currently available and directs users to more resources. See GarageBand 3 Lessons > **x_App_B_Jam Packs.**

Index

The Apple Training Series

The best way to learn Apple's hardware, Mac OS X, and iLife applications!

The Apple Training Series serves as both a self-paced learning tool and the official curriculum of the Apple Training and Certification Program. You can work through this book as a self-paced course or attend a class at an Apple Authorized Training Center. To find an authorized center near you, go to www.apple.com/training

Mac OS X Support Essentials
0-321-33547-3 • $49.99

Mac OS X Server Essentials
0-321-35758-2 • $54.99

Desktop and Portable Systems, Second Edition
0-321-33546-5 • $54.99

Mac OS X System Administration Reference, Volume 1
0-321-36984-X • $59.99

Mac OS X System Administration Guide, Volume 2
0-321-42315-1 • $54.99

iWork '06 with iLife '06
0-321-44225-3 • $34.99

iLife '06
0-321-42164-7 • $34.99

GarageBand 3
0-321-42165-5 • $39.99

The Apple Pro Training Series

The best way to learn Apple's professional digital video and audio software!

Final Cut Pro 5
0-321-33481-7 • $49.99

Advanced Editing Techniques in Final Cut Pro 5
0-321-33549-X • $49.99

DVD Studio Pro 4
0-321-33482-5 • $49.99

Aperture
0-321-42276-7 • $49.99

To see a full list of Apple Pro Training Series, visit: **www.peachpit.com/appleprotraining**